NOAH

STUDIES ON PERSONALITIES
OF THE OLD TESTAMENT
JAMES L. CRENSHAW, *Editor*

DANIEL IN HIS TIME
by André LaCocque

JOSEPH AND HIS FAMILY: A LITERARY STUDY
by W. Lee Humphreys

EZEKIEL: THE PROPHET AND HIS MESSAGE
by Ralph W. Klein

NOAH: THE PERSON AND THE STORY IN
HISTORY AND TRADITION
by Lloyd R. Bailey

NOAH

THE PERSON AND THE STORY IN HISTORY AND TRADITION

Lloyd R. Bailey

University of South Carolina Press

First Edition

Manufactured in the United States of America

Library of Congress Cataloging-in-Publication Data

Bailey, Lloyd R., 1936–
   Noah : the person and the story in history and
tradition.

   (Studies on personalities of the Old Testament)
   Bibliography: p.
   Includes index.
   1. Noah (Biblical figure)   2. Deluge.   3. Noah's ark.
I. Title. II. Series
BS580.N6B35   1989   222'.11095   88-27781
ISBN 0-87249-571-X
ISBN 0-87249-637-6 (pbk.)

Grateful acknowledgment is made to the following publishers for permission to reprint copyrighted material:
James B. Pritchard, ed., *Ancient Near Eastern Texts Relating to the Old Testament*, 2nd edition.
Copyright 1950, 1955, © 1983 renewed by Princeton University Press.
Thorkild Jacobsen, *The Sumerian King List*, The Oriental Institute of The University of
Chicago, *Assyriological Studies*, No. 11 (Chicago, 1939).
Thorkild Jacobsen, *The Treasures of Darkness*, Yale University Press, New Haven and
London, Copyright © 1976 by Yale University Press. All rights reserved.
James Darmesteter, *The Zend-Avesta*. Vol. 4 of the Sacred Books of the East, ed. F. Max
Müller. Oxford: The Clarendon Press, 1895.
Edmond Sollberger, "The Rulers of Lagas." *Journal of Cuneiform Studies*, 21, 1967.
J. Van Dijk, *LUGAL UD ME-LÁM-bi NIR-GÁL*. 2 vols. E. J. Brill, Leiden, The Netherlands, 1983.
Scripture quotations unless otherwise noted are from the Revised Standard Version of the
Bible, copyright 1946, 1952, 1971, 1973 by the division of Christian Education of the National Council of the Churches of Christ in the U.S.A.

CONTENTS

CONTENTS

CONTENTS

ILLUSTRATIONS

MAPS

CONTENTS

TABLES

PREFACE

In those instances where readers of the present volume might be helped by reading other sources, I have cited *The Interpreter's Dictionary of the Bible*, four volumes (*IDB*), and its *Supplementary Volume* (*IDBS*) wherever possible. This I have done, not necessarily because their articles are the most recent or detailed on every subject, but because the volumes are quite reliable and will be readily available, to the average reader, in public and church libraries.

Chapter 5 has been published previously as *Where Is Noah's Ark?* (Nashville: Abingdon Press paperback, 1978). Gratitude is hereby expressed to the Press for return of the original copyright, and the material is published herein with but slight modification.

I wish to thank the Research Council of Duke University for financial assistance, which made available to me one of the sources cited herein.

ABBREVIATIONS

AASOR:	*Annual of the American Schools of Oriental Research*
ANF:	Ante-Nicene Fathers (of the Church) series
Antiq.	Josephus, *Antiquities of the Jews* (Whiston, translator)
BAR:	*Biblical Archaeology Reader*, 4 vols. (Selected articles from *Biblical Archaeologist*; not to be confused with the periodical entitled *Biblical Archaeology Review*)
B.C.E.:	Before the Common Era (i.e., B.C.)
Ber. Rab.:	Bereshit Rabbah (Genesis Rabbah)
BM:	(text in the) British Museum
CAD:	*Chicago Assyrian Dictionary* (multi-volumes; in process)
CBS:	Cuneiform texts in the University of Pennsylvania Museum
C.E.:	Common Era (i.e., A.D.)
Col.:	Column, of a text cited
CSCO:	Corpus Scriptorum Christianorum Orientalium series
D:	Pentateuchal Source (Deuteronomy)
E:	Pentateuchal Source (the Elohist)
ETL:	*Ephemerides Theologicae Louvanienses*
IB:	*The Interpreter's Bible* (12 vols.)
ICR:	The Institute for Creation Research (San Diego, Calif.)
IDB:	*The Interpreter's Dictionary of the Bible*, 4 vols.
IDBS:	*IDB, Supplementary Volume*
IO–VC:	*The Interpreter's One-Volume Commentary on the Bible*
J:	Pentateuchal Source (the Yahwist)
JAOS:	*Journal of the American Oriental Society*

JASA:	*Journal of the American Scientific Affiliation*
JB:	The Jerusalem Bible (translation)
JNES:	*Journal of Near Eastern Studies*
KJV:	King James Version of the Bible
l, ll.:	line(s), of the text cited
LXX:	Septuagint
NAB:	New American Bible (translation)
NEB:	New English Bible (translation)
NIV:	New International Version of the Bible
NJB:	New Jerusalem Bible (translation)
nv:	"I have not seen (the source cited)"
P:	Pentateuchal Source (the Priestly writer)
PCC:	Patrologia Cursus Completus (series)
PEQ:	*Palestine Exploration Quarterly*
Praep. Evang.:	*Preaparatio Evangelica*, by Eusebius of Caesarea
RSV:	Revised Standard Version of the Bible
sec.:	section, of a text cited
Tan.:	Tanhuma (homiletic Midrash)
TEV:	Today's English Version of the Bible
trans.:	translated by
v., vv.:	verse(s)
VAB:	*Vorderasiatische Bibliothek*
VT:	*Vetus Testamentum*
W–B:	Weld-Blundel Text, of the Sumerian King List
ZA:	*Zeitschrift für Assyriologie*
ZDMG:	*Zeitschrift der deutschen morgenländischen Gesellschaft*

EDITOR'S PREFACE

Critical study of the Bible in its ancient Near Eastern setting has stimulated interest in the individuals who shaped the course of history and whom events singled out as tragic or heroic figures. For example, Rolf Rendtorff's *Men of the Old Testament* (1968) focuses on the lives of important biblical figures as a means of illuminating history, while Fleming James's *Personalities of the Old Testament* (1939) addresses the issue of individuals who function as inspiration for their religious successors in the twentieth century. Other studies restricted to a single individual—e.g., Moses, Abraham, Samson, Elijah, David, Saul, Ruth, Jonah, Job, Jeremiah—have enabled scholars to deal with a host of themes and questions: psychological, literary, theological, sociological, and historical. Some, like Gerhard von Rad's *Moses*, introduce a specific approach to interpreting the Bible, hence provide valuable pedagogic tools.

As a rule, these treatments of individual figures have not provided books accessible to the general public. Some such volumes were written by thinkers who lacked an expert's knowledge of biblical criticism (Freud on Moses, Jung on Job) and whose conclusions, however provocative, remain problematic. Others were targeted for the guild of professional biblical critics (David Gunn on David and Saul, Phyllis Trible on Ruth, Terence Fretheim and Jonathan Magonet on Jonah). Few such books have succeeded in capturing the imagination of a wide audience in the way fictional works like Archibald MacLeish's *J.B.* and Joseph Heller's *God Knows* have done.

The books in this series are written by specialists in the Old Testament for readers who want to learn more about biblical personalities without becoming professional students of the Bible themselves. The volumes throw light on the imaging of deity in biblical times, clarifying ancient understandings of God. Inasmuch as the Bible constitutes human perceptions of God's relationship with the world and its creature, we seek to discern what ancient writers believed about deity. Although not necessarily endorsing a particular understanding of God, we believe such attempts at making sense of reality contribute something worthwhile to the endless quest for knowledge.

James L. Crenshaw
Duke Divinity School

INTRODUCTION

There was a fellow by the name of Noah,
   built an ark.
Everybody knows he built an ark.
You say, "What did Noah do?"
[Everybody] says, "Well, he built an ark!"

Thus did comedian Bill Cosby begin a classic sketch.[1] The success of his performance (measured in terms of audience laughter and subsequent imitation by hearers) resulted not merely from his skill but also from the common knowledge of the story on the part of the audience. Noah is one of a very few biblical characters concerning whom contemporary hearers would have sufficient knowledge in order to understand a good joke.

Cartoons, in current popular publications, are perhaps an adequate indicator of society's knowledge of a particular subject. Thus most political cartoons are funny today, but opaque after a year or so as readers forget the proper background information. Measured by the large number of Bible-subject cartoons that I have collected over the last decade (from both ecclesiastical and secular magazines), it appears that only Adam and Eve, Noah, Moses, and Jesus have sufficient name-recognition to make the scene. Of those, Noah received by far the largest measure of attention.

There was a time when the list of biblical stars was not quite so small. During previous centuries, the United States was affirmably biblically literate. Proper names from its pages, even of minor persons, were given to children and were recognized as such: Keziah (Job 42:14), Achsah (Judg. 1:12), Obadiah (he of the book by that title), and Uriah (2 Sam. 11:3), among others. Such names have now vanished from Western North Carolina where I grew up, and the descendants of such persons will refer to them erroneously as "Axie," "Cuziah," and "O. B. Diah." Noah, however, continues in full vigor as a namesake.

The Noah story has had a more serious impact upon our society in the last few decades. Press reports and books have announced that remains of "the flood" have been discovered by archaeologists, and that remains of Noah's boat are yet to be seen on an impressive mountain in eastern Turkey. More recent still is the claim (made mostly in scholarly circles) that the biblical narrative of the flood, long considered by most academic interpreters to be composite, is in reality the product of single authorship (just as the church had affirmed all along).

Perhaps it is in order, then, to review what is known or may plausibly be conjectured about this ancient, revered, and popular character, as well as about the composition and meaning of the traditions that have kept him in the public mind.

ONE

CATASTROPHE STORIES AROUND THE WORLD

Many peoples have preserved a story of how, in primeval time, the known human race was threatened with extinction by a natural disaster. Usually one or more human couples survived and repopulated the world.

In a few accounts, the disaster takes the form of a great fire. For example, the Arawaks of British Guiana relate what happened when the great "Dweller on High" (Aiomun Kondi) became dissatisfied with the evil doings of human beings.

> Those men who believed in the warning of the coming fire dug deep into the sand-reef, and formed a retreat therein, consisting of a roof of timber, supported by massive pillars of same. This they covered with layers of earth, and a thick upper coating of sand. Having removed everything combustible from the neighborhood, they then remained quietly in their subterranean abode, till the flame which swept the earth's surface had passed by them.[1]

The Hodesum of Bengal relate a similar story, which begins with the creation of human beings.

> And after the world was peopled, [the deity] Sirma Thakoor destroyed it once, with the exception of sixteen people, because people became incestuous, and unmindful of God, or their superiors. (Some say he destroyed it with water, some say with fire.)[2]

5

The sacred literature of the Zoroastrians of ancient Persia (now Iran) relates the threat of a great freeze, likewise to be survived in an underground enclosure. Since it has remarkable similarities to the Mesopotamian accounts of the great deluge, it is appropriate to delay discussion of it until the end of chapter 2, below.

Usually, however, the near destruction of humanity results from a great flood. Indeed, so numerous is this type of story that one modern collection contains 302 texts from around the world,[3] including Mesopotamia, Egypt, Greece, Syro-Palestine, Europe, India, eastern Asia, New Guinea, Central America, North America, Melanesia, Polynesia, Micronesia, Australia, and South America. How does one account for such widespread attestation? A popular conjecture runs as follows:

> ... every branch of the whole human race ... have traditions of a Great Deluge that destroyed all mankind, except one family, and which impressed itself on the memory of the ancestors of all these races before they separated. All these myths are intelligible only on the supposition that some such event did actually occur. Such a universal belief ... must be based on a Historical Fact.
>
> [Halley, p. 75]

At first glance, this might seem to be a plausible argument. A few moments of reflection, however, may raise a number of questions, among them the following.

First, does the widespread attestation of flood stories necessitate the conclusion that they originated from a single source? Instead, is it possible that a number of local floods have given rise to independent stories, just as a regional fire or freeze may have led to stories about them? After all, catastrophic flooding occurs in most areas of the world. The answer would depend, in part, upon the similarities in the various flood stories. How similar could they be if each had arisen as a description of a local inundation? How different could they be and still have arisen from a single occasion? What is the possibility that once independent stories have later influenced each other, so that they now sound as if they might have had a common origin when in fact they do not?

How similar or different the flood stories are depends upon how widely one casts the net in collecting them. If it is limited to accounts from the "Lands of the Bible" (Syro-Palestine and Mesopotamia), for example, one may be struck by their similarities and suspect a common origin (see below, chap. 2). However, if the accounts are gathered from around the world, one may be struck far more by their divergencies than by their similarities! It is important that such collections have been gathered without regard for their support for a single, universal flood. It would be easy to rule out those that sound dissimilar, and then to be amazed at how similar the remainder are!

When a great number of flood stories is read, at least the following differences will be noticed (based on those in Gaster, pp. 82–131).

1. *What is the cause of the flood?* God desired to kill a certain jackal (India); conflict between giants (Iceland); God is offended at human wickedness (Egypt, and elsewhere); the gods retaliate against noisy humans (Mesopotamia); a crab is offended by a bird (China); a human kills a giant snake (Borneo); a god is offended by the slaughter of his alarm clock, a bird (Fiji); two wise men recite an incantation for rain (New Zealand); a frog disgorges water, which it had swallowed, when thirsty animals tickle it (Australia).

2. *Who escaped from the flood?* No one (Greek Syria); a single male (India); sixteen people (India); a brother and sister (Burma, China); two men and a woman (Philippines); eight persons (Fiji); eighty persons (Armenia); a man and a coyote in separate boats (North America); a man and a female dog (Mexico).

3. *How did humans escape the waters of the flood?* By climbing a high mountain (North America, Borneo, Indonesia, Greece); by use of a god's boat (Egypt); in a nutshell, which a god had dropped from the sky (Lithuania); by clinging to a clod of earth, which a deity dangled from above (Indonesia); by entanglement in a tree when a woman's hair got caught in it and kept her from being swept away (Sumatra); by a boat (Mexico, Borneo, the Near East); by an eagle (Philippines); rescued by a pelican in a boat (Australia); by floating on a ball of resin (North America); by climbing trees (Brazil).

4. *How was the earth flooded?* The sea arose (Indonesia, Asia Minor); a local lake overflowed (Wales); blood from a slain giant (Iceland); rainfall (most areas).

5. *By what means was the earth repopulated?* Natural birth from the survivors (most areas); stones turned into people (Greece); mud images of humans were activated (Greek Syria); dairy products merged to create a female (India); a dead male returned to life when a female survivor struck him (Sumatra); the surviving male formed wives from stone and wood (Borneo); a female dog became a woman (Mexico).

7

6. *Where did the survivors disembark?* Usually very near to where the story is popularly known. It is sometimes said that one can be taken there and shown remains of the boat (see below, chap. 4).

7. *Was the entire earth covered by the flood?* Not in all accounts.

8. *Has there been more than one such flood?* In a few accounts.

Is it plausible that all such differences will have arisen in the process of transmission, as the story of a single event was retold by the scattered descendants of Noah?

In some instances, such changes in the story might well have taken place: the number of survivors (the change from "eight" to "eighty," e.g.); how the earth was flooded (societies adjusting it to their own geography: a rise in sea level for those along the coast, e.g.); where the survivors landed (pride in having it nearby, if not in the interest of the tourist trade!).

In other instances, changes in transmission seem a bit surprising: the change from a universal to a local flood, for example. In yet other instances, corruption of the story becomes difficult to conceive: the means of repopulation (stones, dairy products, a dog); the means of survival (there is some distance between Noah's boat and a woman's hair caught in a tree, e.g.).

In the remaining instances, the corruption would be so total as to destroy the point of the story: if more than one flood is proclaimed, then the covenant (Gen. 9) is unknown; the "punch line" has been lost, including the symbolism of the rainbow. And finally, there is the fact that some flood stories lack a theological context, that is, deity does not play a role in them.[4]

Second, even if the various stories could be traced back to a common source, is that within itself evidence of a historical basis for the event that the story relates? After all, riddles, fables, and legends can spread throughout the world, as have, for example, the fables of Aesop. (Note: the question being asked here is not, "Is the biblical account true?" but rather, "Does universal belief arise only from historical fact?" as Halley seems to imply.)

Consider the following similarly widespread belief. The story that the first human being was both male and female (an androgyn: *IDBS*, pp.25–27) is told in such widely separated areas as Australia, Oceania, Iran, Mesopotamia, and Greece.[5] Would one want to argue, on that basis, that this story represents the true biological history of human beginnings, taken throughout the earth by the descendants of that being when it was divided into male and female? One could argue, perhaps, that even the Bible has echoes of the idea: the first being (Adam) gave rise to a female by division of its body (Gen. 2:21–22). Or is it not more likely that such stories have arisen in many locations from the observation of hermaphrodites who are born in all societies from time to time?

Similarly, does the widely attested story of a universal flood of necessity attest to anything more than local experience of catastrophic flooding, expressed in poetic terms? The answer may depend, in part, upon how one views the Bible: Where, in its pages, does it intend to depict the beginnings of pure "happenedness," of "just the facts"? (To that issue we shall turn in chap. 5, below.) The answer may also depend upon the amount of "evidence" one assumes to exist from the disciplines of archaeology and geology for such a deluge. (To that issue we shall turn in chap. 3, below.)

Third, even if some widely separated flood stories are so similar that one must suspect that they describe the same event, does that indicate that they were distributed by the sons of Noah after the Genesis flood? That is, wherever human beings settled, was the flood story initially a part of their sacred tradition?

In some cases, one may trace the emergence of a flood story within a given culture: it became known there only long after human settlement. For example, the story does not appear in Sanskrit literature until after the arrival in India of elements of Aryan civilization (Gaster, p. 96). Knowledge of the story among the Lolos people of China is attributable to the nearly forgotten missionary activity of the Nestorian Christians (Gaster, p. 355, sec. 38, n. 6). Mesopotamian influence upon an already existing flood story among the Greeks has been well charted (Westermann, p. 398).[6] Christian missionary activity in the eighteenth and nineteenth centuries has taken the biblical account to the ends of the earth, where it was then available for "discovery" by later travelers to whom it seemed an independent confirmation of the story of Noah.[7]

Fourth, is it true that "every branch of the whole human race" has a tradition of a great deluge (so Halley)? Apparently not, to judge from the previous paragraph. More to the point is the *IDB* article (II: 280), speaking to the claim that the widespread distribution of flood stories supports the historicity of the biblical accounts.

> This notion has necessarily been given up. We know, e.g., that numerous peoples have no flood legend in their literature. Flood stories are almost entirely lacking in Africa, occur only occasionally in Europe, and are absent in many parts of Asia. They are widespread in America, Australia, and the islands of the Pacific. . . . Many do

not know a world-wide flood at all, but only a local inundation. . . . Often the heroes save themselves . . . without intervention by the gods. Further, only a few of the flood stories give the wickedness of man as the cause of the flood. . . . Facts of this kind disprove the claim that the biblical account is the parent of all flood stories.

TWO

FLOOD STORIES IN THE ANCIENT NEAR EAST

Although flood stories from around the world vary widely in their content, those from Syro-Palestine and Mesopotamia (the so-called lands of the Bible) are strikingly similar. While it is difficult, if not impossible, to believe that the former descended from a single source (or describe a single event), the reverse may indeed be the case in the Ancient Near East. It is, after all, an area given to regular and catastrophic flooding, for which adequate archaeological and geological evidence has come to light (see chap. below, 3). Furthermore, it is an area through which the story of "the flood" could easily spread: it is geographically small and well defined (the so-called fertile crescent), its inhabitants spoke closely related Semitic languages, there was occasional political unity of the whole (under Assyrians, Babylonians, and Persians), and commerce was widespread throughout at all periods.

The major flood accounts, four in number, are as follows. An English translation of many of them, with notes, may be found in the various editions of Pritchard's volume, and there is a brief discussion in *IDB* (II: 278–84). One should be aware, however, that new materials have come to light since these works were published and that the understanding of them may have changed. This is especially true of the Atrahasis Epic (Lambert and Millard).

1. *The Sumerian account of the deluge*, or the story of Ziusudra. This is the oldest version yet known, with the single surviving copy (CBS 10673) dating to the first half of the second millennium (about 1600 B.C.E.?). Only

about one third of this broken text has survived and thus the account is so sketchy that it can be understood only with the aid of other sources. From elsewhere we learn that Ziusudra was king of the Mesopotamian city of Shuruppak, and that the place was destroyed by a great flood. For this event there is even archaeological evidence (for which, see chap. 3, below), and we learn of it from another flood story as well (the Gilgamesh Epic). A brief summary of the Ziusudra text may be found in table 1.

2. *The Akkadian text of the Gilgamesh Epic*, which, in Tablet XI, contains the story of how Utnapishtim and his family survived the flood (see Heidel; also Tigay). The fullest form of the epic comes from the famous library of King Ashurbanipal at Nineveh and apparently was written around the beginning of the first millennium B.C.E. Substantial fragments have been found in both Old and Middle Babylonian, and copies existed in the Hittite and Hurrian languages.

The larger account tells of the search for immortality by Gilgamesh, king of the city of Uruk in southern Mesopotamia. He learns that such status has actually been achieved by one Utnapishtim ("he who found life") of Shuruppak, and sets out to find him and learn the secret of eternal life. From the latter he then hears the story of the great deluge. It apparently was an independent story, which the creator of the Gilgamesh Epic has incorporated into the larger account.

This flood story contains the closest parallels to the biblical account, for which see the summary on Table 1. No reason for the deluge is given, since that is not relevant in the larger epic of which the flood story is now a part: ". . . their heart led the great gods to produce the flood." Utnapishtim is made to relate that event as part of his personal experience, and thus its larger significance is not reported.

3. *The Atrahasis Epic*, long known only from quotations in Greek and Latin writers. Then, in the mid-nineteenth century, fragmentary cuneiform texts began to emerge from excavations at Nineveh and elsewhere. However, it would be a century later before the dozens of fragments (some in Old Babylonian and others in Neo-Assyrian) would be arranged in the proper (original) sequence and the coherence of the story emerge (as in Lambert and Millard).

As was the case with the Gilgamesh Epic, this flood story is part of a much larger account. Now, however, it is an earlier and entirely different one, which may be traced back to the first part of the second millennium (1700 B.C.E.?). It includes the creation of human beings' and resultant divine dissatisfaction with them, and thus it has similarities with the account in Genesis 2–9. It is similar to the much briefer and fragmentary Sumerian account (Ziusudra), and apparently the Gilgamesh Epic is dependent upon it. The name of the hero (Atrahasis, traditionally thought to mean "the exceedingly wise one") is applied to Utnapishtim as well.

4. *The account of Berossus*, a Babylonian priest of the third century B.C.E. His history, entitled *Babyloniaka* (in Greek), has not survived, save in secondhand quotations by later writers.[2] The Jewish historian Josephus (first century C.E.) seems to have read it (*Antiquities*, I.iii.6). According to Berossus, Xisouthros (i.e., Ziusudra) was warned in a dream that a disastrous flood was impending, was told to write a history and bury it for preservation in the city of Sippar (in southern Mesopotamia), and was commanded to build a boat, which he should stock with animals and then ride out the deluge with family and friends. He releases birds in order to check on the withdrawal of the waters. When he (along with wife, daughter, and a navigator) disembark in Armenia, they suddenly disappear, apparently in keeping with the older cuneiform accounts of the survivors becoming immortals and thereafter dwelling beyond the known earth. Nonetheless, they are able to tell others in the boat to recover the buried history book. Those survivors then journey to the city of Babylon and rebuild it, while the boat remains visible for many years in the mountains of Armenia.

Berossus' account deviates from the cuneiform sources in only two regards: he gives a specific calendric date for the beginning of the deluge (as does the Bible), and he related the burying of a pre-flood history. It is plausible that he learned his account from the priests of Sippar (where the history was to be deposited) and then adapted it to a Babylonian setting (i.e., the command to rebuild Babylon).

In addition to the aforementioned major accounts, there are occasional references to "the flood" in other compositions, thus attesting its popularity. Among them are the following (with no systematic effort having been made to find them all).

The Gilgamesh Epic, although not primarily concerned with the flood, nonetheless opens with a description of its hero as one who "brought intelligence of (the days) before the flo[od]" (I, i,*l. 6*, trans. Heidel).

Ashurbanipal, the learned king of Assyria (669–633 B.C.E.), remarks, "I study stone inscriptions from before the flood, which are obtuse, obscure and confused" (*VAB*, vii. 256, 18–19; trans. Lambert and Millard, p. 26).

The Sumerian King List (W–B Text 444; ca. 1900–1800 B.C.E.), after enumerating five cities were eight kings reigned for 241,200 years, concludes (apparently speaking to the city of Shuruppak): "The Flood swept thereover" (i,*l.* 39; trans. Jacobsen, p. 77; Pritchard, p. 265). For a flood deposit at this site, see below, chapter 3.

The so-called Babylonian World Map (600 B.C.E.; see Beek, p. 75, for photo) refers to the residence of Utanpishtim (the flood hero) at the edge of the world.

A list of postdiluvian rulers in the city of Lagash (BM 23103), possibly a response to the Sumerian King List, begins:

> After the Flood had swept over
> and had brought about the destruction of the land—
>
> [Obverse, *ll.* 1–2; trans. Sollberger]

Naram-Sin, a famous king of ancient Akkad, reports, "I made the land of Akkad (look) like (after) the Deluge of water that happened at an early time of mankind" (from the so-called Cuthean Legend; *CAD*, vol. A/1, p. 77).

The overall similarities and differences in these various accounts (including the Bible, but excluding Berossus) may be grasped with the aid of table 1.

TABLE 1   COMPARISON OF FLOOD STORIES

GENESIS	ATRAHASIS	GILGAMESH	ZIUSUDRA
	(versifications are those of Lambert and Millard)	(versifications are those of Pritchard)	(versifications are those of Pritchard)
	The junior gods (the Igigi) complain to the senior gods (the Anunnaki) that they are being overworked in the maintenance of the world. [Tablet I, *ll.* 33–181]		
A human being is created and placed in God's garden "to till it and to keep it." This the deity does by breathing into a model made	Human beings are created in order to relieve the junior god in their labors. This is done by mixing clay with the blood of a		Brief mention of the creation of humans and animals (the text is broken before and after). [*ll.* 47–50]

TABLE 1 (continued)

GENESIS	ATRAHASIS	GILGAMESH	ZIUSUDRA
of clay. A female, called "The Mother of all Living" is fashioned from the rib of the prior creature. [2:4a–23]	slaughtered god and moulding it into a human shape. Seven pairs of humans were thus created. The goddess who was involved in the process (Nintu) is sometimes called "The Lady of the womb." [Tablet I, *ll.* 189–339]		
The wickedness of humans "was great in the earth" and the Lord decides to destory them with a great flood. [6:5–7, 11–13]	The human race multiplies and their noise irritates the senior gods. The latter try various means of population control (e.g., infertility and famine), but they are not effective. They finally decide upon a great flood. [Tablet I, *ll.* 352–416; II, col. i, *l.* 1–col. viii, *l.* 37]	The city of Shuruppak "was ancient . . . when their heart led the great gods to produce the flood." [Tablet XI, *ll.* 8–19]	The gods have decided to bring a great deluge. [*l.* 101; details in subsequent lines, 102–37, but they are missing]
Noah finds "favor in the eyes of the Lord," builds a boat in seven days according to given specifications, and takes aboard his family and the required animals. [6:8, 14–22; 7:1–10]	The god Enki (Ea) decides to save his devotee Atrahasis. He instructs him to build a boat from the reeds of his house, since the flood is to begin in seven day. This is done, and Atrahasis, his family, and various animals enter the boat. [Tablet III, col. i, *l.* 1–col. ii, *l.* 55]	The god Ea decides to save Utnapishtim, and gives him details for the construction of a great boat, which is to be completed in seven days. He then enters the boat with "all my family and kin . . . beasts of the field . . . (and) the craftsmen." [Tablet XI, *ll.* 20–95]	A deity warns Ziusudra of the impending destruction. [*ll.* 152–60; discussion of a boat likely in the missing section, *ll.* 161–200]
Rain falls for forty days and forty	A fierce storm rages, terrifying even the	The flood lasts until the seventh day,	The flood lasts for seven days and

TABLE 1 (continued)

GENESIS	ATRAHASIS	GILGAMESH	ZIUSUDRA
nights. The waters cover the high mountains, and all nonmarine life perishes. After five months, the ark comes to rest. Noah sends out a raven, a dove, then another dove, to see if dry land has appeared. [7:11–8:12]	deities. It lasts for seven days and seven nights. [Tablet III, col. iii–iv, *l.* 48; the landing of the boat was apparently related in a missing section thereafter]	during which even the deities lament. "All of mankind had returned to clay." The boat comes to rest on Mount Nisir. Utnapishtim sends out a dove, a swallow, and a raven (the last of which does not return). [Tablet XI, *ll.* 96–154]	nights. It "swept over the land" (i.e., Sumer). Ziusudra opens a window when the sun again appears. [*ll.* 201–5]
Noah and his family leave the ark, and offer sacrifice to the Lord. [8:15–20]	Atrahasis disembarks and offers sacrifice. Various deities continue to complain about the destruction. [Tablet III, col. v, *l.* 30–col. vi, *l.* 4]	Utnapishtim offers various cultic acts in gratitude (libations, burning cedarwood). Various deities continue to complain about the destruction. [Tablet XI, *ll.* 155–69]	Ziusudra slaughters an ox and a sheep. [*ll.* 206–11; the text is broken thereafter]
The Lord guarantees the continuation of humanity and a reliable realm of nature. [8:21–22; 9:8–17] However, severe restrictions are now placed upon the race. [9:1–7]	The god Enlil (who had ordered the flood) is angered that some humans have ascaped. He decides to accept the continuation of the race, but takes steps that will limit its ability to multiply and to thus disturb the gods. [Tablet III, col. vi, *l.* 5–col. vii, *l.* 11]	Enlil is angry that some humans have escaped. He keeps his oath to destory all mortals by granting immortality to the survivors, who are to live thereafter beyond the known earth. [Tablet XI, *ll.* 170–96]	Ziusudra is given "life like (that of) a god," and taken to "the land of Dilmun, the place where the sun rises." [*ll.* 251–61]

FLOOD STORIES IN THE ANCIENT NEAR EAST

I. SIMILARITIES IN THE ACCOUNTS

The similarities between the biblical account and one or more of the others include at least the following particulars.

1. The Genesis account, although it may once have been an independent piece of literature (see below, chap. 5), is now part of a larger narrative of primeval happenings. This is true of the Atrahasis Epic as well, although the larger context is both alike and different (Frymer-Kensky). The Ziusudra text is apparently similar to Atrahasis. Such is not the context, however, of the flood story within the Gilgamesh Epic. There it is related as part of the exploits of the king of Uruk, and thus it is depicted within history rather than in primeval time. Of necessity it has been changed by the editor into a first-person account by Utnapishtim. Contrast "Noah . . . went into the ark" (Gen. 7:7) and "he (Atrahasis) sent his family on board" (III.ii.42) with "All my family and kin I made to aboard the ship" (Gilgamesh, XI, *l.* 84).

2. The deluge happens as the result of divine displeasure with human beings. (However, the cause of that displeasure differs from one account to the next.)

3. The animals arrive by divine command (Genesis and Atrahasis, but not in Gilgamesh).

4. A deity intervenes in order to save a family of humans. (This is not the case in some flood stories elsewhere in the world.)

5. Attention is given to the dimensions of the boat (Genesis, Gilgamesh), and it is to be caulked with pitch (Hebrew: *koper*; Akkadian: *kupru*).

6. The destruction is to begin within seven days of the divine disclosure.

7. The flood results from rainfall. (Genesis also mentions that "all the fountains of the great deep burst forth," 7:11.)

8. Specific mention of closing the door to the boat.

9. The entire world is covered by the waters (stated in Genesis, implied in Atrahasis and Gilgamesh; Ziusudra speaks of "the land").

10. The boat comes to rest on a mountain (section is missing from Atrahasis; not so stated in Ziusudra).

11. A window is opened in the boat, in order to check on the withdrawal of the waters.

12. Birds are released, in order to see if they will return (Genesis and Gilgamesh; other texts broken).

17

13. Sacrifice is offered when the survivors disembark; the deity is said to "smell" it.

14. A divine concession to humans is expressed at the end. (However, its nature varies from one account to the next.)

II. DIVERGENCIES IN THE ACCOUNTS

Although the similarities are often close and their number is significant, there are divergencies as well. The following list is not necessarily exhaustive.

1. Monotheism (one deity) in Genesis versus polytheism in all the others. In the Mesopotamian accounts, not all the members of the divine council are in favor of the destructive flood. One of them (Enki/Ea) takes surreptitious steps to ensure the survival of a few humans. Later, various of the deities will express regret at what they have allowed to happen (Atrahasis).

2. The cause of the divine displeasure. In Genesis it is human "wickedness" (murder, according to Frymer-Kensky); in Atrahasis it is noise resulting from overpopulation (Kilmer). However, Utnapishtim merely states to Gilgamesh that "their heart led the great gods to produce the flood" (i.e., the precise cause has been deleted from this account, since it is not essential to the story line). The Ziusudra text is broken.

3. Noah is depicted as a common citizen, whereas Ziusudra is stated to be a king (we learn from elsewhere that his city was Shuruppak).

4. From Berossus and the Sumerian King List[3] we learn that there were ten generations of rulers prior to the flood. Noah is the tenth generation of humans prior to the flood in Genesis. Nonetheless, a total of 457,200 years[4] is involved in the Sumerian account but only 1,656 years[5] in Genesis. The former is based upon the sexagesimal system, i.e., base-60, and thus may be expressed as $(60^3 \times 2) + (60^2 \times 7)$. This suggests that the figures are "ideal" rather than "actual." (For a general discussion, see app. 3, and for other illustrations, see immediately below and in chap. 5.)

5. At the beginning of the flood, Ziusudra has reigned for 36,000 years, while Noah is aged 600 years. Nonetheless, the two figures are related in a way that cannot be accidental, since they are based on multiples of 60 (the Mesopotamian system, whereas Israel's numerical reckoning was in base-10, as in our modern system). Ziusudra's age is $60^2 \times 10$, and Noah's age is 60×10. This is our first occasion to wonder if

certain of the biblical figures might not be "ideal" rather than "actual," as are the Mesopotamian ones.

6. Noah gives no explanation to his neighbors concerning the structure that he is erecting, but both Atrahasis and Utnapishtim indulge in clever explanations with a double meaning, which were meant to deceive. Later accounts, however, have Noah exhort his neighbors to repent (see below, chap. 6).

7. The downpour lasts forty days in Genesis, but a mere seven days in the other accounts.

8. The boat comes to rest in Armenia (Ararat) in both Genesis and the account of Berossus, but east of Mesopotamia in Gilgamesh (the other texts are broken; see below, chap. 4, for full discussion of the locations).

9. The boat is made of "gopher wood" in Genesis (see *IDB*, II: 441), but of reeds in the Atrahasis Epic.

10. In Genesis, the dimensions of the boat are 300 cubits long, 50 cubits wide, and 30 cubits high. Allowing about 18 inches for an Israelite cubit (*IDB*, IV: 837), this would yield 450 × 75 × 45 feet. Utnapishtim's boat is a cube, 120 cubits per side. Allowing 19.7 inches for a Babylonian cubit (*IDB*, IV: 836), this would yield 197 feet each side. Thus the volume of Noah's boat is 56,250 cubic yards, while that of Utnapishtim is 283,162 cubic yards, that is, the latter is about five times as large.

The dimensions of the Mesopotamian boat again reflect a preoccupation with the "ideal" number 60: it is 60 × 2 cubits per side, and its volume is thus $(60 \times 2)^3$ cubic cubits. Noah's boat reflects the same system, but only in part: its length is 300 cubits (i.e., 60 × 5), its height is 30 cubits (i.e., half of 60), and its volume is 450,000 cubic cubits (i.e., $[60^3 \times 2] + [60^2 \times 5]$).

11. Noah's boat contains a total of eight persons (four couples). The number in Atrahasis' family is not stated; one fragment (DT 42) contains instructions to take aboard also "your kith, your kin, and the skilled workers." Utnapishtim took along "all my family and kin," and possibly a "boatman" named Puzur-Amurri.[6] Late tradition in Armenia is that Noah's boat contained eighty persons (see below, chap. 4 and app. 1).

12. Noah's boat is to have three decks, while that of Utnapishtim is to have six (each of which is divided into nine parts).

13. Noah is to take aboard seven pairs of "clean" animals, but only a single pair of those that are "not clean" (Gen. 7:2–3). A bit later, we read that "two and two of all flesh" entered the ark (7:13–16), and mod-

ern interpreters have long suspected that two different accounts have been combined. (See below, chap. 5, on the composition of the early chapters of Genesis.) Utnapishtim is instructed to preserve "the seed of all living things" (Tablet XI, *l.* 27). The Atrahasis test, in a broken section, mentions "Clean (animals) . . . Fat (animals) . . . winged (birds of) the heavens. The cattle . . . The wild (creatures) . . ." (III.ii.32–37; fragments help clarify).

14. Utnapishtim and Ziusudra are granted immortality, but Noah remains a mortal. This would be a deliberate departure from the Mesopotamian account, apparently. (However, see below, chap. 6.) The Atrahasis text is too broken to interpret.

15. After the flood, the Lord renews the divine commitment to creation: the regularity of nature will not again be interrupted, and humans are again to "multiply, and fill the earth" (Gen. 9:1, with reaffirmation of 1:28). In the Atrahasis Epic, the deities, having brought on the deluge in order to reduce human commotion caused by overpopulation, take steps to retard human fertility: they institute sterility, stillbirth, and celibate classes of persons. (Thus the story has been shaped, apparently, by the different sociological realities of Israel [underpopulation?] and Mesopotamia [overpopulation]. This should caution the modern reader against accepting such primeval stories as "pure history." This issue will be explored at length in chap. 5, below.)

III. DEPENDENCIES BETWEEN FLOOD STORIES

The similarities between the biblical and the Mesopotamian flood stories are so striking and so numerous that it is impossible to escape the suspicion that they are somehow related (Heidel, pp. 260–69; Cassuto, II: 23–29). (For comparison of Mesopotamian accounts, see Tigay; also Harmatta.) The discussion has usually revolved around three options:

First, the Genesis account (G) is the oldest, and those of Mesopotamia (M) have deviated from it with the passage of time. G was brought to Palestine, likely as part of the Patriarchal migration, around the beginning of the second millennium (2000 B.C.E.). That migration had its beginning in "Ur of the Chaldeans" (Gen. 11:31), in southern Mesopotamia, and involved a period of time at Haran (far to the north), near the "mountains of Ararat" where the ark came to rest (11:31; 8:4). The account was then handed down to Moses (or whoever it was that compiled the materials in the book of Genesis: see below, chap. 5–6).

Usually this position, rather than resting upon historical and literary arguments, is stated in stark religious terms: "Christian scholarship . . . unanimously assets that Genesis gives us God's inspired record of that great catastrophe, while the Babylonian epic . . . showing by its gross polytheism the serious corruption of the original facts . . ." (Whitcomb and Morris, p. 488).

Second, the Genesis account is derived from the Mesopotamian one. The account may have been transmitted to Israel by diplomats or merchants during the period of the monarchy, and especially might one expect such literary influence during the period of Judean exile to Babylonia (587–39 B.C.E.). This position has seemed plausible, since the Mesopotamian account was committed to writing sometime around 2000 B.C.E., almost a millennium before the earliest biblical materials may have taken their present shape.

Third, both G and M have evolved from a common source. Since a number of versions of the flood story are already known, there is no reason to assume that all of them have come to light, including a possible ancestor of all the others. In that case, there would be no necessity to assume that either G or M is the "original" and that the others have resulted from changes (either deliberate or accidental) in the process of transmission. Thus, both G and M could develop local variations over the centuries, in accordance with the needs and style of the local audience.

How is one to evaluate, in the most general terms, there various possibilities? At least the following factors might be relevant: (*a*) In the case of the third suggestion, above, may one assume that there must be *a common ancestor*? Is it not also possible that the description of an event took various shapes right from the beginning, much as an event in the present can give rise to differing eyewitness accounts?

(*b*) Ancient authors and editors may not have had the modern mentality of discovering and reporting the mere "facts." (In the case of Genesis, this issue will be examined in chap. 5, below.) Note, for example, how they felt free to take traditional stories and place them in an entirely new context: the story of the flood was removed from primeval time (as in Atrahasis) and placed within the life story of Gilgamesh, even changing it to a first-person account. Even in its primeval setting, it arguably reflects the social realities of its intended audience: Atrahasis reflects overpopulation (a reality in the Tigris-Euphrates valleys), and

Genesis underpopulation (a reality in the hill country where the Israelites settled at the time both of the conquest and of the return from exile).

(c) When numbers are involved in M (either for dimensions of the boat or for ages of persons), they are clearly idealized, based upon exact multiples of the prevailing sexagesimal system. Since the biblical figures reflect the same base-60, it is difficult to say that M is a "corruption" of G. It is much more plausible that G is a deliberate modification (reduction) of M.

(d) At least one of G's divergencies from M seems to reflect the sociology of Palestine rather than of Mesopotamia: "be fruitful and multiply" (G) versus reduction of overpopulation (M). It is therefore plausible to suggest that M has the older context for the flood story. This may be true concerning the flood-hero's explanation of the boat as well: it looks as if G has repressed an aspect of the story that, from the point of view of monotheistic Yahwism, it found objectionable. This would also provide a basis for the later portrait of "Noah the Preacher" (see below, chap. 6). To be sure, the opposite approach is just possible: that both M and Judeo-Christian tradition (including the New Testament) asked the question "What did the hero tell his neighbors?" and both then conjectured an answer.

(e) What kind of literature is G (see below, chap. 5)? Is the story a unity (see below, chap. 6)? And what is its purpose (see below, chap. 7)? All those questions must be studied before one can decide whether it is necessary to conclude, on grounds of faith, that G is the basic (accurate) account. In any case, "Christian scholarship' does *not* "unanimously assert" what Whitcomb and Morris claim (noted in the first suggestion, above), unless one limits the definition of such scholarship to those who make the assertion.

(f) Is geological and archaeological evidence relevant to the inquiry, and if so, what is the nature (see below, chap. 3–4)? Does it suggest a local flood or a universal one, and which is more in keeping with the accounts in G and M?

IV. Repeated Seasonal Flooding

Finally, it is important to realize that not all references in Mesopotamian literature are to *the* flood. Flooding in the valleys of the Tigris and Euphrates is seasonal and has been catastrophic on a number of occasions (see below, chap. 3, for the archaeological evidence). In addition to the flood that seems to be the basis for the accounts of Ziusudra, Atrahasis, Utnapishtim, and Noah (?), the following may be mentioned (see *CAD*, vol. A/1, pp. 80–81).

A Sumerian text (BM 120011) relates that "When the rain had rained, when walls had been demolished," Father Heaven impregnated Mother Earth and created a troublesome *numun*-plant. In a way that is not clearly stated, the plant causes the shepherd Dumuzi to offend the goddess Inanna, who then unleashes a devastating flood:

> When the rain had rained, when walls had been demolished,
> When boiling hot hailstones had rained,
> . . . .
> Stalls were demolished, sheepfolds were ripped out,
> Vicious floodwaters were hurled against the rivers,
> Vicious winds were hurled against the marshes,
> By (?) the . . . of the Tigris and Euphrates,
> . . . .
>
> [Trans. Kramer, 1980]

The Sumerian Gudea, king of Lagash (twenty-first century B.C.E.), reports a dream in which the deity Ninurta (Ningirsu) appeared, "according to his wings the Indugud bird, according to his lower parts a flood" (i.e., a vast thundercloud?). Gudea then describes him:

> Your heart, rising as (rise the waves in) mid-ocean,
> crashing down as (crash) the breakers,
> roaring like waters pouring out (through a breach in a dike),
> destroying cities like the flood wave.
> [Cylinder A, viii, *ll.* 23–26; trans. Jacobsen, *Treasures*, p. 132]

Presumably the deity is the force behind the rising tributaries of the Tigris, which after heavy rainfall come roaring down from the foothills of the Zagros range to the east. In a related text ("Ninurta and the Anzu Bird"), we apparently see Ninurta's power as the raging river becomes a wave, sweeping into the marshes near the river's mouth and threatening the temple of the god Enki at Eridu.

The Sumerian composition "Enmerkar and the Lord of Aratta" relates the journey of Enmerkar, king of Uruk, to Aratta, perhaps in southwestern Iran. An obscure passage mentions what may have been a catastrophic local flood (or even *the* flood of Mesopotamian literature):

> After the violence of the flood had raged
> Inanna, the queen of the lands,
> Because she greatly loved Dumuzi,

Sprinkled the water of life on them,
Produced trees for them everywhere in the land.

[*ll.* 573–77; trans. Kramer, *Enmerkar*, p. 43]

The catastrophic flooding of the Tigris and Euphrates, fed by spring rainfall and melting snow at the headwaters, not only laid waste cities along their banks (see below, chap. 3), but caused the rivers to change their courses from time to time (see fig. 1; see also Beek, p. 99, for maps). Cuneiform texts speak of "the old Tigris," for example.

Medieval historians record that floods destroyed entire villages, creating vast swamps where they once were located.[7] Even modern excavators have observed the dangerous consequences of exceptionsl rainfall combined with runoff from snow in the mountains:

... the country would have been submerged beneath hundreds of miles of lake, as happened for the last time in 1954, before the con-

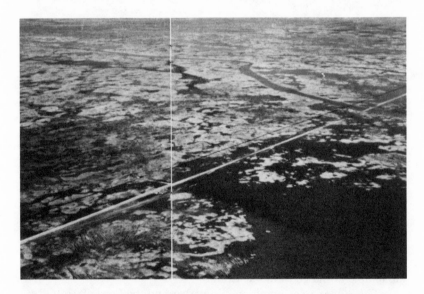

Figure 1. Aerial photograph of the great flood near Badanah in November, 1985. It illustrates clearly the sudden, massive destruction that can take place in the Near East. The caption reads: "From the Trans-Arabian Pipe Line Company plane it was an almost incredible sight: the northern deserts of Saudi Arabia, usually one of the driest areas in the world, transformed into a vast swampland, waves splashing against the pipeline, a great river flowing majestically past lakes and ponds and nibbling hungrily at the edges of the Tapline Road." Courtesy of Aramco World Magazine *(from the issue of March–April, 1968, pp. 32–33).*

struction of the Samarra barrage and dam which now enables sur-
plus Flood-water from the Tigris to be diverted into the Wadi
Tharthar.

[Mallowan, p. 64][8]

V. THE FLOOD FREEZES?

Let us return now to the ancient Iranian account of a great freeze
(see above, chap. 1), since comparison can now be made with the flood
stories of nearby Mesopotamia and with that of Genesis.

The sacred literature of the ancient Zoroastrians (*IDB*, IV: 963;
related to the Magi of the nativity story in Matt. 2:1–12, *IDB*, III:
221–23), contains a work of some length known as the Vendidad.[9] In
chapter 1 it relates that the good deity's (Ahura Mazda's) creation was
attacked in various ways by his evil opponent (Angra Mainyu). In chapter 2 we are introduced to a human in primeval time, named Yima.
Although a mortal, he lives in a world that does not yet know death, and
is appointed by Ahura Mazda to oversee the created order (". . . to nour-
ish, to rule, and to watch over my world," v. 4). So successful was Yima
that, after 300 years, the earth had reached the saturation point. Thereupon Yima enlarged the earth with the aid of implements given to him
by the deity, and the process of fertility continued (vv. 10–11). The en-
largement happens twice more at 300-year intervals, and still the multi-
plication of humans and beasts continues (v. 16). Then (presumably
after another 300 years),[10] Yima is informed by Ahura Mazda of a decision of the heavenly beings:

> 22. O fair Yima. . . . Upon the material world the
> evil winters are about to fall, that shall bring
> the fierce, deadly frost; . . . that shall make
> snow-flakes fall thick, even an *aredvi* deep
> on the highest tops of the mountains.
> 23. And the beasts that live in the wilderness,
> and those that live on the tops of the mountains,
> and those that live in the bosom of the dale shall
> take shelter in underground abodes.
> . . . .
> 25. Therefore make thee a *Vara* [underground enclosure]
> . . . and thither bring the seeds of sheep and oxen, of men, of
> dogs, . . .
> . . . .

25

28. Thither thou shalt bring the seeds of
every kind of tree, of the highest of size
and sweetest of odour on this earth. . . . two of
every kind, to be kept inexhaustible there,
so long as men shall stay in the *Vera*.
. . . . . .

30. . . . thou shalt make nine streets, six in
the middle part, three in the smallest.
. . . That *Vara* thou shalt seal up . . . and thou
shalt make a door, and a window self-shining
within.
. . . .

32. And Yima did as Ahura Mazda wished. . . .

[Trans. Darmesteter]

The following parallels with the "catastrophe" stories of nearby societies have been noticed.[11]

1. The creation of humans is followed by a period of rapid expansion to the point of overpopulation, with which one might compare
Atrahasis (as interpreted by Kilmer).

2. A single human is warned of impending destruction by one
among a group of deities, as is the case in the Mesopotamian accounts
(and by the sole deity in Genesis).

3. This takes place, apparently after a period of 1,200 years (as
noted above; see also n. 10, this chap.). Compare Atrahasis, "Twelve
hundred years had not yet passed when the land extended and peoples
multiplied" (I, *ll.* 352–53). It is interesting to note that, in Genesis 6:1–4,
there is mention of a period of 120 years before the flood (60 × 2, rather
than 60 × 20), but this may be accidental (see app. 5, n. 1).

4. The deity addresses the human directly as in Genesis (but in contrast to Mesopotamian accounts).

5. The *Vara*, an underground enclosure, is square, with which one
might compare the cubic boat of Utnapishtim. Its height is not stated,
although commentaries set all its sides at about two miles.

6. The *Vara* seems to have three levels, as does the boat of Noah.

7. The largest part of the *Vara* is to have nine streets, and the levels
of Utnapishtim's boat are to be divided into nine parts.

8. The mention of "window" and "door" is comparable to Genesis.
Utnapishtim mentions a door and "hatch." However, Yima's "window"
supplies artificial light, since the *Vara* is underground.

9. The command to preserve animals is common to all sources, but

the specification of pairs is found only for animals in Genesis and for seeds in the Vendidad. The Vendidad specifies the saving of 1,000 humans in the upper part, 600 in the middle part, and 300 in the smallest part (v. 30, apparently a division along class lines).

There are other, less evident parallels, such as "the bird Karshipta" (v. 42), a resident of the heavens, "who brought the Religion of (Ahura-) Mazda into the *Vara*." This may be a raven, reminiscent of the birds sent out by both Noah and Utnapishtim (so Schwartz).

On the other hand, the differences are considerable, not merely in the nature of the impending catastrophe (and thus of the means of surviving it), but also in how long humans remain inside their instrument of salvation. The residence in the *Vara* is expected to be long: every forty years, each couple bears a pair of children, a male and a female (v. 41). The lifespan, according to other sources, is 300 years. Presumably, the "great freeze" is an eschatological event, which the inhabitants of the underground enclosure still await in safety.

Given all the parallels, what is the possible relationship of this story to those of Mesopotamia that relate a great deluge? It is possible, on the one hand, that the harsh climate of northern Persia gave rise to the perception that the deities would bring a deadly and sustained winter upon the world. Then the conviction was given literary from through the influence of the Mesopotamian "catastrophe" literature. On the other hand, it is possible that the flood story became known in Persia (either from the Bible or from Babylonian sources) and was adapted to local meteorological realities. In any case, the parallels between the Zoroastrian religion and that of the Hebrew Bible (Old Testament) are far wider than the stories of Yima and Noah.[12]

THREE

IS THERE PHYSICAL EVIDENCE
OF NOAH'S FLOOD?

Acting under the assumption that the biblical account (Gen. 6–9) is a reliable record of what once happened, or at least that a modest historical event gave rise to the present account, some modern interpreters have suggested a variety of causes and pointed to supporting evidence for the reality of Noah's flood. Indeed, it is not unreasonable to suppose that a catastrophic worldwide deluge would have left behind debris that might endure to the present time! The goal of such interpreters, then, has been to establish the date, the extent, and the mechanism by which that great flood came about. In addition, the goal for some of the interpreters has been to prove that the Bible is true in all areas of its description, or at least to strengthen their faith in God.

Two types of evidence have been introduced, archaeological and geological, and they are described in the present chapter. A related topic, "Has Noah's Ark Survived?" will be treated in the next chapter and in appendix 4.

I. ARCHAEOLOGICAL EVIDENCE?

A number of sites (mounds containing ancient habitation) in Mesopotamia, when excavated in the early twentieth century, have yielded a substantial layer of alluvium (i.e., sediment that has been deposited by flowing water). Evidence of human occupation was found both above and below these layers of silt, indicating that a disruption has taken place. Since the age of the deposits[1] corresponded roughly to the time when Noah might be supposed to have lived,[2] it was inevitable that a connection be made with "the flood." Furthermore, these sites were appropriately located, since the biblical account suggested that Noah was a resident of Mesopotamia: Eden was in the vicinity of Assyria and the headwaters of the Euphrates River (Gen. 2:10–14), and Noah's descendants inhabited "the land of Shinar" (Gen. 11:1–2).[3]

Specifically, the following sites produced such layers of alluvium and led to a proposed connection with Noah's flood.[4]

A. Ur

Ancient Ur (the modern Tell al-Muqayyer) was, according to the biblical tradition, the hometown of Abraham (Gen. 11:28, 31). There, during the course of his excavations in 1928–29, Sir Leonard Woolley discovered a layer of "clean water-laid" silt. It varied in thickness[5] up to eleven to twelve feet, and thus perhaps was of such magnitude as to require a deluge of the proportions that Genesis had described! Woolley dated it to the middle of the fourth millennium (i.e., about 3500 B.C.E.) and attributed it to "the Flood of Sumerian history and legend, the Flood on which is based the story of Noah."[6] Less careful descriptions of the layer as evidence of "the Flood" created a sensation around the world.

B. Kish

This lesser known site (the modern Tell al-ʿOheimir) was excavated by Stephen Langdon and Charles Watelin. During the 1928–29 season, they uncovered four alluvial deposits, the uppermost (most recent) of which was about one foot thick.[7] Langdon thought that this layer derived from about 3300 B.C.E. and attributed it to "the Flood of Sumerian legend." The date seemed compatible with that of Woolley's discovery at Ur and thus added to the publicity that remains of "the Flood" had indeed been found.

C. Shuruppak

It was at Shuruppak (the modern Tell Fara) that, according to Sumerian tradition, "the Flood swept thereover."[8] It is not surprising, therefore, that this city was the residence of Utnapishtim, the flood-hero of the Gilgamesh Epic (see above, chap. 2). Eric Schmidt, in the course of the 1930–31 season of excavation here, found an alluvial deposit that was two feet in thickness and that seemed to date from the beginning of the third millennium (i.e., about 3000 B.C.E.).[9]

D. Nineveh

Nineveh (the modern Tell Quyunjik) was once the capital of the Assyrian empire. At this vast site several strata of mud and riverine sand were uncovered, totaling six feet in depth. The excavators (R. C. Thompson and M. E. L. Mallowan) discovered them some fifty-four feet beneath the surface of the mound, during the course of the 1931–32 season. They designated them as evidence of a "pluvial interval" (rather than of "the flood") and assigned them to the fourth millennium.[10]

Other sources are sometimes added to this list of "flood sites," although their excavators were more cautious in the way they described their findings.

E. Uruk

Uruk (the modern Warka) is called "Erech" in the English Bible (Gen. 10:10; Ezra 4:9). This site, near the Persian Gulf, was excavated by Julius Jordan. In the course of the 1929 (?) season, he encountered a "sterile stratum," five feet in depth, which he dated to the beginning of the third millennium B.C.E.[11]

F. Dar i Khazineh

The remains of an ancient village have been uncovered at this location, northeast of the delta on the Karun River in modern Iran. It has been dated by ceramic evidence to the period 4000–3000 B.C.E., and apparently close to the end of that period. Laminated silt, gravel, and sand now cover it to a depth of eight feet. It apparently was occupied for a long period of time ("perhaps thousands" of years), during which an alluvial plain built up around it (suggesting repeated flooding from a stream nearby that is now dry). Finally, flooding made it uninhabitable. (Investigated by R. A. Harmer and A. N. Thomas, as reported in Lees and Falcon, pp. 31–32.)

G. Lagash

At Lagash (the modern Tello, or Tell Luh), André Parrot, in the course of the 1930–31 campaign, uncovered a "sterile layer." He interpreted it as a "sub-foundation of packed soil prepared for subsequent building . . . of one of the temples of Lagash," and assigned it to the early third millennium B.C.E.[12] Nonetheless, one sometimes reads that he there encountered a "flood layer" (see *IDB*, II: 286b: "Alluvial layers similar to those at Ur and Kish have been found at Uruk, Fara (ancient Shuruppak), Telloh (ancient Lagash), and Nineveh.")

H. Evaluation of the Evidence

It is hardly surprising, in view of the number of "sterile" deposits, of their comparable antiquity, and of the considerable thickness of some of them, that Noah's flood not only would come to mind as an explanation, but also that the claim would be made that the biblical account now had independent verification. Thus, Halley's widely read *Pocket Bible Handbook*, having stated that the account in Genesis was handed down by a son of Noah ("He told it as he saw it," p. 73), claims that ". . . an Actual Layer of Mud, evidently deposited by the Flood, has been found in three separate places: Ur, . . . Fara, . . . Kish, . . . possibly, also at a fourth place, Nineveh" (p. 77).[13] Similarly, the popular *Thompson Chain-Reference Bible*, in its fourth improved edition updated (1982), contains an (antiquated) "Archaeological Supplement" in which one reads of Ur: "The most significant find for Bible students was an eight foot water-laid strata of clean clay and sand" (p. 366) and then the author quotes the excavator (Woolley) to the effect that this is evidence of "the flood" that is reflected in the story of Noah.

Early astonishment that these various strata might reflect a single event was soon replaced, in many quarters, by caution if not skepticism. Among the problems that began to emerge were the following.

First, had all of the deposits resulted from the action of water? The excavator at Lagash clearly did not think that this was true of his site. As for the most famous of them, at Ur, an early analysis had raised the possibility that it was eolian (i.e., deposited by wind, as drifting sand) rather than alluvial in origin. A well-known atlas had taken this point of view,[14] but later analysis did not sustain it.[15]

Second, how widespread was the evidence of catastrophic flooding? Did it extend not only throughout Mesopotamia, but beyond into, say,

Syro-Palestine? A number of other sites in Mesopotamia, of equal or greater antiquity, have been excavated down to virgin soil, and no evidence of flooding came to light at them. Perhaps the most important of these is Eridu, located only about seven miles away from Ur. Equally serious is the fact that no site in Syria or Palestine, where archaeologists were equally active during the early part of the present century, has yielded a "flood layer." "In these two countries some of the oldest towns in the world have been excavated . . . (and) show no evidence of a flood . . ." (Bright, *BAR*, I: 33–34).

Third, what was the source of the alluvium? Were there indications that it had been deposited by fresh water (e.g., rainfall and river overflow), as opposed to salt water (e.g., a tidal wave, or a mixing of heavy rainfall with the waters of the oceans in a universal flood)? Microscopic analyses of the silt from Ur indicated that it was "fresh water silt . . . (of) riverine origin."[16] Mud from Kish was characterized by "the absence of fresh-water molluscs as well as by the absence of contemporary marine organisms, and by the presence of terrestrial molluscs" (Mallowan, pp. 74–75; i.e., the deposit likely originated from soil run-off, upstream). The excavators at Nineveh characterized the strata there as "mud and riverine sand" (A. Parrot, p. 51).

That these various "flood deposits" might indeed be riverine is suggested by the location of the sites. All are in close proximity to a major source of flowing water: Nineveh is beside the Tigris; the others are on the course of the Euphrates, or major (but long-vanished) canals, or streams that have since dried up (at Dar i Khazineh; see maps 1 and 2).

If such flooding of the water channels of Mesopotamia actually took place, and with catastrophic consequences for human settlement, we should not be surprised to find abundant literary attestation to it, as has been provided in chapter 2, above.

Further evidence of the source of the flooding to which the alluvial deposits attest, as well as of its limited extent, is provided by the fact that some of the sites were not totally inundated. To be sure, the extent of the flooding at a given site is not always clear, since the excavations were conducted in small areas of the giant mounds rather than removing the entire surface a layer at a time. In the case of the most publicized and substantial of the deposits (at Ur), it became clear from several "trial pits" that the flooding had not overflowed the entire city. The excavator concluded that the city had been situated on an elevation in a marshy area, and that the rising water had caught it most heavily on the side that was exposed to the flow: ". . . the mud was heaped up against the

Map 1.   Map of Mesopotamia, showing places connected with major flooding. From André Parrot, The Flood and Noah's Ark, *p. 33. Courtesy of SCM Press.*

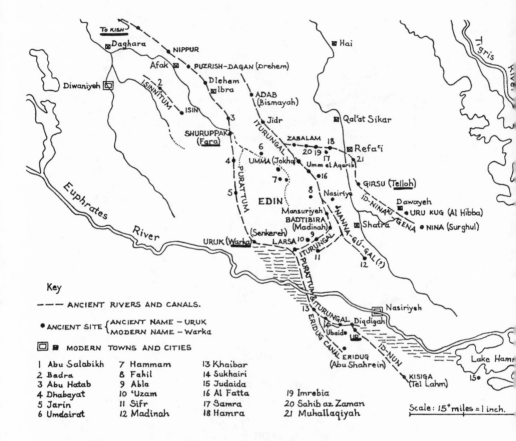

Key

- - - - ANCIENT RIVERS AND CANALS.

● ANCIENT SITE { ANCIENT NAME – URUK
                MODERN NAME – Warka }

▢ ▣ MODERN TOWNS AND CITIES

1 Abu Salabikh	7 Hammam	13 Khaibar
2 Badra	8 Fahil	14 Sukhairi
3 Abu Hatab	9 Abla	15 Judaida
4 Dhabayat	10 'Uzam	16 Al Fatta
5 Jarin	11 Sifr	17 Samra
6 Umdairat	12 Madinah	18 Hamra

19 Imrebia
20 Sahib az Zaman
21 Muhallaqiyah

Scale: 15⁺miles = 1 inch.

Map 2. Map of Sumer, showing the course of ancient rivers and canals. Underlining has been added to t
sites with flood deposits. Reproduced from Iraq, 26 (1964), *Plate XVIII, courtesy of the British School of*
Archaeology in Iraq.

north slope of the town mound which, rising above the plain, broke the force of the flood waters; on the plain east and west of the mound we should probably have found nothing"[17] (see fig. 2).

Fourth, do the various flood deposits attest to a single catastrophe, such that all of lower Mesopotamia might have been inundated? Was there a substantial local event, which might have given rise to the Mesopotamian (if not the biblical) accounts?

While the alluvial deposits at Shuruppak, Uruk, and Kish (its earliest one) may be dated to about 2800 B.C.E. on the basis of ceramic evidence,[18] those at Ur and Nineveh are close to 3500 B.C.E. for the same reason.[19] In particular, Langdon seems to have dated the great deposit at Kish too early by several centuries: rather than 3300 B.C.E. as he suggested, an acceptable date among some archaeologists is now approximately 2600 B.C.E.[20] These results (shown in fig. 3) make it quite clear that there is no archaeological evidence for *the* flood, but rather for *floods*.

Now the question becomes: Which of these floods may be (in Woolley's words) the source of "the Flood of Sumerian history and legend"? That is, with which of these various layers may one connect the accounts

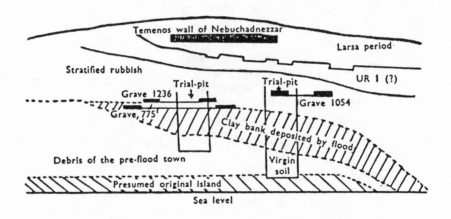

Figure 2. Stratigraphic section of Woolley's excavation at Ur, showing the limited extent of the flooding. From André Parrot, The Flood and Noah's Ark, *p. 46. Courtesy of SCM Press.*

PERIODS	DATES	Ur	Kish	Shuruppak	Uruk	Lagash	Nineveh
Early Dynastic	2470 / 2800		▬		▬	/////////	
Jamdat Nasr	2800 / 3000						
Uruk	IVth Millennium						
Obeid		▬					▬
Halaf							

Figure 3. Comparative chronology of Mesopotamian sites which contain flood deposits. From André Parrot, The Flood and Noah's Ark, *p. 52. Courtesy of SCM Press.*

of Ziusudra, Atrahasis, and Utnapishtim? If the deposit at Ur is to qualify (as Woolley proposed), then one must ignore the claims of the literature itself.

> Shurippak–a city which thou knowest,
> (And) which on Euphrates' [banks] is situate—
> That city was ancient, (as were) the gods within it,
> When their hearts led the great gods to produce the flood.
> [Gilgamesh XI, *ll.* 11–14; Pritchard, p. 93]

This location seems reflected in the Sumerian King List as well.

> . . . kingship to Shuruppak was carried.
> (In) Shuruppak Ubar-Tutu(k)
> became king and reigned 18,600 years.
> 1 king reigned its 18,600 years.
> [In all] five cities were they [Eridu, Bad-tibira(k), Larak, Sippar, and Shuruppak]
> 8 kings reigned their 241,200 years.
> The Flood swept thereover.
> [W–B 444, i, *ll.* 31–39; Jacobsen, *King List*, pp. 75–77]

Since, according to the conception of the author of the King List, "king-ship" resided only in one city at a time, one may well conclude that "swept thereover" refers to Shuruppak where kingship resided at the time (*l.* 31), rather than to the entirety of the previous five cities. Thus we read, in the following lines (40–42):

> After the Flood had swept thereover,
> when the kingship was lowered [again] from heaven
> the kingship was in Kish.

It should be noted, of course, that Woolley made his statement of identification in 1929, at least a year before the excavations at Shurup-pak and well before it was realized that Langdon had assigned a date to the deposit at Kish that was several centuries too early. If Kish, Shurup-pak, and Uruk attest the same catastrophic event, it would not be unreasonable to see that flood as the basis of the Mesopotamian accounts.

Not everyone is convinced that Woolley was necessarily wrong, however. It has been argued by Raikes that an annual flood of the Euphrates, however unusual in magnitude, could not have produced the legendary flood: "The argument has been used, and has considerable weight, that a flood of such size that it became part of the legend of Mesopotamia must have had entirely exceptional causes" (p. 61). Furthermore, flowing water does not deposit alluvium of the depths recorded at Ur and Shuruppak; rather, "long sustained and deep flooding," with still waters, would be required (p. 60). "Still water conditions would only be achieved by impounding the water through the operation of some hitherto unidentified phenomenon. This could have taken the form of either local uplift or local subsidence" (p. 62). (For more cautious statements by Raikes, see below, this chap., "Geological Evidence.")

I. NOAH'S FLOOD

What may be said about the account in Genesis, based solely upon the available archaeological evidence that has been presented above?

On the one hand, if the biblical account is to be accepted as historically accurate in its details (e.g., the flood was worldwide), and if one is to accept the "traditional" date of that event as computed by Archbishop

Ussher (2349 B.C.E.; see n. 2), then one must conclude either *(a)* that the flood happened as stated and has left no archaeological remains in Mesopotamia or Syro-Palestine, or *(b)* that the biblical account has no basis in fact. The former conclusion would strain the credulity of the unbiased person. The latter conclusion is unduly skeptical, given what is known about the early chapters of the Bible (for which, see below, chap. 5).

On the other hand, if the "traditional" date is a miscalculation of the biblical data (on which, see below), then one might propose either *(a)* that the date be set back a few centuries, and thus it could coincide with the flood-layers and literature of Mesopotamia, in which case one could speak of a historical event, although local in scope, or *(b)* that the date be set back several millennia, in support of which geological evidence might be introduced, some of it attesting to flooding on a global scale.

It is the second of these options (i.e., revision of Ussher's chronology) that almost all modern interpreters have chosen. There remains, however, a spirited debate between advocates of the two approaches within it. Perhaps the majority of biblical scholars within "main-line" Protestantism and within Roman Catholicism prefer the "local-flood" option. Perhaps the majority of those biblical scholars who would characterize themselves as "conservative" advocate a "universal flooding" (and some, a "universal flood").

Has, then, archaeology given us evidence of "the flood"? On the one hand, noted biblical historian John Bright remarks, "Archaeology has given us no trace of it" *(BAR*, I:37). On the other hand, well-known archaeologist M. E. L. Mallowan states concerning the early flood-deposits at Kish: ". . . one of them may have been the . . . Genesis Flood" and concerning that at Shuruppak: ". . . identifiable with the . . . Genesis flood" (plate XX). It all depends upon how one defines "the flood."

II. GEOLOGICAL EVIDENCE?

If one felt that the "traditional" chronology (Ussher's) for the events in Genesis 1–11 was a miscalculation, or that it was entirely unreliable, then one could propose that Noah's flood happened at a much earlier time than excavation of Mesopotamian mounds might attest. As for Syro-Palestine, excavations at Jericho have revealed that the earliest occupation there was prior to 8000 B.C.E. (*IDBS*, pp. 472–73), with no evidence of disruption by a great flood. Was it prior to that?

On what basis could one continue to trust biblical chronology, and yet reject Ussher's calculations? The following proposals have been offered (Whitcomb and Morris, pp. 474–89).

First, Ussher based himself upon (English?) texts of the Bible, which would reflect the Masoretic (Hebrew) tradition. However, the Greek Bible (Septuagint) has an "extra" generation: the name Cainan appears between Arpachshad and Shelah at Genesis 10:24, reflected in the New Testament at Luke 3:36.[21] (For further discussion of this "extra" generation, see below, chap. 5.) If one generation has been skipped over, might there be many more?

Second, the expressions "begat" and "the son of" may sometimes denote more remote descendants than the very next generation, and this would allow for "gaps" in the genealogies. For example, Matthew 1:8 records that "Joram (was) the father of Uzziah," whereas the line of descent actually was: Joram-Ahaziah-Joash-Amaziah-Uzziah (Azariah), according to 2 Kings 8:24; 11:2, 21; 12:21; 14:21. That is, there were three additional generations. TEV handles the matter adeptly by stating: "the following ancestors are listed," and thus deleting the many usages of the word "father."

Third, one might conclude that the major purpose of the genealogies in the early chapters of Genesis "was more than simply chronological . . . it is unnecessary to press them into a rigid chronological system" (Whitcomb and Morris, p. 477).

With such revisions of Ussher's chronology in mind, it has been proposed that a universal flood occurred "several hundred thousand years ago," or that a modest flood (which still destroyed all human life) occurred at least 15,000 years ago, or that a catastrophic local flood (without destroying all humans on earth) occurred a bit less than 10,000 years ago,[22] or that a universal deluge indeed destroyed all life on earth (save for Noah's family and sea creatures) less than 10,000 years ago (the choice of Whitcomb and Morris, pp. 488–89). (For further discussion of the nature of the genealogies in Gen. 1–11, see below, chap. 5 and app. 3.)

Those interpreters who have turned to geological and paleontological evidence for an early date for the flood (of whatever extent) have made at least the following proposals for the mechanism by which the deluge came about.

A. Earthquake and Tidal Wave

Edward Suess (professor of geology at the University of Vienna), working in conjunction with a well-known expert in Ancient Near Eastern literature (Paul Haupt, of Johns Hopkins University), proposed that a violent storm coincided with an earthquake and generated a devastating tidal wave, which struck lower Mesopotamia.[23] He suggested that the following data supported such an interpretation of the biblical account. First, "The fountains of the great deep burst forth" (Gen. 7:11). Jets of water, sometimes shooting many feet into the air, are a common occurrence during earthquakes. "Such phenomena have never been observed on any great scale except in extensive low-lying districts, where subterranean water is present, nor would they be explicable under any other conditions." That is, the Mesopotamian plain would qualify well. Second, the coincidence of cyclone and earthquake is otherwise attested in the Pacific area (e.g., in 1737 and 1780 C.E.), resulting in thousands of deaths. Third, the Mesopotamian flood stories suggest that the ark was driven by the storm in a direction contrary to the flow of the Tigris and Euphrates. That is, Utnapishtim's boat was constructed at Shuruppak and came to rest on Mount Nisir (Gilgamesh XI, *ll.* 141–44). The mountain is likely the modern Omar Gudrun/Pira Magrun (see below, chap. 4, sec. III, A, 3) and thus the boat was driven toward the north, from the direction of the Persian Gulf. Fourth, Mesopotamia is geologically unstable, and thus has often been the location of earthquakes.

It should be noted that Suess' proposal was made in 1885, and thus before the aforementioned archaeological evidence came to light. That evidence, uncovered in the 1920s and 1930s, indicates that the flood levels are of riverine origin and were largely local in scope. It does not support a massive and widespread calamity such as a tidal wave would have produced.

Why, then, would the story of Utnapishtim's flood have depicted the ark as having floated to the north, against the flow of the rivers? Likely because that is the direction of the high mountains atop which the boat was *assumed* to have lodged. Otherwise, it would have followed the overflowing rivers out into the Persian Gulf.

B. Glacial Melt

The last Ice Age, which apparently began about 30,000 years ago, caused northern Europe and much of North America (as far south as

Ohio) to be covered with an ice cap that was hundreds of feet thick. Consequently, the accumulation of water in the cap resulted in a drop of sea level around the world to nearly 400 feet below where it now stands. The subsequent melt may not have been uniform and gradual, but rather, may have reached a sudden peak about 11,600 years ago. This is said to be evident from a sudden and massive infusion of fresh water into the Gulf of Mexico at that time. This reduced the Gulf's salinity and produced a measurable and datable change in the chemical composition of one-celled marine organisms known as Foraminifera, whose fossils survive to the present time.

The resultant sudden rise in sea level could have been catastrophic along the gently sloping shelves of the Persian Gulf. "Man was forced to move inland, and this universal migration might have created the memory of a universal flood."[4]

However, the traditional interpretation has been that the glacial melt was gradual, perhaps no more than a foot in sea-level rise in twenty to thirty years. Moreover, how would one account for the statements (in both Mesopotamian and biblical literature) that the waters of the flood remained in place for some time (as a tidal wave would not) and that the flood-heroes had plenty of warning of impending disaster (which neither sudden glacial melt nor tidal wave would produce)?

Such questions led petroleum geologist Walter S. Olson to offer a variation on the Ice Age explanation (in *Zygon*). About 19,000 years ago, the sea stood about 390 feet lower than at present. United States Navy hydrographic charts of the Persian Gulf area can be used to plot the shoreline as it then would have existed (i.e., the 65-fathom contour). At that depth, two basins emerge, each much smaller than the present Gulf, and separated from each other by a ridge, which crests at about the 35-fathom line (i.e., about 180 feet down from the present surface). About 11,500 years ago, the glacial melt pushed the rising sea northward over the lower basin until it approached the top of the ridge that separated it from the upper one. When the sea overflowed the ridge, it quickly eroded a deep channel (still visible on the contour map) and allowed a sudden and massive infusion of water to race up the upper basin until its depth reached the contour of the channel on the ridge. Survivors might have fled to the mountain heights to the east (the foothills of the Zagros range), where settlement seems to have begun about 9000 B.C.E. (according to archaeological remains). The Gulf continued to rise, reaching its present level around 5000–4000 B.C.E.

Data on sea-level changes in the area of the Persian Gulf over the last 18,000 years may be found in Brice (chap. 15). The figures are not substantially different from those of Walter Olson (see map 3).

Olson's original and plausible conjecture of an early flood in the area of the Gulf leaves several questions unanswered with respect to the flood literature. Is this the flood of Utnapishtim, which has been transferred to a much later time and localized at Shuruppak? How could such a tradition have survived, in oral form, for some 6,000 years? Why not have the survivors escape on foot to the high mountains, as some flood accounts do (see above, chap. 1), if that is in fact what happened? If the Mesopotamian accounts refer to much later and riverine flooding, is the catastrophe in the upper basin of the Gulf uniquely remembered as Noah's flood?

An interesting textual support for a glacial-melt explanation for Ancient Near Eastern flooding has recently emerged in J. Van Dijk's interpretation of a Sumerian composition known as *Lugal-e ud melambi nirgal*.[25] The title means "King, Storm, the Glory of which is Noble" and is commonly shortened by modern interpreters to *Lugal-e*. Its hero is the god Ninurta (whose connection with the flooding of the river Tigris has been mentioned above, in chap. 2). Therein, one reads of his role in bringing fertility to the land of Sumer (Tablet VIII, *ll.* 1–25).

A standard interpretation sees this section of *Lugal-e* as a myth, which "humanizes the power behind the yearly flood into a young king undertaking major irrigation works."

> At that time the waters of the earth coming from below
>   did not come pouring over the fields,
> (nay!) as ice long accumulating they rose in
>   the mountains on the other side.
> The gods of the country who were stationed there,
>   who carried pickaxes and baskets
> and whose assigned tasks were thus,
> poured it, according to what they had first
>   chopped off (from it), on a man's field.
> The Tigris, for which a great fate (was decreed?),
>   did not rise in flood,
> its outlet did not take it straight into the sea,
>   did not carry sweet water.
> At the quay no one dipped (?) a water pail,
>   in dire famine nothing was produced,
> [Trans. Jacobsen, *Treasures*, p. 130]

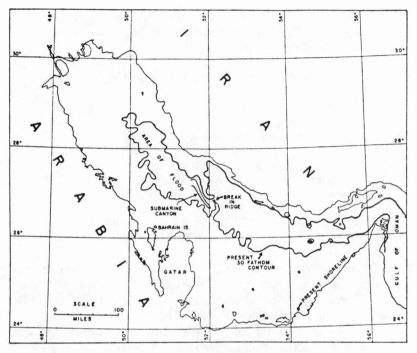

Map 3. Map of the Persian Gulf, showing the area flooded catastrophically by a rise in sea level. (Based on interpretation of bathymetric data from Hydrographic Chart H.O. 3647 of the Persian Gulf.) Reproduced from Olson, courtesy of Zygon.

43

Ninurta, in order to remedy the situation, erects a great stone wall (the Zagros Mountains?), which channels the fertilizing waters of the Tigris southward through the land of Sumer.

> The Lord directed (his) great intelligence to it,
> . . . .
> He made a heap of stones in the mountains—
> . . . .
> The mighty waters followed along the stone.
> . . . .
> what in the mountains had been consumed by swamps
> he gathered and threw it into the Tigris.
>
> [Trans. Jacobsen, *Treasures*, p. 131]

The resultant irrigation projects allowed for the production of food in abundance, earning for Ninurta the adulation of humans and deities alike.

The text, apparently composed at the time of King Gudea of Lagash (Jacobsen, *Treasures*, p. 131), would thus be concerned with the establishment of the annual hydraulic cycle, a portrait of Ninurta likewise expressed in the king's vision-report (see above, chap. 2).

Quite a different interpretation has been proposed by Van Dijk (1983), as part of his reconstruction of *Lugal-e* from some 200 scattered tablets and fragments, producing a sequentially numbered work that is more than 700 lines long. He regards the aforementioned section (*ll.* 333–58 of his text) as crucial to the whole, and sees therein a reference to "le déluge" (see I: 31–34).

> 334. At that time, when the salubrious water no longer left the
>   earth, it did not rise over the fields,
> 335. since the ice, which was packed everywhere, on the day it
>   started to melt, caused destruction in the Mountain,
> 336. (and) since because of that the gods of the country were
>   subjected to servitude,
> 337. thus they had to carry the axe and the basket,
> . . . .
> 340. The Tigris in its plain had not (yet) r[isen] its flood.
> . . . .
> 334. Nobody (yet) cleaned the canals, nobody dredged the silt,
>   [Trans. Lloyd Bailey, from the French of Van Dijk, I: 93–94][26]

To Van Dijk, this is not a myth (which he defines as personification of concepts) concerning the annual cycle of nature, but rather, is "semi-history": the situation it describes "corresponds well with the development of agriculture following the last postglacial period" (I: 34).

He bolsters his interpretation by pointing to a number of other texts that seem to depict the beginnings of agriculture as part of a "second creation" following a flood (beginning with BM 23103, cited above in chap. 2):

1. After the Flood had swept over
2. and had brought about the destruction of the land—
. . . .
13. (and) they had not (yet) established (for)
             the countless overwhelmed people
. . . .
22. Canals were not dug,
23. dyke-ditches were not dredged;
. . . .
56. they established for the people
57. the spade, the hoe, the basket, (and) the plough
. . . .

[Trans. Sollberger, pp. 282–83]

Van Dijk then concludes: "It seems to me also that the two texts [*Lugal-e* and BM 23103] refer to the same flood . . . which preceded the 'second creation,' which is known from the accounts of Gilgamesh, the Bible, Atrahasis, etc." (I: 31). Such a deluge, preceding the postglacial evolution of agriculture in Mesopotamia, obviously would have no connection with the alluvial strata at sites such as Ur (I: 33).

Van Dijk refers only obliquely to Noah's flood. Presumably he does so because of the following sequence of events, parallel to the texts that he cites:

The sons of Noah who went forth from the ark were Shem, Ham, and Japheth. . . . Noah was the first tiller of the soil.

[Gen. 9:18, 20 RSV]

Concerning Van Dijk's interpretation, a foremost Sumerologist (Samuel Noah Kramer) has this to say: "The two lines on which Van Dijk's conclusions are largely based, lines 334–335, pose numerous problems in both reading and meaning . . . Van Dijk's rendering which is justified by two brief notes only . . . has much in its favor, and may turn out to be correct, but still needs further corroboration."[27] He speaks of the adequacy of the translation, not of its reference to a known historical event.

C. Tectonic Activity

The crust of the earth beneath the Mesopotamian plain is pressed from either side by the masses of Arabia and Iran. This has produced a line of fold mountains to the east and has caused the floor of the plain to undulate, which has resulted generally in subsidence. Such tectonic activity allowed the head of the Persian Gulf to progress northward as early as the Pliocene Era (about 13 million years ago). This is evident from core (drilling) samples, which reveal considerable levels of marine fossils at some distance from the present Gulf. Nearly one hundred miles inland, for example, such deposits may be found thirty-five feet below the present surface of the plain (Lees and Falcon, p. 37). Such inundations usually were gradual, and the Gulf has been pushed back by alluvial deposits from the rivers and by wind-blown soil from the surrounding areas.

If the flooding at Ur and simultaneously (?) at other nearby lowland sites evidences "deep flooding by still water," which brief river overflow could not provide, then a dramatic subsidence might have provided the occasion (Raikes). However, Lees and Falcon had already stated that there is no evidence of marine incursion since very ancient times (the Pliocene Era) and subsequent studies of the deltaic sediments have verified their opinion (Larsen and Evans, p. 238). At most, then, tectonic forces might have produced a slight uplift, which impounded part of the rivers' water, deepened the marshes in the delta, and made low-lying villages uninhabitable.

D. A Vapor Canopy

The geological evidence cited thus far would account for a worldwide inundation of only coastal areas, or for a sudden catastrophe only regionally (the Persian Gulf). It cannot be used to support an event of the magnitude that Genesis describes: ". . . all the high mountains under the whole heaven were covered . . . covering them fifteen cubits deep" (Gen. 7:19–20).[28] If that claim is not to be set aside as hyperbole (exaggeration)[29] or otherwise not allowed by the nature of the literature in the "primeval story" (see below, chap. 5), then a major problem arises. The normal hydrological cycle (evaporation and condensation of water vapor) would not be sufficient to account for the flood: "If all the water in our present atmosphere were suddenly precipitated, it would only suffice to cover the ground to an average depth of less than two inches" (Whitcomb and Morris, p. 121).

How, then, might the amount of water sufficient to meet the requirements of Genesis have been provided? Perhaps by a "great vapor canopy," which could have surrounded the earth. It would not initially have contributed to the earth's rainfall, since its height might have been such that atmospheric particles (the necessary nuclei for condensation as rain) had not reached it. Could this be the implications of Gen. 2:5-6, "... the Lord God had not caused it to rain upon the earth ..."? How long could that situation have prevailed? "... there is no mention made of any change in this meteorological phenomenon ... so it evidently continued until the time of the Deluge" (Whitcomb and Morris, p. 241). Then, presumably at God's bidding, nuclei for condensation were introduced into the vapor canopy, precipitating the great flood: "... possibly the passage of the earth through a meteorite swarm or the sudden extrusion of large amounts of volcanic dust into the air" resulted in the biblical report that "the flood-gates of heaven were opened" (Whitcomb and Morris, p. 258).

The concept of a vapor canopy as the source of Noah's flood goes back at least to Isaac N. Vail (1840–1912), who published a number of papers on the subject.[30] He based his idea (which has come to be called "the Vailian Ring-Canopy Theory") upon what he perceived to be the requirements of the early chapters of Genesis, and apparently upon telescopic observations that the planets Jupiter and Saturn were surrounded by bands of darkness and light (allowing him to project a parallel with a young earth).

It is the more recent (and self-styled) "Creationists" who have developed the "canopy theory" into a full-scale explanation for the biblical flood.[31] Advocates Whitcomb and Morris have proposed that the earth itself is only a few thousand years old, and that God created it "with an appearance of age," which has misled others into thinking that it is billions of years old. As for the flood, to date it as much as 5,000 years before Abraham "stretches Genesis 11 almost to the breaking point" (p. 489). Thus, while allowing a date as early as 7000 B.C.E., Morris believes that "there is nothing really impossible or unreasonable about the traditional date of 4004 B.C." for creation (i.e., Ussher's date).[32]

From this point of view, evidence of Noah's flood abounds in fossilized animal remains, in thick water-laid rock layers in the earth, and in evidence of violent disruption of the rock strata. All of these, it is proposed by Creationists, have been commonly misunderstood by geologists and paleontologists who have transformed them into "a supposed rock record of gradual organic evolution" (Whitcomb and Morris, p. 271). Thus the various methodologies that have been used by such scientists to

47

fix the age of the earth at billions of years are each said to be conceptually or methodologically flawed and thus to be unreliable (pp. 331–78). (Such methods include the measurement of radioactive decay [e.g., the disintegration of uranium and thorium into lead, or potassium into argon], radiocarbon dating [for which see below, chap. 4, sec. VI, A], the Doppler Effect in relation to galactic motion, the erosion of deep gorges by running water, the depth and extent of sedimentary deposits in river deltas, the accumulation of deposits in caves and lake beds, and so on.)

As for the close literary parallels between the biblical and the Mesopotamian flood stories (see above, chap. 2), the latter apparently tied to local floods of riverine origin, Whitcomb and Morris remark: ". . . Genesis gives us God's inspired record of that great catastrophe," whereas the Mesopotamian account is "a serious corruption of the original facts . . ." (p. 488).

E. An Extraterrestrial Origin

The Bible relates two episodes that, if the description is accurate in its particulars, might lead a modern interpreter to siphon off some of the geological data that Creationists attribute to the flood and then to apply them in explanation of those episodes. I speak of, first, the plagues that befell Egypt at the time of Moses (Exod. 7–12), namely, waters of the Nile turning to blood, frogs, gnats, flies, disease of cattle, boils, hail, locusts, darkness, and death of people, and, second, the twofold reversal of the sun's motion in the sky, as observed on the sundial of King Ahaz (Isa. 38:7–8).

Immanuel Velikovsky (b. 1895), with university studies in medicine (M.D.), law, history, and natural sciences, noticed references in a wide range of ancient literature that he thought described those same two biblical events. That is, the events were not local, but were part of worldwide cataclysms. In addition, there was a vast amount of geological and paleontological evidence for widespread natural catastrophes: fractures and uplift of the earth's strata, reversals of the earth's magnetic pole, earthquakes and volcanic activity, massive extinction of life-forms, and so on. Could such evidence be compressed into a few great events and then related to the literary evidence?

Velikovsky thus proposed that, during the fifteenth century B.C.E., the planet Jupiter had spun out a large mass of material, which then assumed a cometlike form and passed through the orbit of the earth.

48

This slowed the earth's rotation, resulting in earthquakes, tidal waves, meteorites, and (as the earth passed through the tail of the comet) darkness. This was, then, the basis of the series of plagues that befell Pharaoh's kingdom, and this seemed especially compelling, since (according to the "traditional" chronology of Archbishop Ussher), the exodus from Egypt was to be dated to the middle of this same century.

The "pillar of cloud" by day and the "pillar of fire" by night were the tail of the comet (see Exod. 13:21–22). Carbon and hydrogen from the comet combined with material in the earth's atmosphere to produce "manna," which rained down upon the Hebrews as they journeyed through the Sinai Wilderness (Exod. 16:13–21).

The comet's erratic orbit soon produced another near collision with the earth: at the time of Joshua, it affected the earth's rotation, making the sun and moon appear to "stand still" (Josh. 10:12–14), causing earthquakes and volcanic action, and resultant tidal waves around the world. The comet then settled into orbit and became what is now known as the planet Venus. It was not its present, regular orbit, however, but a much larger and erratic one, which would lead it into later collision with other planets.

In the eighth century B.C.E., Venus thus collided with Mars and changed both orbits. Mars then came near the earth a number of times, resulting in great natural disasters, an elongation of the earth's year, and a shift in the inclination of the earth's axis. This is reflected, in the Bible, in the account of the sun's shadow being displaced on the sundial of King Ahaz of Judah.

Such radical ideas about astronomy[33] and geology,[34] combined with unusual literary interpretations and a radical revision of the chronology of the Ancient Near East,[35] produced a storm of negative reaction from scholars in each field (including astronomers who later confessed to not having read Velikovsky's works and biblical scholars who attempted to organize a boycott against his publishers).[36] However, his ideas were sometimes well received in the popular press, and admirers founded magazines in which to discuss his ideas (e.g., *Pensée; Kronos; Society for Interdisciplinary Studies Review*). Subsequent realization of Velikovsky's serious misunderstanding of ancient texts, as well as of his serious scientific errors, has eroded his influence even among ardent admirers, both religious[37] and secular.

Thus the geological and paleontological evidence, which Creationists had introduced in support of Noah's flood, Velikovsky usurped for his own purposes. What, then, had he to say about the causes of that great deluge? Apparently he had planned to write a volume on this very topic. He remarks, *"Worlds in Collision* comprises only the last two acts of the cosmic drama. A few earlier acts—one of them known as the Deluge—will be the subject of another volume of natural history"* (p. xvi of *Worlds*). More than two decades later, with that promised volume not completed, he remarks: "In my understanding, less than 10,000 years ago, together with the Earth, the moon went through a cosmic cloud of water (the Deluge) and subsequently was covered for several centuries with water, which dissociated under the ultra-violet rays of the sun, with hydrogen escaping into space."[38]

An extraterrestrial origin for the flood-waters was likewise proposed by Donald W. Patten.[39] He suggested that an "astral visitor," either surrounded by ice-rings or accompanied by an ice satellite, passed near the earth. A superior gravitational field could have resulted in the transfer of the ice to the earth, and especially to its poles (if the crystals had become electrically charged). Subsequent melt, combined with a decay of a vapor canopy, plus "water from the foundations of the deep," produced Noah's flood.

Such suggestions, repeatedly laced with "if," have had a very narrow hearing.

F. Dust, Rather Than Rain

Quite a different geological approach to the origins of the Mesopotamian flood story has been proposed by J. V. Kinnier Wilson. He points to the remains of a massive landslide, presumably triggered by an earthquake, which took place about 9500 B.C.E. on the Saidmarreh (Kharkheh) River in the foothills of the Zagros Mountains to the east of Mesopotamia. Several cubic miles of debris were propelled down the slope, some of it coming to rest as much as ten miles from its point of origin, and damming the courses of the river's tributaries.

There is reason to believe that the area of the landslide (now called Kabir Kuh) was the ancient Mount Ebih, the location of events in a Sumerian mythological text known as "Inanna and Ebih." The goddess Inanna's attack upon the area is described in terms that may be associated with earthquake imagery. Wilson's proposal is that memory of a natural event has been preserved in the mythological text and also in many other texts that deal with divine conquest of "the rebel land." In one of them *(Lugal-e)* the god Ninurta controls dangerous flood waters by building a great stone wall (the damming of the river by the landslide?). One of the weapons in the divine battle was a "storm" (Sumerian: *amaru*; Akkadian: *abubu*), possibly referring to the cloud of dust, natural gas, and smoke that must have arisen from the landslide, and which blotted out the sun and was destructive to life in a wide surrounding area. But, suggests Wilson, since the term *abubu* can also mean a rainstorm, "the early story-tellers no longer believed in a huge cloud of smoke and dust which turned day into night for seven days, and began to retell the story in terms of a cloud of rain" (p. 112).

Wilson's innovative interpretation of Sumerian mythological texts has failed to win acceptance for a variety of reasons. Among them are the following: the difficulty of oral transmission of the story for 6,000 years (also assumed by other explanations, above); the assumption that jets of flaming natural gas accompanied the landslide, producing smoke (for this there is no geological evidence, and Wilson apparently has suggested it in order to meet the requirements of certain of the descriptions in the texts); and the attempt to explain a great number of apparently unrelated texts by this single natural phenomenon.[40]

G. Conclusions

Is there geological evidence for "the flood"? That glacial melt (at the end of the last Ice Age) produced flooding of coastal areas around the world is apparently widely accepted. That such melt may have led to a sudden and catastrophic flooding in the area of the Persian Gulf is plausible in view of contour lines beneath the present level. However, evidence of a worldwide inundation of the magnitude that Genesis describes is lacking, in the opinion of the vast majority of modern interpreters (be they "secular" or "religious" in orientation).

Such "evidence" for Noah's flood emerges only if one rejects the methodologies and conclusions of modern astronomers, geologists, and paleontologists, namely, that the earth is a few billion years old; and if one assumes that the Bible was intended to be a textbook in those very areas (i.e., that its "inspiration" is inseparably related to those topics). To the nature of the early chapters of Genesis we will turn in chapter 5, below.

Has the latter point of view heavily influenced the Creationist position, outlined above? Morris (and others) strenuously deny that their approach is anything other than scientifically objective: so-called Scientific Creationism (also called Creation Science) is based upon physical data only, and leads independently to the same conclusions as so-called Biblical Creationism.[41] Statements such as the following, however, may lead one to wonder if this is so.

But if we are willing to accept in faith the account of Creation as simple, literal truth, then we immediately have a most powerful *tool for understanding all the facts of geology* in proper perspective.

[Whitcomb and Morris, pp. 238–39; italics added]

. . . the *instructed* Christian knows that the evidences for full divine inspiration of Scripture are *far weightier than the evidence for any fact of science.* When confronted with the consistent Biblical testimony to a universal Flood, the believer must certainly accept it as unquestionably true.

[Whitcomb and Morris, p. 118; italics added]

It becomes very important, therefore, for Christians to re-study and re-think the great mass of geological and paleontological data . . . to determine wherein . . . it is at variance with the Biblical record of creation and the Flood. If this geological scheme is basically fallacious, *as we have had to decide that it must be,* then we need to try to understand why . . . a great body of responsible scientists have accepted it as true.

[Whitcomb and Morris, p. 119; italics added]

In view of such statements, it is hardly surprising that U.S. District Court Judge William R. Overton enjoined the Arkansas Board of Education from implementing the "Balanced Treatment for Creation-Science and Evolution-Science Act," on January 5, 1982. The judicial opinion stated that the Act "was simply and purely an effort to introduce the Biblical version of creation into the public school curricula. The only inference which can be drawn from these circumstances is that the Act was passed with the specific purpose by the General Assembly of advancing religion."[42]

A similar statute, enacted by the State of Louisiana, was struck down by the Federal District Court. The State appealed to the United States Supreme Court, which ruled decisively on June 19, 1987, that statutory requirement for equal time for "creation science" in the public schools was unconstitutional under the Establishment Clause.[43]

FOUR

HAS NOAH'S ARK SURVIVED?

I. Preliminary Considerations

The belief that the great boat (ark) in which a family had escaped the waters of a worldwide flood could still be viewed at its original landing site began to be attested in the Near East in the late pre-Christian period. Reports of its survival continued through the Middle Ages and have intensified in the Christian West in the nineteenth and twentieth centuries. A number of books have appeared in the 1970s and 1980s, some of them best sellers, offering detailed reasons for believing, not ony that the ark of Noah had survived relatively intact atop a mountain in eastern Turkey, but that parts of it had been recovered and were on display in France. A large number of articles concerning this matter have appeared in newspapers (e.g., *New York Times; Grit*), magazines (e.g., *Life; Reader's Digest*), and religious publications (e.g., *Christian Century*). Even wider interest has been generated by a number of movies, one of which has been shown on prime-time network television (*In Search of Noah's Ark*, NBC, May 2 and Dec. 24, 1977). It probably is safe to say that there are few persons in the United States who are unaware of this topic.

Some of those who are actively involved in the search for the ark have, with a mixture of humor and seriousness, coined the term "arkeology" to describe their activity, and they have organized a number of expeditions to the upper reaches of "Mount Ararat." This mountain, which they believe to satisfy the geographical requirements of Genesis

53

8:4, is a spectacular 16,950-foot peak near the Turkish border with Russia and Iran. It is called Büyük ("Big") Ağri Daği (or Dağ) by the Turks (pronounced: äri̇ däi̇), Jabal al-Harith by the Muslim historians, and Masis by the ancient Armenians.[1]

Evidence for the ark's survival, as presented in the various popular publications and movies, usually is of four types: (1) ancient reports that it could still be seen, beginning as early as the third century B.C.E., and continuing thereafter in Jewish, Christian, and Muslim sources; (2) modern eyewitness accounts that an intact wooden structure stands at the snow line on "Mount Ararat" (at about 13,500 feet), and that its dimensions agree with the biblical description of Noah's ark; (3) photographs, allegedly showing a boat-shaped structure said to be located high on the mountain, taken from the ground, from aircraft, and by satellite; (4) hand-hewn beams said to have been recovered from beneath a glacier at the snow line and to have been assigned an age of 5,000 years by supposedly reputable agencies, thus allowing the beams to be old enough to meet the requirements of a literal biblical chronology for the flood.

While this topic has understandably caught the popular interest, biblical scholars at major academic institutions have almost totally ignored it. Consequently, there is scarcely a source to which interested persons can go for an informed, calm, nonpolemical investigation of the claims that are being made. It is crucial that such an investigation be undertaken, since some of the books by ark-searchers (a term that this writer will use hereafter instead of "arkeologist") are flawed by misunderstandings and misuse of the ancient sources, by the use of "evidence" that most other investigators have discredited, and by a failure to investigate the accuracy of some of the tests used to arrive at an age of 5,000 years for the "ark wood." It is also obvious that some of the ark-searchers seem to have made up their minds prior to an objective examination of the evidence.

Among the questions that must be asked concerning the claim that parts of the ark have been recovered from "Mount Ararat" are the following:

1. The ark came to rest upon "the mountains of Ararat." First of all, where is "Ararat"? Is the "Mount Ararat" that is the focus of modern investigation (Büyük Ağri Daği) the same site as indicated in Genesis 8:4? Do the early reports of the ark's survival all point to the same site? How many Noah's arks have been discovered, and where?

2. What do the ancient reports say? Do they all deal with the biblical Noah? Have any of the writers personally seen the remains? Is the

mentality and worldview of the ancient reporters so congenial with our own that their word can be accepted without question?

3. Are the recent eyewitness accounts in general agreement? Are the witnesses still living so that they may authenticate the stories attributed to them? If not, have the stories been reliably transmitted? Have some of them been exposed as fabrications? How well do their details accord with the known geography of the mountain?

4. Are the objects in the photos undeniably a boat, or is there disagreement? Are all of the photos genuine?

5. How reliable are the testing methods that resulted in an age determination of 5,000 years? Are all the results in agreement? Has evidence appeared since the last popular presentation, that is, since the movie?

6. If there is a wooden structure of considerable age near the top of Büyük Ağri Daği, is it automatically to be acknowledged as Noah's ark? Are there reasonable options to this conclusion? What ancient reports are there of other structures on this mountain?

7. How might a massive structure, regardless of its nature, have got to such a difficult height? Since there are no trees on Büyük Ağri Daği, should one reasonably conclude that the heavy timbers must have floated there from a great distance? What do we know about the mountain in antiquity? Was it always barren?

II. WHERE WAS BIBLICAL ARARAT?

The ark, says the writer of Genesis, came to rest "upon the mountains of Ararat." Presumably we have on the best evidence (it says so in the Bible) a definite landing place for Noah's ark. But note that there are several mountains involved; "Mount Ararat" as such never appears in the Bible.

Problems arise immediately, however, when we ask "Where was Ararat?" What did the biblical writers have in mind by the term? Is there any way we today can discover just what they meant? Fortunately, we can get some clues. Genesis 8:4 is the only place in the Bible where the landing place of the ark is mentioned, and it is clear that an individual peak is not singled out. This is in agreement with other biblical writers, who use the term "Ararat" to indicate a considerably larger area. The assassins of Sennacherib, king of Assyria, flee northward from Meso-

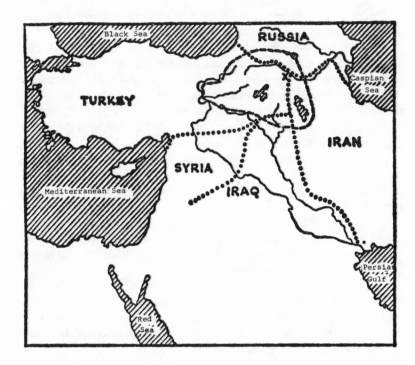

Map 4. Boundaries of the ancient kingdom of Urartu (the "Ararat" of the Bible), super-imposed upon modern boundaries.

- - - - - -   *Ancient boundary of Urartu*

. . . . . .   *modern boundaries*

x   *location of the mountain Ağri Daği*

potamia to "the land of Ararat" (2 Kings 19:37; Isa. 37:38). Jeremiah summons "kingdoms" from the north for war against the Babylonians: "Ararat, Minni, and Ashkenaz" (Jer. 51:27).

Ararat would thus seem to be a mountainous area of some extent, a political "kingdom" north a Mesopotamia, bordering the ancient lands of Minni and Ashkenaz. A precise location cannot easily be assigned to Ashkenaz. Its people seem to have been nomadic Scythians from beyond the Caucasus Mountains who settled in the plain of the Araxes River and northward. But the kingdom of Minni is known from Assyrian records (where it is called Manna) to have been southeast of Lake Urmia. Thus the kingdom of Ararat likely would be located between

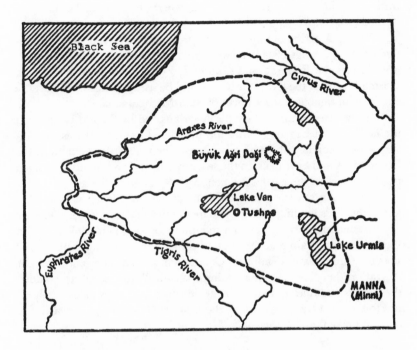

Map 5.   Boundaries of the ancient kingdom of Urartu. Tushpa is the capital city. Note the location of Büyük Ağrı Daği, the modern "Mount Ararat." Based upon Boris Piotrovsky, The Ancient Civilization of Urartu *(New York: Cowles Book Co., 1969).*

Assyria and Minni, somewhere around lakes Van and Urmia in modern Turkey.

Ararat is itself mentioned in Assyrian records, where it is called Urartu. In the thirteenth century B.C.E., Shalmaneser I uses this term to refer to a group of small kingdoms located southeast of Lake Van. Twelfth-century records (Tiglath-pileser I) refer to a kingdom west of the lake as Nairi; by the ninth century this Nairi has been incorporated into Urartu. Thus the boundaries of the kingdom of Urartu became, generally, the Euphrates River on the west, the crest of the western Taurus Mountains on the south; and the borders with the kingdom of Manna in the upper reaches of the Zagros Mountains to the southeast of Lake Urmia. The northern boundary is uncertain, but it may have extended to the plain of the Araxes River. It is clear that political concentration was in the vicinity of Lake Van where the capital, Tushpa, was located (see maps 4 and 5).[2]

During a period of military strength in the ninth and eighth centuries B.C.E., the kings of Urartu were able to expand their borders westward across the Euphrates and southward into Syria as far as Aleppo. During this time, the term "Ararat" could be used to indicate almost the entire mountainous district north of Syro-Mesopotamia.

In the late eighth century the Assyrians, led by Sargon II, invaded the heartland of Urartu/Ararat and plundered its cities. It was then invaded by nomadic tribesmen from across the Caucasus Mountains, the Cimmerians and Scythians, in the seventh century, and finally destroyed by the Medes in the early sixth century.

As we can now see, the Genesis flood narrative is not very specific about the ark's landing place. "The mountains of Ararat" seems to refer not to a mountain peak but to a mountainous kingdom. How then did the tradition develop that the ark had come to rest upon a specific peak? Possibly through a misreading of Genesis 8:4, so that is becomes "Mount Ararat" rather than the "mountains of Ararat." To this must be added the understandable human desire to locate holy places as precisely as possible (e.g., some persons seek the exact spots where Jesus was born, tried, crucified, and buried).

A. Ararat Becomes Armenia

The Armenians, mentioned as early as the Behistun inscription of Darius I of Persia (522–486 B.C.E.), may have migrated to the Urartu/Ararat area from Phrygia.[3] Their first settlement seems to have been at the headwaters of the river Halys, and Herodotus, in the fifth century B.C.E., clearly distinguishes them from part of the older population, which he calls Alarodians. (His "Alarod" seems to be a linguistic variation of "Ararat/Ararad."[4]) As the new Armenian population moved east and north, the Alarodians (Araratians) were increasingly pushed toward the plain of the Araxes.[5] This situation is reflected in the administrative divisions of the Persian empire: the thirteenth satrapy (a political area) included the Armenians and had its capital at the city of Van, just east of the lake, while the eighteenth included the Alarodians and was situated to the northeast on the Araxes.[6] Thereafter, Ararat (called Airarat by the Armenians) became just a northerly sudivision of the Arsacid kingdom of Armenia (during the second and third centuries C.E.).[7] Thus Jerome in the fourth century C.E. can remark, commenting on Isaiah 37:38, "Ararat is a region in Armenia on the Araxis . . . at the foot of the great Taurus Mountain."[8]

Around the beginning of the Cristian era, readers of Genesis would probably understand the word "Ararat" in terms of the geography of their own day, rather than that of the Genesis narrator. That is, they might restrict the term to the small district on the Araxes, the Ararat of their time, rather than properly equating it with the much larger ancient kingdom of Urartu. The result would be that one tall mountain in this area, Ağri Daği, rising dramatically from the plain of the Araxes, would become a prime candidate for "Mount Ararat."

Many of the earliest translations of the Bible, done in the centuries just before and after the beginning of the Christian era, render the term "Ararat" as "Armenia."[9] This was entirely proper, since the Armenia of the translators' day was roughly equivalent in size to the ancient kingdom of Urartu/Ararat. The area had gained a measure of independence in the early second century B.C.E., and was divided into Greater and Lesser Armenia. The former extended eastward as far as the Caspian Sea and northward to the river Cyrus; the latter extended westward to the river Halys (see map 6). After 80 B.C.E., Greater Armenia sometimes expanded southward to include an area along the Tigris River, and area called Qardu by the Semites, and Gordyene (Gordyaea) by the Greeks and Romans.[10] It is in this mountainous area (Qardu/Gordyene), in the extreme south of Ararat/Armenia, that ancient tradition will locate another possibility for the ark's landing place.

While Armenia was a country of considerable size and with fluctuating boundaries, its religious and administrative center was to the north in the Airarat district, on the Araxes River, centering in the cities of Armavir and Artaxata (Artashat). Indeed, Armenian tradition stressed that Haik, the ancestor of the entire group, had first settled in this very area. Thus even the term "Armenia," when encountered in the early translations of the Genesis flood story, might suggest more to some readers than Greater Armenia. It could be taken to mean Armenia par excellence, the heartland on the Araxes. If so, then the ark's landing place ("in the mountains of Armenia") would again be restricted to a narrow area, and again one mountain, Ağri Daği, would become a prime candidate.

But here it must be stressed that even some of the early translations of the Bible—for example, the Syriac Peshitta and the Aramaic Targums—understand the word "Ararat" in the wide sense, and translate it in a way that exempts Ağri Daği as the prime candidate for the ark's landing place. These translations say that the ark landed "in the Qardu (Gordyene) Mountains," south and east of lakes Van and Urmia, but still within the boundaries of Ararat.

B. Conclusions

During the period when the traditions in Genesis took their final shape, the term "Ararat" meant a rather extensive area with slightly fluctuating boundaries. This area can be equated with the kingdom of Urartu, known from Assyrian records. In general, the kingdom of Urartu was concentrated in the extensive Qardu/Gordyene Mountains around lakes Van and Urmia.

No one mountain is singled out in the Genesis account as the ark's landing place. Rather, a mountainous area is specified, and this is a more apt description of the Qardu area (where the Taurus and Zagros ranges collide) than of the more northerly valley of the river Araxes where Ağri Daği is located. Hence some of the ancient translations of the Bible translate "mountains of Ararat" by "mountains of Qardu."

By the beginning of the Christian era, the boundaries of Armenia were roughly those of ancient Ararat/Urartu, so that some translations of Genesis justifiably read that the ark came to rest in "the mountains of Armenia." But the phrase "mountains of Ararat," found in the Hebrew original and in some other ancient translations, might lead to a misunderstanding. By then Ararat was only a small, northerly district of Armenia. Undue emphasis might then be placed on the possibility that the ark landed in the north, in the vicinity of Ağri Daği.

By the time of the conversion of Armenia to Christianity (fourth century) and the introduction of an alphabet, so that the Bible could be translated into Armenian (fifth century), Armenia was a semi-independent kingdom whose religious and administrative centers were concentrated in the northern part of the country.[11] Thus when some persons read in the early translations that the ark had come to rest in "the mountains of Armenia," and when Armenians in particular read this in their own Bible, they might understand it in a much more restricted sense than the writer of Genesis intended. Attention would be focused too narrowly toward the north where Ağri Daği was located.

Our study thus far has not enabled us to decide whether the authors of the Genesis flood story had a specific site in mind when they referred to the "mountains of Ararat." But it has helped to establish the geographical boundaries within which specific sites could legitimately be proposed; it has indicated the plausibility of a southern location, that is, in the Qardu (Gordyene) Mountains, as suggested by some ancient translations; and it has given some of the reasons why a specific mountain farther to the north, Aǧri Daǧi, would later be singled out by some people as the landing place of Noah's ark.

III. ANCIENT REPORTS OF THE ARK'S SURVIVAL

It is a very natural human desire to want to locate—and visit—historic and holy places. Throughout the centuries men and women have made pilgrimages, and paid fees, to see the "place where it happened."

Although, as we have seen in the last section, the Bible does not specify the exact landing place of Noah's ark (nor does it make any mention of the ark surviving), natural human curiosity has led to a wide variety of proposals. Particularly during the Byzantine era there were ark speculations and searches.[12] The fact that there are many proposed ark landing sites is often ignored by some modern-day ark-searchers, who indiscriminately gather all ancient reports and present them as if every mention of "Mount Ararat" automatically meant Aǧri Daǧi.

A. Often-Discussed Landing Sites

1. *Jabal Judi*, in the Arabian peninsula (see map 6 and fig. 4) is mentioned in the Qur'ān (11.44). It is located in the 'Aja' range, whose peaks rise almost perpendicularly to a height of 5,600 feet from the edges of the great Nafud Desert in the Najd,[13] and it was famous for its pre-Islamic temples.[14] The Muslims may have picked up the ark tradition for this mountain from Syrian Christians, since Bishop Theophilus of Antioch (second century) reports, "The remains of the ark are to be seen in the Arabian mountains to this day."[15] It is possible, however, that Theophilus is referring to Arabia Deserta (which extended to the upper limits of the Mesopotamian plain) rather than Arabia Felix (Arabia proper), and if so he would be referring to the Qardu Mountains just beyond the Tigris (see map 6, site 3b). In any case, the tradition still survives in Arabia, since "In the town of Chenna, in Arabia Felix, says the traveller Prevous, is a large building, said to have been erected by Noah; and a large piece of wood is exhibited through an iron grating, which is said to have formed a portion of his ark."[16]

Map 6.   Traditional Landing Sites for Noah's Ark.

< < < < < < < <   mountain range

- - - - - -   boundary of Armenia (Major), first century, B.C.E.–1st
century, C.E. Armenia Minor is to the west, between the
Euphrates and Halys rivers.

numbers 1-5   ark landing sites, corresponding to the numbered
discussion in the text.

　　　　　　　　　　1. Jabal ("Mount") Jūdī (of the Quran)
　　　　　　　　　　2. Mount Baris (?)
　　　　　　　　　　3a. "in Adiabene" (Pir Omar Gudrun?)
　　　　　　　　　　3b. "in Gordyene" (Mt. Qardu, later called Jabal
Jūdī)
　　　　　　　　　　4. "near Celaenae," in Phrygia
　　　　　　　　　　5. Büyük Ağri Daği (Masis; "Mount Ararat")

Muslim tradition includes the belief that the ark sailed seven times around the Ka'aba in Mecca before traveling on to its final resting place.

2. *Mount Baris*, "above Minyas in Armenia, where, as the story goes, many refugees found safety at the time of the flood, and one man, transported upon an ark, grounded upon the summit, and relics of the timber were for long preserved; this might well be the same man of whom Moses, the Jewish legislator, wrote."[7] Mount Baris is not otherwise mentioned in ancient records, and location of Minyas is uncertain.[8] In any case, there is no real reason to identify it with Ağri Daği. Indeed, one may wonder if Mount Baris might be Mount Elbruz, the highest peak of the Caucasus range, 18,465 feet tall, and at the northern limit of Armenia.[19] The identification of Mount Elbruz with Baris is perhaps strength-

Figure 4. The northwest spur of the 'Aja' range (Arabia) from the northeast, which contains Jabal Jūdī of the Quran. From Alois Musil, Northern Neğd, p. 147. Courtesy of The American Geographical Society.

ened by a similar tradition, which is still current in Armenia,[20] that Noah and his family were not the only survivors of the flood. While his ark rested on Ağri Daği, other persons had climbed to the top of a still higher mountain *to the north*, which remained above the waters.

3. Somewhere in the mountains of modern Kurdistan (the upper Zagros range, northeast of Mesopotamia), with the possibility that more than one site is indicated.

3a) In *Adiabene*—roughly between the Upper and Lower Zab rivers, tributaries of the Tigris (see map 6). In the first century C.E. Josephus, discussing the royal family at Adiabene, remarks, "in a district called Carra [Carron][21] . . . the remains of the ark in which report has it that Noah was saved from the flood . . . to this day are shown to those who are curious to see them."[22] In the third century Hippolytus wrote: "The relics of this ark are . . . shown to this day in the mountains called Ararat, which are situated in the direction of the country of the Adiabene."[23]

Figure 5. Aerial photograph of the Zagros range, showing the conspicuous peaks Shaikh Bakh (center) and Pir Omar Gudrun/Pira Magrun (right). From C. J. Edmonds, Kurds, Turks, and Arabs, *Frontispiece. Courtesy of Oxford University Press.*

And possibly Julius Africanus, also writing in the third century, has this location in mind: "and the ark settled on the mountains of Ararat, which we know to be in Parthia."[24] This site may be the same as that of the Gilgamesh Epic (11:140), where Utnapishtim's boat comes to rest on Mount Nisir, which is likely the spectacular Pir Omar Gudrun (called Pira Magrun by the Kurds), just south of the Lower Zab River (fig. 5).[25]

3b) In *Gordyene* (Gordyaea), the mountainous area between the Tigris and the Upper Zab rivers, south and southeast of Lake Van (see map 6). Thus Strabo, after having discussed the city of Nisibis in upper Mesopotamia, says: "Near the Tigris lie the places belonging to the Gordyaeans, whom the ancients called Karduchians; ... [they were] held in subjection by the king of the Armenians."[26]

This area is called Qardu(n) in Aramaic and Syriac sources; "the mountains of the Karduchi" by Xenophon;[27] and "the Gordian Mountains" by Ptolemy.[28] It was part of the Armenian province of Korčaik (Gord-Haïk) and particularly of the canton called Gordouk (see below, site 5, and maps 7 and 8). It is part of the area still known as Kurdistan. (Note that the sounds *g*, *k*, and *q*, are easily interchanged in the languages of this area.)

Several of the Targums (Aramaic translations of the Bible: Onkelos, Neofiti, and Pseudo-Jonathan A) render the "mountains of Ararat" in

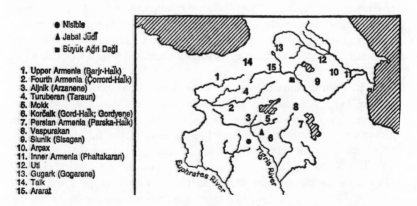

● Nisibis
▲ Jabal Jūdī
■ Büyük Ağrı Dağı

1. Upper Armenia (Barjr-Haïk)
2. Fourth Armenia (Çorrord-Haïk)
3. Aljnik (Arzanene)
4. Turuberan (Taraun)
5. Mokk
6. Korčaik (Gord-Haïk; Gordyene)
7. Persian Armenia (Parska-Haïk)
8. Vaspurakan
9. Slunik (Sisagan)
10. Arçax
11. Inner Armenia (Phaltakaran)
12. Uti
13. Gugark (Gogarene)
14. Taik
15. Ararat

Map 7. Map of the provinces in Armenia (fifth century, C.E.), based on Heinrich Hübschmann, Indogermanische Forschungen, 16 (1904). Note the location of the province whose name is spelled variously as Korčaik/Gord-Haïk/Gordyene/Qardu. It is no. 6, where classical sources put the ark's landing place. By contrast, note the location of the modern "Mount Ararat (Büyük Ağri Daği).

Genesis 8:4 as the "mountains of Qardu(n)," as do the Peshitta (the Syriac Bible) and other Jewish and Christian sources.[29]

The idea that Noah's ark landed in this area may come from Berossus, a Babylonian writer of the third century B.C.E., who, telling how the ancient Sumerian flood-hero Ziusudra survived the deluge, says: "There is still some part of the ship [of Ziusudra] in Armenia, at the mountain of the Gordyaeans; and some people carry off pieces of the bitumen . . . and use (it) as amulets." Josephus, who quotes these remarks,[30] happily identifies Ziusudra with the biblical Noah and does not seem to remember that he has located the ark in two or three different places (sites 2 and 3a). It may be, however, that the adjoining territories, Adiabene and Gordyene, were roughly the same in his mind, as indeed they were to others. For example, Pliny[31] places Nisibis in Adiabene. Less excusable are modern ark-searchers who quote Berossus as if he supported their view that the ark had landed on Ağri Daği (see map 6, site 5).

Theophilus of Antioch may have had this location in mind when he mentions that the ark came to rest in the Arabian Mountains (see site 1, above).

Epiphanius, bishop of Salamis in the fourth century, trying to make it clear that Gordyene falls within the area of biblical Ararat/Armenia, reports that the ark rested "in the mountains of Ararat, [i.e.,] in the midst of [the mountains of] Armenia and [of] Gordyene."[32] An alternative translation might be "between the mountains of Armenia and those of Gordyene," in which case he might be trying to harmonize the geographical terms. In another passage, however, Epiphanius says unambiguously that "the remains of Noah's ark are still shown in the land of the Gordians."[33]

An attempt to harmonize the various traditions seems to be the reason for Targum Jonathan's explanation of Genesis 8:4. This translation suggests that the mountain had two peaks. The ark came to rest "on the mountains of Qardun [Gordyene]: the name of the one mountain is Qardunia, and the name of the other mountain is Armenia."

The Nestorian (Syriac-speaking) Christians put the specific landing place on a conspicuous mountain that rises just north of the Tigris at the edge of the Gordyene/Qardu range: a 6,800-foot peak, now called by the Turks Cudi Dağ. (It may have been called Mount Nipur by the Assyrians,[34] and perhaps revered by them, since King Sennacherib carved massive reliefs there about the year 700 B.C.E.)[35] The Nestorians built several monasteries on the mountain, including one on the summit called the Cloister of the Ark. This was destroyed by lightning in 766 C.E.[36]

The Muslims, who conquered this area in the seventh century C.E., accepted the Nestorian tradition of the ark's landing on Cudi Dağ and erected a mosque on the site of the Cloister of the Ark. Several explanations have been offered for the fact that they came to call this mountain Jabal Jūdī, thereby creating confusion with site 1, above: (a) the Assyrians had called this area "the land of Guti" (Kutu), and that terminology may have survived as "Jūdī" until the Islamic period,[37] (b) Jūdī/Cudi is a corruption of Gardu/Qardu, that is, the consonant r has been lost;[38] (c) the name has been transferred from the Jabal Jūdī in Arabia (site 1, above),[39] earlier believed to be the landing place.

During the early Islamic period, Jews, Christians, and Muslims are in general agreement that this mountain is the ark's landing place:

> The ark rested on the mountains of Ararat, that is, Jabal Judi near Mosul.
>
> > [Eutychius, Bishop of Alexandria (Saʿid ibn-Bitrik), ninth century][40]

> The ark came to rest on Jabal Judi . . . 8 parasangs from the Tigris. The place . . . is still to be seen.
>
> > [Al-Masʿudi, tenth century][41]

> [I traveled] two days to Jezireh Ben ʿOmar, an island in the Tigris, on the foot of Mount Ararat . . . on which the ark of Noah rested. ʿOmar Ben al-Khatab removed the ark from the summit of the two mountains and made a mosque of it.
>
> > [Benjamin of Tudela, twelfth century][42]

> In order to see the place where the ark landed, he [the emperor Heraclius, seventh century] climbed Jabal Judi, which overlooks all the land thereabout.
>
> > [Al-Makin, thirteenth century][43]

That wood said to have come from the ark was recovered from atop the mountain—indeed, that a Muslim sanctuary had been constructed there from it—is reported in the thirteenth century by the Muslim geographer Zakariya ben Muhammad al-Kazwine.[44]

On the slopes of the mountain there was, according to the ancient sources, a village called Themanin, meaning in Syriac "Eighty": "And when they came out of the ark, they built themselves a city and called it

Themanin, according to their number, for they said, 'We are eight.' "[45] Again, "Judi is a mountain, near Nisibis. . . . At the foot of it there is a village called Themabin; and they say that the companions of Noah descended here from the ark, and built this village."[46] The village is now called Betmanim, or Heshtan.[47] According to the biblical account, the ark contained eight persons: Noah, his wife, their three sons, and their wives. In Nestorian Christian and Muslim tradition, the eight *(themane)* has become confused with eighty *(themanin)*, giving rise to the tradition that Noah's family was accompanied by a group of persons totaling eighty.

Relatively recent visitors to the mountain report that the ruins of the Nestorian monasteries are still visible, as well as a structure (mostly of stone) called Safinat Nebi Nuh ("the Ship of the Prophet Noah").[48] Annually, on September 14, representatives of all faiths in the area— Christians, Jews, Muslims, Sabians, Yezidis—gather to commemorate Noah's first sacrifice atop the mountain (see fig. 6).[49]

There is still one other ancient attestation to the Gordian/Qardu Mountains as the ark's landing place, although previous books by arksearchers have failed to realize it: Faustus of Byzantium (see below, site 5).

4. Near *Celaenae in Phrygia*. This location seems to reflect the combining of Semitic and Greek flood stories. Julius Africanus, after giving his own opinion (see above, site 3a), mentions that others prefer this location. It is also mentioned in the Sibylline Oracles (200 B.C.E.–500 C.E.): "There is in Phrygia . . . a steep tall mountain, Ararat . . . thence streams of the great River Marsyas spring . . . there . . . the ark of Noah abode."[50] At the nearby city of Apameia (Apamea),[51] also called Kibotos (Cibotus; κιβωτός—"box; ark"?—in any case, it is the term used in the Greek Bible for Noah's ark; but the meaning could be something like "treasury"),[52] coins of the fourth century C.E. were struck apparently depicting this scene. A couple seem to be looking out a window of a boat; another couple is outside. There are two birds, one approaching the boat with a tree branch in its claws, and an inscription on the side of the boat reads ΝΩΕ ("Noah"?) (see fig. 7).

5. *Ağri Daği* (Büyük Ağri Daği; Masis in Armenian) is the Mount Ararat of present-day ark-searchers (see fig. 8). Armenian tradition has placed a number of Noah-related stories in the vicinity of this spectacular mountain: the Garden of Eden; Noah's first grapevine (still bearing fruit until it was destroyed in the earthquake of 1840 C.E.); the burial place of his wife (at Murand) and of Noah himself (at Nakhichavan);

Figure 6. Photo of "The ship of the Prophet Noah" (safinat Nebi Nuh), a stone structure on the crest of Jabal Judi (Cudi Dağı/Mt. Qardu), where various faiths (Christian, Jew, Muslim, Zoroastrian) meet annually to commemorate Noah's sacrifice upon leaving the ark. From Gertrude Lowthian Bell, Amurath To Amurath, fig. 184. (1911).

No. 4

No. 5

No. 6

Figure 7.   Reverse side of coins minted in the Phrygian city of Apameia Kibotos. The scenes show Noah and his wife inside the ark (Greek: kibotos), with a dove returning overhead with an olive branch. Then, to the left, the couple has emerged from the ark, with arms upraised in a prayerful stance. Note, in scenes No. 4 and 5, that the word "Noah" (NΩE) is inscribed on the ark. Beneath, the inscription reads: "Of the people of Apameia." The city was founded by Antiochus I of Syria (280–261 B.C.E.). Reproduced from Calmet's Dictionary of the Holy Bible, with the Biblical Fragments, *by Charles Taylor. Seventh Edition; London: Samuel Holdsworth, 1838, at Vol. V, Plate IX. A photograph of a similar coin in the Israel Museum, with helpful discussion, may be found in Yaakov Meshorer, "An Ancient Coin Depicts Noah's Ark,"* Biblical Archaeology Review, *September/October, 1981, pp. 38–39.*

Figure 8. *Photograph of Büyük Ağri Daği (Masis; the "Mt. Ararat" of modern ark searchers). Courtesy of* Aramco World Magazine *(from the issue of March–April, 1973, p. 21).*

the spot where he first stepped from the ark; and the location of his house.[53] Most important and basic to all of the foregoing traditions is the claim that his ark came to rest on the mountain and that it survives there largely intact to this day. While few persons would doubt that these traditions have grown over the centuries and that some of them are less than historical (the grapevine and the burial places are certainly doubtful), the idea that this is the genuine landing place of the historical Noah has recently been ardently proclaimed.

By now it should be clear that traditions from the Ancient Near East are not unanimous in saying where the flood-hero's boat landed. The accounts examined thus far that specifically mention Noah are either very general as to location (e.g., in the mountains of Ararat/Armenia, a vast area with several possible locations) or seem to point to specific mountains other than Ağri Daği. Thus the basic question becomes: How old is the tradition that says Noah's ark landed atop this majestic peak?

An attempt to trace it to the first century C.E. is made by quoting Josephus: "The ark rested on the top of a certain mountain in Armenia ... both he [Noah] and his family went out ... the Armenians call this place 'The Place of Descent' ('Αποβατήριον) . . . the remains of the ark are shown by the inhabitants to this day."[54] While Josephus is thus not very specific, his translator, William Whiston (1737 C.E.), in a clumsily worded note, seems to identify this "place of descent" with a city at the foot of Ağri Daği, namely, with Ptolemy's Naxuana,[55] Moses of Chorene's Idsheuan, and modern Nachidsheuan (i.e., Nakhichavan in the U.S.S.R., which name, he says, means "the *first* place of descent"). The problems with Whiston's often-quoted identification are several and serious. They may be summarized as follows (points *a* through *h*).

a) Josephus here merely uses the general term "Armenia." Elsewhere (sites *3a–b*, above) he has more specifically placed the landing site in that part of Armenia called Adibene or Gordyene (Qardu), far removed from Ağri Daği, and there is nothing in the present passage to contradict this.

b) Just as several of the traditional locations have recently yielded wood that has been taken as evidence to support the claim (sites 1, *3b*, 5), we need not be surprised if more than one of them, indeed each of them, included a spot formally named "the Place of Descent." Thus the same name found in Josephus and in the vicinity of Ağri Daği would not prove that Josephus was referring to the latter.

c) Since a variety of ark traditions that originated at other locations have been transferred to Ağri Daği (see below), it is possible that this one originated elsewhere as well. Indeed, the Armenians may have borrowed it from Josephus' account, since his works were translated into Armenian in the fifth century C.E.

d) There are two cities named Idchavan (= Whiston's Idsheuan?) in Armenia: one in the province of Taik, the other in the province of Airarat, whereas Nakhichavan is in the province of Vaspurakan.[56] Thus the two names cannot refer to the same place.

e) Moses of Chorene, at least in his *History*, does not even mention a place called Idsheuan.[57]

f) There is a controversy surrounding the date of Moses of Chorene and his various writings. His *History* is an account of his native Armenia from its legendary beginnings down to the year 440 C.E. and is dedicated to Prince Isaac, who died in 481. Understandably, therefore, he has traditionally been dated to the fifth century. However, modern critical studies have seriously undermined that date, as well as his accuracy as a historian.[58] Specifically, the work seems to refer to a number of events that happened much later, most of them in the sixth and seventh centuries (e.g., the provincial divisions made by Justinian in 536 C.E., and the monastery of Zwartnots, which was not built until 654). The problem seems resolved to the extent that experts in the field have recently confined their debate almost entirely to whether Moses' work is to be assigned to the eighth or even the late ninth century.[59] The very existence of the scholarly debate is often ignored by popular writers who are out to prove that the ark survives atop Ağri Daği.[60] Matters are not helped by the fact that the debate is often printed in hard-to-obtain sources and in such languages as Armenian and Russian.

g) Early Armenian tradition does not identify the landing place with Ağri Daği, but rather, with the Gordyene/Qardu Mountains far to the south. For example, in an eighth-century account, King Tiridates ascends to the summit to get stones with which to build a chapel. There is no indication that the mountain should not be climbed or that an angel was thought to guard anything, to say nothing of the ark! (See app. 2, below.)

h) The earliest form of the place name "Nachidsheuan" is Naxcavan, which, contrary to the often quoted opinion of Whiston, does *not* mean "the place of first descent" and thus cannot be equated with anything in Josephus' text. Rather, the name consists of a place name, *Naxč* (or *Naxuč*) plus *avan*, "market town."

Since the last two points are crucial for rejecting the claim that Josephus' remarks support Ağri Daği as the ark's landing place, it is necessary that they be developed in greater detail. The relevant information can be found in a little-known article, written in German seventy-five years ago by a respected grammarian of the Armenian language, H. Hübschmann. An English translation of this article is given in appendix 1. Now, however, another claim must be considered.

Faustus of Byzantium is sometimes cited as a fifth-century, C.E. witness that Ağri Daği was the ark's landing place.[61] He related that Saint Jacob (or James), bishop of Nisibis (modern Nusaybin) on the river Habur in upper Mesopotamia, desired to see the ark. "[He] left his village and journeyed to Mt. Sararad[62] in the Armenian Mountains in the region of Airaratic control (domain) in the Canton of Gordukh. . . . Having arrived, he asked God to let him see the preserved ark that Noah had built, which had come to rest on this mountain at the time of the deluge" (*History*, III.10). After a difficult climb, he fell asleep near the summit, only to be awakened by an angel who informed him that it was not God's will that he ascend higher. In compensation for not being allowed to see the ark, he was given a small piece of it, "which is preserved to this day."[63]

Concerning Faustus' report, ark-searchers would do well to ponder the following points.

Had he meant to refer to Ağri Daği, Faustus presumably would have used its well-known Armenian name, Masis, as he does elsewhere (e.g., at III.20).

Faustus uses the unique expression "in the region of Airaratic control," which is not the same as the province of Airarat where Ağri Daği is located (he uses the latter term at III.7, 12, 14; IV.24; V.6; VI.1, 6).

Faustus specifically places the mountain in "the Canton of Gordukh." A canton is a smaller division of a province, and it is agreed by writers ancient and modern that Gordukh lies in the province of Korcaik[64] (Gord-Haïk; Gordjaik: see map 7), that is, in the mountainous area between the Tigris and Lake Van,[65] the same area which Semitic writers call Qardu and which classical writers call Gordyene (see map

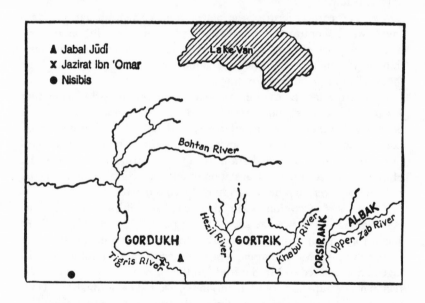

Map 8.   "Cantons" of the province of Korčaik (Gord-Haïk; Gordyene; the Qardu region of semitic authors), in the fifth century, C.E. Note that Faustus of Byzantium placed the landing place of Noah's ark in the "canton" of Gordukh (that is, at Jabal Jūdī), whereas the modern "Mt. Ararat" (Büyük Ağri Daği) is far to the north, beyond Lake Van. (Map based upon Heinrich Hübschmann in Indogermanische Forschungen, 16 [1904].)

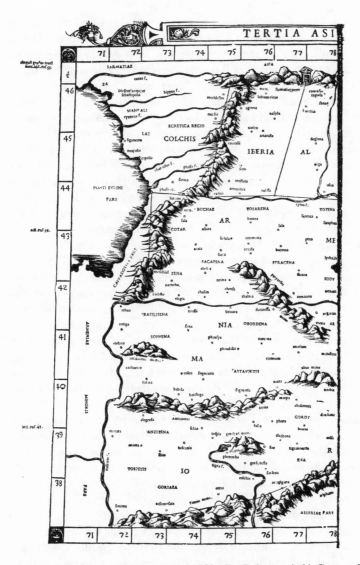

Map 9. Map based upon the coordinates of Claudius Ptolemaeus in his Geography *(second century,* C.E.*). Note that he located the Gordian Mountains at the headwaters of the Tigris River (75° longitude and 39.5° latitude), while the Paryardes Mountains (containing Büyük Ağri Daği, the modern "Mt. Ararat") are at the headwaters of the Euphrates and Araxes rivers (77° longitude and 42° latitude). From* Claudius Ptolemaeus Geographia, *"Tertai Asiae Tabula." Venice, 1511.*

6). Indeed, Gordukh is the canton nearest the Tigris and thus almost within sight of Saint Jacob's hometown of Nisibis (see map 8). This is clear not only from Armenian sources but from Muslim geographers who relate that the canton of Bakarda (or Kardai), which is the Armenian Gordukh, included the city of Jazirat ibn ʿOmar, located on an island in the Tigris.[66] It is quite clear, then, that Faustus' mountain is far removed from Aǧri Daǧi in the province of Airarat. Rather, it should be identified with Jabal Jūdī in Gordyene (site 3b, above; app. 2).

Furthermore, Ptolemy, in his *Geography*, separates the area in which Aǧri Daǧi is located from the Gordian Mountains by 3 degrees latitude,[67] which, in his system of reckoning, is a distance of 150 miles (see map 9). The city of Naxuana, which Whiston sought to identify with Josephus' Ἀποβατήριον and with Armenian "Nachidsheuan," is separated by the same distance from the Gordian Mountains.

Ark-searcher John Montgomery, who argues that Aǧri Daǧi is the landing place, avoids this fatal testimony from Faustus and Ptolemy, and indeed uses both to support his position. He, apparently mistakenly, assumes that Faustus' reference to Airarat means the province; he identifies Faustus' "Gordukh" with a "Cortaea" in Ptolemy, said to be mentioned at *Geography*, V.13.[68] Unfortunately, however, the present writer cannot find a place named "Cortaea" in critical editions of Ptolemy's Greek text.[69] It presumably is a misreading[70] from a Latin translation, either of "Coriaea"[71] or of "Cotaea."[72] Cotaea is at the same latitude as the Gordyene Mountains, and Coriaea is one degree even further south, and so both are totally unrelated to Aǧri Daǧi.

Faustus' account is evaluated in the article by Hübschmann (see app. 1). Hübschmann's conclusion is that the older Armenian writers all understood the Gordian (Qardu) Mountains to be the ark's landing place. This was true of Faustus as well. Only after the eleventh/twelfth century C.E. was the location shifted to Aǧri Daǧi. Thereafter, the name of the nearby city Naxcavan ("Naxcville") was reinterpreted to mean "the first settling place" (Naxijavan or Nachidscheuan).

Hübschmann does not exhaust the evidence that the original geographical setting of Faustus' story was the Gordian/Qardu Mountains, perhaps Jabal Jūdī in particular. Additional information seems to support that conclusion.

First, people who still live in the vicinity of Jabal Jūdī tell a story that is very similar to the adventure of Saint Jacob. A holy man had vowed to visit the remains of the ark on Jabal Jūdī, but he was discouraged by an evil spirit who gave him the false report that the summit was still a month's journey ahead.[73]

Second, it would certainly be surprising if the Syrian Saint Jacob, resident of Nisibis and thus within sight of the Qardu Mountains—the very range which the Bible, in the local Aramaic and Syriac translations, indicated as the ark's landing place—ignored that area and journeyed instead to the edge of the known world. Had he done so, he would have been denying the traditions and indeed the Scriptures of his community, a community that he served as bishop.

Third, Saint Ephraem the Syrian (Ephraem Syrus), described as Jacob's student and lifelong companion, several times refers to the resting place of Noah's ark as "the mountains of Qardu."[74] If Jacob had set out to find the ark on Ağri Daği, and if his belief had been confirmed by an angel, it is scarcely believable that Ephraem would have ignored all this and continued to proclaim that the ark was nearby in the Qardu Mountains.

Fourth, Bar-Hebraeus, the revered Syriac theologian and philosopher (1226–86) who lived in this same area, would presumably have been aware of a successful journey that Bishop Jacob had taken to Ağri Daği to recover the ark. Yet he continued to affirm that the landing place was Mount Qardu.[75]

By the twelfth century, however, it is clear that many Armenians had come to assume that Faustus' story was about an area near Ağri Daği. For example, there is the report of Vincent of Beauvais:

> Mount Arach, where Noah's ark rests, . . . (is near) the river Arathosi [Araxes], which . . . empties into the Caspian Sea. . . . It is said that no man has ever ascended it, except for one monk. . . . When he had climbed part of the way, he would fall asleep. . . . Finally, however, the Lord gave in to his persistence. . . . When he returned he brought one of the beams from the Ark back with him.[76]

The description of the surrounding territory suggests that the Arakad Mountains (Mount Aragats; Ala-Göz), 12,000 feet high and perpetually snow-covered, are meant. A hermitage (named Hreshtakabnak, "House of the Angel") on the flank claims to possess a fragment of the ark and the hand of Saint Jacob (see app. 2). It is a mistake, therefore, to emend Vincent's text from "Arach" to "Ararat" as is commonly done (e.g., by Montgomery, *Quest*, p. 81).

What brought about this transfer of Faustus' story from Jabal Jūdī to Arach, and then to Ağri Daği? We can make a few educated guesses.

a) Faustus' "region of Airaratic control" could be taken, erroneously, to indicate the province of Airarat on the Araxes, in which Ağri Daği was located. *(b)* The spread of Christianity to upper Armenia, attributed to Saint Gregory the Illuminator,[77] was assisted by Saint Jacob, who sent there a large shipment of his own writings.[78] Perhaps among the material sent was the story of Jacob's search for the ark on Mount Ararat, which, to local ears, would suggest the nearby province of that name. If so, the identification of the mountain with the spectacular Ağri Daği would be pretty much a matter of course. *(c)* The city of Jazirat ibn Omar, at the foot of Jabal Jūdī, had close commercial ties with the interior of Armenia.[79] Thus there would be plenty of opportunity for stories to be transferred from one place to the other by caravaneers.

Such a transference of stories and legends would also have been greatly assisted by the geographical factors outlined in sec. II, above—particularly, the shrinking of the ancient kingdom of Ararat (Urartu) to a small province (Airarat) in the north; and the fact that the heart of Armenia was located in the Araxes plain.

Such transfer of traditions to Ağri Daği can be illustrated from sources other than Faustus. For example, Keryat Themanin ("the Village of the Eighty," originally "Eight": see site 3*b*, above), located on the flank of Jabal Jūdī, was, according to Christian and Muslim traditions, founded by Noah. At least by the thirteenth century, the tradition has been transferred to Ağri Daği—with the Semitic name of the town intact. William of Roubruck reports:

> Near this city [of Naxua] are mountains in which they say that Noah's ark rests; and there are two mountains, the one greater than the other; and the Araxes flows at their base; and there is a town there called Cemanum, which interpreted means "eight," and they say that it was thus called from the eight persons who came out of the ark, and who built it on the greater mountain.[80]

The eighty/eight variation occurs at both locations, supporting the dependence of one story upon the other.

Ağri Daği and Jabal Jūdī have other ark traditions in common—although which derived from which (if any) is not so evident. For example, it was said that the ark, floating north, temporarily came to rest on a peak, then journeyed on to its final resting place. In the case of Jabal

Jūdī, the ark stopped first at Jabal Sinjar;[81] on its way to Aǧri Daǧi it stopped at Suphan Daǧ.

In addition, it should be noted that both mountains were the site of monasteries connected with the ark story (Saint Jacob and Saint Gregory on Aǧri Daǧi; the Cloister of the Ark, and others, on Jabal Jūdī)[82] and that the grave of Noah is shown near the foot of each.[83]

B. Other Sites of Ark Landings

The book of Jubilees (second century B.C.E.) states: "And the ark went and rested on the top of Lubar, one of the mountains of Ararat" (5:28; cf. 7:1; 10:15). Since Jubilees sometimes supplies names for places that are left nameless in the Bible, we cannot be sure that, in geography of its times, there was a specific peak called Lubar, and if so, where it was located. Epiphanius, however, continuing in a passage cited above (site *3b*), assigns a location: the ark came to rest "in the mountains of Ararat, in the midst of [or, "in between"] the mountains of Armenia and of Kurdistan [Gordyene], on a mountain called Lubar." There is a real possibility that he is merely combining various names or locations rather than relating personal knowledge of a mountain by this name. The same designation is mentioned in Jewish Midrashic literature[84] and in the Byzantine historians Georgius Cedrenus in the eleventh century and Georgius Syncellus in the ninth century.[85]

The possibility that the word "Lubar" might be related either to the word "baris" or to "Elbruz" (site 2, above) has been noted in passing by a few scholars.[86]

According to Samaritan tradition (but not in the Samaritan translation of the Bible), the ark landed in Ceylon, or Serandib. In Islamic tradition as well, a number of biblical episodes are localized in Ceylon.[87]

One tradition locates the ark in Persia (modern Iran). It was said to have landed on Alwand (Elwand) Kuh, an 11,700-foot peak in the Zagros range near Ecbatana (Hamadhan), which is also connected with Paradise.[88] Map 10 shows the ark atop this mountain (?), which it calls "Mont Ararat." Another tradition points to Mount Demavand, a spectacular 19,000-foot peak in the Elburz range just south of the Caspian Sea. Jews living in this area trace their ancestry back to the exiles who were settled there by Shalmaneser of Assyria (2 Kings 17:6).[89] Some modern scholars identify Nicolas of Damascus' "Mount Baris" (above,

Map 10. Map showing Noah's ark atop Alwand Kuh (?) in modern Iran. From A. Calmet's Dictionnaire historique, critique, chronologique, géographique et littéral de la Bible, *Vol. A–D, 1730.*

site 2) with this mountain.⁹⁰ It should be added that Iranians who live in the vicinity of Aǧri Daǧi accept it as the ark's landing site, calling it Kuh-i-Nuh ("the Mountain of Noah").

A few nineteenth-century scholars located the ark in Afghanistan—in Hindu Cush, an offshoot of the Parmir-Himalaya range.⁹¹

C. Summary and Conclusions

Which one of the various landing places mentioned in ancient sources in the "correct" one? At present, any answer is pure guesswork. The biblical writer does not name a specific site; rather, a vast geographical area is given (Ararat/Urartu), within which several of the proposed sites fall. If the matter is ever to be decided definitely, it will have to be by means other than the ancient reports.

Many of the ancient sources not only say that the ark has survived to the present; they also introduce wood from the ark as evidence. Thus, such claims for Aǧri Daǧi (or any other site) are not unique; indeed, they are precisely what we would expect.

None of the ancient writers claims to have seen the ark or any part of it, or to have visited a landing site—or even to have conversed directly with anyone who has. They only quote someone else, usually ending with the cliché, "It is said that the remains of the ark are to be seen to this day." This they report, even if centuries have passed since the original source.

Various groups, believing their area to have been the cradle of civilization, or the center of the earth, point to the most conspicuous mountain in the vicinity as the ark's landing place. For some Arabs in the Arabian peninsula, it would be Jabal Jūdī in the 'Aja' range (site 1); for Jews in Babylonia, Mount Nisir (?) in the Zagros (site 3a); for Jews and Christians in upper Mesopotamia, Jabal Jūdī in the Gordian/Qardu Mountains (site 3b). In Armenia, after the introduction of Christianity and the translation of the Bible into Armenian, it would be Arach or the spectacular Masis—Aǧri Daǧi. Among these ancient traditions, the one associated with Aǧri Daǧi seems to be very late—likely the latest, since it dates to the eleventh/twelfth centuries C.E. at the earliest.

In sum, while the ancient reports are interesting and point to literary and archaeological phenomena that merit further investigation, they are not, within themselves, convincing evidence that the ark has survived. Less problematic evidence will need to be produced, as even ark-searchers admit: "The total number of such accounts does not overly impress the researcher; and by no means do these accounts provide conclusive proof that the Ark has survived."[92]

IV. SOME RECENT EYEWITNESS ACCOUNTS OF THE ARK

Those who set out to conquer Ağri Daği had to face a fearsome climb—snowstorms, poisonous snakes, and treacherous footing were just a few of the hazards. In addition, there was the local Armenian belief that a terrible demon lurked on the upper heights. It is hardly surprising, therefore, that a firm conviction grew that no one could reach the summit.[93]

Thus from the Middle Ages until comparatively recent times, we have only the hearsay kind of ark evidence that the ancient reports contained. "But at the summit a great black object is always visible, which is said to be the Ark of Noah" (Jehan Haithron, thirteenth century). "Near this city [of Naxua] are mountains in which they say that Noah's ark rests" (William of Roubruck, thirteenth century). "The Armenians . . . are of the opinion that there are still upon the said mountain some remainders of the ark. . . ." (Adam Olearius, seventeenth century). "Twelve leagues to the east of Erivan one sees the famous mountain where almost everyone agrees that Noah's ark landed—though no one offers solid proof of it" (John Chardin, seventeenth century).[94]

During the eighteenth century, such "it-is-reported" evidence was not good enough, apparently. John Warwick Montgomery remarks: "Not surprisingly, the 18th-century age of 'Enlightenment' provides no additional accounts of Ark sightings: the rationalists and deists of the time were not inclined to seek confirmation of biblical revelation in scientific and historical matters."[95] But such an evaluation of the silence is hardly to the point, since the Bible itself makes no claim that the ark survived, even briefly—to say nothing of claiming that it landed on Ağri Daği.

The first verifiable ascent to the summit was made in the year 1829, by J. J. Friedrich Parrot and a company of five other persons.[96] Soon thereafter, the old hearsay evidence is replaced by direct, eyewitness accounts. It is claimed that the severe earthquakes that shook the mountain in 1840[97] and in 1883 exposed Noah's ark, which previously had been largely hidden beneath the ice cap.[98]

The case for the ark's survival, as presented in current books and movies, depends heavily upon the eyewitness accounts. Unlike the ancient reports, there is no doubt as to which mountain is meant. Instead of "a great black object" seen from a distance, the claim is now made that the ark has actually been touched, entered, and explored and that it accords exactly with the description in Genesis. It is imperative, thereafter, that such accounts be both taken seriously and scrutinized carefully. Some of the more famous ones will be outlined below, followed by brief observations. (It must be emphasized that the present writer has not interviewed persons or sought to verify the existence of the documents alleged to contain eyewitness accounts, but is, rather, dependent upon the accounts as they are given in books authored by ark-searchers.)

A. The Account of the Old Armenian

First is the strange story attributed to an Armenian Seventh-Day Adventist, Haji Yearam, related in his seventy-fifth year after a near fatal illness. As a youth (about 1856?) he and his father had guided "three vile men who did not believe the Bible" to the intact ark high on Ağri Daği. It had several floors and contained animal cages with the bars still in place. The men, enraged that the Bible thus appeared to be vindicated, tried to destroy the structure but found that they could not do so. It was too massive; the wood had become "more like stone than any wood" and could not be burned. Thereupon they descended the mountain, threatening their guides with torture and murder should they ever reveal what had been found.

Harold Williams, who cared for Yearam during his illness, says that about 1918, near the time of Yearam's death, he saw a newspaper report of the death of an "elderly scientist" in England. The scientist had confessed, just before dying, that he had participated in an adventure identical to that related by Yearam. And thus the account of the ark's discovery would seem to be verified in a remarkable and unquestionable fashion.[99]

The following curiosities about this story should be noted: (a) Williams apparently made little mention of Yearam's adventure until 1952 — remarkable in view of the sensational nature of the case. (b) Williams' report is prefaced by a troublesome "If I remember correctly. . . ." (c) Where would the "vile" scientists have learned of the ark's location? Known written reports are confined to obscure seventeenth-century (or earlier) travelers. Would English scientists be moved to undertake such a lengthy and hazardous journey to combat such hearsay evidence? Although there was a British expedition to the mountain in 1856, it cannot be connected with Yearam's three "scientists." It was a company of five, led by Major Robert Stuart. They were guided up the mountain by Kurds, not Armenians, and had no interest in trying to find the ark.[100] (d) The reason for guiding the Westerners up the mountain, put in the mouth of Yearam's father, sounds precisely, and surprisingly, like the thought of modern American ark-searchers. It goes something like this: "God had hidden the ark until now, but the time has come to confound unbelievers." Does this suggest that Yearam's story has been embellished as it was retold? If so, to what extent? (e) The ark was described as covered with "varnish or lacquer," a curious state of affairs for wood long aged by the elements of nature. This sounds more like a subsequent attempt to explain why the wood had survived than an accurate, on-the-spot observation. In any case, other eyewitnesses have described the wood as covered with moss (Hagopian) or as very soft (J. Bryce). (f) Why would the men have tried to silence their guides, when apparently the location of the ark was already well known, especially to the inhabitants of the area? Or why would they think that a family in remote Armenia would have such access to Western news media that the episode would become known? (g) Yearam died in 1920 at the age of eighty-two.[101] The scientist, who was "much older than he," allegedly told the story about the same time, so he must have been over 100 years old. (h) The scientists have never been identified, nor has a copy of the newpaper that Williams quotes ever been produced, despite a diligent search.

B. Bryce's Wood

In 1876 the Englishman James Bryce found a timber at the 13,000-foot level, "about four feet long and five inches thick, evidently cut by some tool."[102] It was easy to cut (in contrast to the reports of Yearam and others), and he severed a piece of it with his ice-axe and carried it away. Bryce, a careful observer, considered it possibly to be a part of Noah's ark, and his account is often published in support of the ark's survival. However, in a seldom-quoted passage, he reflects: "I am, however, bound to admit that another explanation of the presence of this piece of timber . . . did occur to me. But as no man is bound to discredit his own relic, . . . I will not disturb my readers' minds, or yield to the rationalizing tendencies of the age by suggesting it."[103]

84

C. The Turkish Expedition

An article in the British newspaper *Prophetic Messenger*, dated 1883, is said to quote a news release from Turkey: a governmental expedition, sent to survey the damage to Ağri Daği caused by an earthquake, found a portion of the ark projecting from a glacier. It was forty to fifty feet in height, and contained compartments about twelve to fifteen feet in height.[104]

The report is remarkable for at least the following reasons. (*a*) In order to reach the heights of the mountain, the groups went through a "dense forest." This is in absolute contrast to many detailed descriptions of the mountain, which report that there are no trees at all—to say nothing of a dense forest.[105] (*b*) The group also encountered a stream on the mountain, "wading sometimes waist high in water." Other accounts mention occasional streams from the melting snow of the glacier, but otherwise there is usually no flowing water on the mountain.[106] (*c*) Despite the great age of the wood and the fact that it was "painted . . . with a dark brown pigment," the visitors recognized the species of tree and pronounced it identical with the gopher wood of the Genesis account. This easy identification is in contrast to the later case of Fernand Navarra (see below, sec. VI), whose wood specimens could not be identified with absolute certainty even by the wood scientists who examined them. And as for the biblical "gopher wood," its species remains a mystery. (*d*) The original news release, cited by the *Prophetic Messenger*, has never been produced. (*e*) The story seems to have gathered additional details as it spread from newspaper to newspaper, with the *Prophetic Messenger* version representing a late stage of development. In an earlier report, in a Dutch newspaper dated July 28, 1883, one supposedly can read only that the ark has been found in Armenia in a well-preserved state, that it is made of "gopher wood," and that an American had already made an offer to purchase it.[107]

D. Prince John Joseph

John Joseph, sometimes identified as "Prince of Nouri," "Grand-Archdeacon of Babylon," and "Episcopal Head of the Nestorian Church of Malabar, South India," claims to be another witness. In 1887, after three (or eight, according to some accounts) attempts, he claims to have reached the top of Ağri Daği and found the ark. He entered the structure, which projected from beneath ice and snow, and made detailed measurements that coincided exactly, so he said, with the dimensions of the ark in Genesis. His grand scheme to remove the ark and take it to the Chicago World's Fair of 1893 did not materialize.[108]

The problems with this account include: (a) He reported that the beams of the structure were joined "with long nails." This detail is emphatically denied by others who claim to have been inside the same ark (Hagopian). (b) He was, it seems, unable to verify any of his pretentious titles. Although he was apparently refused ordination as bishop by the Nestorian Patriarch, he continued, for at least ten years, to announce that he was on his way to the ordination service.[109] (c) At public lectures he was unable to convince others of the truth of his claim (even his close friends said that he "almost convinced others"). (d) We are told, on the one hand, that he indeed gained the backing of "Belgian financiers" for his plan to relocate the ark but that the Turkish government refused permission, and, on the other hand, that he was unable to secure such backing.[110] (e) Since the length of a cubit (Gen. 6:15) is not precisely known,[111] it is curious that the dimensions of the structure on the mountain "coincided exactly" with the biblical description. In any case, since the structure was not totally exposed ("wedged in the rocks and half-filled with snow and ice"), one wonders how the measurements were possible. (f) He reportedly was a mental patient at the State Institution in Napa, California.[112] (I have written to the hospital's director for confirmation of this claim, but he refused to respond on the ground that the confidentiality of records is protected by state law.)

E. Another Elderly Armenian

An elderly Armenian immigrant to the United States, Georgie Hagopian, reported that at the age of ten he was taken to the ark by his uncle, around 1902.[113] His observations, based upon two hours of exploring the ark, include: it was 1,000 feet long, 600 to 700 feet wide, and maybe 40 feet high; the wood was so hard that a bullet would not penetrate it; it was joined with wooden dowels, with no nails in evidence; no doors were visible, but one could ascend to the top by means of a ladder.

The following discrepancies with other accounts are immediately evident. (a) Others found the wood easy to cut (Navarra, Bryce, Knight); (b) Nouri observed that it was joined with nails, not dowels. Since both he and Hagopian claim to have spent hours inside the structure, such a difference can hardly be attributed to faulty observation or poor memory. (*c*) Previous visitors found a massive door lying beside the ark (Yearam) or entered through a hole in the side (the governmental expedition of 1883). (*d*) The dimensions are possibly twice those of Genesis, and thus twice the size of Nouri's find.

F. The Russian Aviator

Perhaps the most celebrated sighting is attributed to a Russian aviator named Roskovitsky, who allegedly photographed the ark from the air in 1917. An expedition later allegedly made detailed measurements and photographs. All these documents, however, are said to have perished in the Russian Revolution. According to published accounts—which curiously did not appear until 1940, and then in a magazine entitled *New Eden*, published in Los Angeles, California—the ark was spotted on the shore of a lake, with about one fourth of its length beached. A catwalk was visible down its length. The ground expedition found hundreds of small rooms, some with cages made of iron bars. Nearby was a small shrine at which Noah had offered his sacrifice after leaving the ark.

Even ardent ark-searchers now admit that this story is almost entirely fiction, including the name Roskovitsky.[14] Apparently, however, there is a historical nucleus to the story, which has been related by relatives of now deceased Russian soldiers of the expedition. From the air, something was spotted in a lake; a ground party could not reach a wooden structure in a swamp because of snakes. But unfortunately for even this alleged nucleus, no one has yet been able to authenticate such terrain on the mountain; indeed, all geographical knowledge contradicts it. The only known swamps on Ağri Daği are at the foot of the mountain. As for the alleged cages made of iron, it is necessary to remember that this metal was discovered by the Hittites about 1500 B.C.E., far too late for use in Noah's ark.

G. Knight's Expedition

New Zealander Hardwicke Knight found huge timbers projecting from beneath glacial ice in 1936. He "broke off" a piece of wood, which was quite soggy, and carried it away. It deteriorated rapidly.[15] The contrast between the condition of this wood and all the previous specimens should be immediately obvious.

H. The Kurdish Farmer

A Kurdish farmer named Resit is reported to have discovered the ark in 1948.[116] The prow, "about the size of a house," was projecting from beneath the ice "about 2/3 of the way up" the mountain. Its wood, blackened with age, was so hard that a piece of it could not be severed with a knife. Resit's fellow villagers, upon hearing his account, climbed to the site and agreed that it was unmistakably a boat.

The account, reportedly carried by the Associated Press,[117] motivated A. J. Smith, dean of a small Bible college in North Carolina, to journey to the mountain in 1949. His goal was to locate Resit, hire him to serve as a guide, and verify that the ark had at last been discovered. Unfortunately, however, Resit could not be found. A search of villages "for 100 miles around" failed to produce anyone who claimed ever to have seen the ark or even anyone who had heard the story.[118]

La Haye and Morris are so predisposed to believe such secondhand hearsay that they seek to explain away Smith's on-the-spot evidence (or lack of it). They propose that since Resit was a Muslim (a fact that they do not verify), he would not have wanted to cooperate with the Christian ark-searchers, nor would any of the persons for miles around—despite that fact that Smith offered a reward for information. No concrete evidence for such local hostility is offered.

One must be even less charitable toward Balsiger and Sellier, who, thirty years later, still repeat the Resit story as valid evidence for the ark's survival, not even mentioning the fact of Smith's unsuccessful expedition.[119]

I. Summary and Conclusions

Research into this type of evidence for the ark's survival is, like that of the other areas, fraught with difficulties. The sources are often third- and fourth-hand. Years could be and have been spent in trying to verify some of them. The original documents often cannot be found—if in fact they ever existed. Alleged eyewitnesses have died and thus cannot verify the reports attributed to them, or clarify critical details. The reports are filled with discrepancies, some minor but others so substantial as to raise the question of credibility. A few are expressed in such strident, polemical tones as to destroy any claim of objectivity. Without questioning the integrity of some reporters, it appears that details have been added as their observations were retold.

The extent to which these accounts have been and will continue to be believed depends, in some measure, upon what the hearer is already predisposed to believe. To the investigator who is not convinced that the ark has survived on the mountain, that is, who seeks evidence for a decision rather than confirmation of an opinion, perhaps the most that can be said is this: hearsay evidence, in the absence of tangible proof, cannot be convincing. While one might believe that a structure of some sort (or at least timbers) exists on the mountain, its nature and origin cannot be determined from these reports. Based upon this evidence alone, one can at least say that further investigation is merited, but that "harder" evidence is needed in order to reach a decision. To the possibility of such evidence we now turn.

V. RECENT PHOTOGRAPHIC EVIDENCE?

As the old adage has it, "The camera doesn't lie." So if, as is often claimed, there are photographs available of a boatlike structure high on Ağri Daği, they should be convincing proof that Noah's ark has survived. Or should they? An examination of this evidence is now in order.

Photographs of an object alleged to be the ark were reportedly taken during World War I and World War II.[120] These have never been produced for evaluation. Several pictures, however, are available from more recent days.

George J. Greene, an American mining engineer, allegedly took a series of photos from a helicopter in 1952, showing an area on the northeastern flank of Ağri Daği. This is the area of the Ahora Gorge, where most of the other sightings have been reported. The photos were lost when Greene was murdered in British Guiana about ten years later. Nearly thirty persons who claim to have seen the pictures say that a boat was clearly visible, even its planking, and that it was projecting from beneath a glacier. Sketches of the object have been made, based upon the memory of those who saw the photos.[121]

Aerial photos of an area 6,000 feet above sea level and twenty miles south of Ağri Daği, taken in 1959 as part of the Geodetic Survey of Turkey, show an oval-shaped object, which some oservers said was roughly the size of the ark in Genesis. A follow-up investigation on the ground revealed a natural geological formation (see fig. 9).[122]

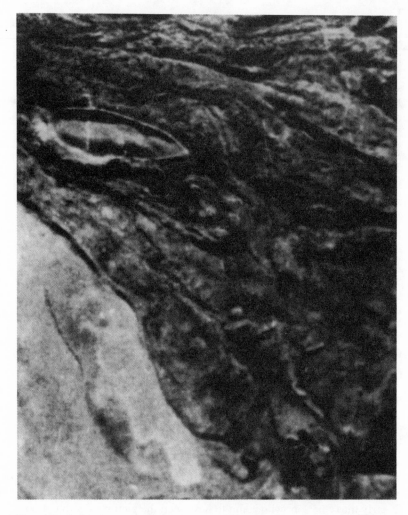

Figure 9. Aerial photograph (1959) of an area of a few miles south of Büyük Ağri Daği, showing the oval-shaped ("boatlike") object which some modern interpreters supposed might be the remains of Noah's ark. Although an expedition concluded that it was a natural (geological) formation, the "ark" claim was renewed in the mid-1980s and was reported on ABC News, "20/20." See Appendix 4. Photo reproduced courtesy of Rene Noorbergen.

A 35 mm. slide of terrain on the mountain was taken by the Archaeological Research Foundation (ARF, a group of ark-searchers) in 1966. When reviewed two years later, it was noticed that the picture contained a small, curiously shaped object near the base of a cliff.[123] Although the photographer, Eryl Cummings, has been very careful to describe the object as unidentified, the photo has been widely publicized as possible evidence for the survival of the ark. In 1972, another group from the Institute for Creation Research (ICR), a small college in California known for its opposition to Darwin's theory of evolution, tried to locate the area shown in the photograph and thereby help identify the object. They "felt they had located the object" in the Ahora Gorge, but it turned out to be "a rock formation, very uniform in shape, giving a finished appearance. Erosion had carved it out of intermittent layers of basalt and volcanic tuft, giving a definite appearance of a catwalk along the top."[124] Rather than concluding that the mystery of the "unidentified object" had been solved, the ICR group decided that the object in the photo must lie elsewhere: "the 'object' has not yet been relocated."[125]

In 1973 a photo of Ağri Daği was taken by the Earth Resources Technology Satellite (ERTS) from an altitude of 450 miles.[126] Subsequently, a "mail room and supply clerk"[127] at the ERTS Center in Sioux Falls, South Dakota, noticed a "peculiar rectangular shape, apparently foreign to the mountain." This was called to the attention of ark-searcher John Montgomery, who saw in it support for the claim that the ark survived atop the mountain.[128] Subsequently a press release was made in 1974 by a United States senator whom Montgomery had contacted, and the matter has thereafter received wide publicity.[129]

Apparently, NASA analysts who have been contacted about this matter agree that an object the size of the ark (300 by 50 cubits, that is, 450 by 75 feet if a cubit is reckoned at around 18 inches[130]) would scarcely be detectable from 450 miles by the ERTS cameras, and if at all only as a single "dot."[131] This seems to have been acknowledged later even by Montgomery, who nonetheless hopes that future satellite photos will prove more helpful in the search.[132]

In either 1974 or 1975, the Holy Ground Mission Changing Center in Palestine, Texas, produced a photo, which they claim shows planking on the sides of the ark. It reportedly was taken high on the mountain with a telephoto lens from a distance of 2,000 feet.[133]

The photo has been criticized by some persons on the following grounds: (a) The "boat" seems to be strangely in-focus (individual "planking" lines are clearly visible), whereas its surroundings are not. A telephoto lens, at that range, should make the focus uniform. Thus some persons regard the photo as composite.[134] (b) "The CIA has analyzed the picture and labeled it as a very amateurish example of a retouched photograph."[135] My inquiry to the Central Intelligence Agency as to whether or not they had indeed examined the photograph produced the following response: "We have looked into your inquiry and are not able to provide any pertinent information." On July 19, 1977, just to make sure that I understood the statement properly, I called the Office of the Assistant to the Director of Public Affairs (who had signed the letter) and was informed that their files contained no information on this matter (see fig. 10).

A. Evaluation and Conclusions

Until the questions surrounding the authenticity of the photo from the Texas center are cleared up by examination of the negative, it should not be used as evidence. In the ERTS photo, the object is too large to be the ark; it likely is a natural formation. At best, the photo by the ARF remains an "unidentified object"; far more likely is the conclusion that it is a natural formation. The object in the aerial photos of 1959 has already been confirmed as a natural formation. That leaves only the photos by Greene, which do not survive for analysis. Hence no conclusions can be based upon them.

But we must raise the following questions concerning Greene's material: *(a)* Was it genuine, or upon close analysis would questions have arisen about it as they have about the Holy Ground photograph? *(b)* Why were the photos not convincing to some of the persons who saw them? Were there differing opinions about what was shown? In any case, Greene failed to arouse interest in an expedition to recover the object. *(c)* Are twenty-five-year-old memories of the photos unquestionably reliable? Is it possible that suggestibility and ark-recovery enthusiasm have influenced the clarity with which the object is remembered to be a boat, with planking intact? To these questions, no answer is possible.

In sum: there is no existing photographic evidence of a boatlike structure on Ağri Daği—to say nothing of evidence for Noah's ark.

VI. WOOD RECOVERED FROM (AND TAKEN UP) "MOUNT ARARAT"

A piece of wood from the ark! To actually see such a relic—perhaps even to own a splinter of Noah's ark—may be the fond hope of amateur

CENTRAL INTELLIGENCE AGENCY

WASHINGTON, D. C. 20505

PUBLIC AFFAIRS

Phone: (703) 351-7676

11 July 1977

Mr. Lloyd Bailey
Duke University
The Divinity School
Durham, N. C. 27706

Dear Mr. Bailey,

This is in response to your letter of 29 June 1977 seeking confirmation that CIA had determined that a photograph allegedly showing a wooden structure high on Mt. Ararat was not authentic. We have looked into your inquiry and are not able to provide any pertinent information. I regret that we cannot be helpful.

Sincerely,

Herbert E. Hetu
Assistant to the Director
for Public Affairs

Figure 10.   CIA letter.

ark-searchers. To the more professional, however, the matter is a good deal more serious. The recovery of wood from Mount Ararat has become a lifetime ambition and adventure.

Before considering in detail the wood found in recent years on Ağri Daği, we should note that over the centuries wood from several arks has been reported. Traidition has it that ark wood was found on Jabal Jūdī in Arabia, on Mount Baris in Armenia, and on an unnamed height in Adiabene. Pieces of ark wood have been displayed in recent times from Jabal Jūdī in Gordyene, from Jabal Jūdī in Arabia, and, of course, from Ağri Daği (see present chap., Sec. III).

It is the Ağri Daği wood that has become famous—featured in the movie *In Search of Noah's Ark* and in most of the popular ark books. And much wood has been discovered on Ağri Daği over the last 1,500 years. To summarize briefly, the following persons have reported finding wood on that mountain: the Dutch traveler Jans Struys in 1670; the English diplomat James Bryce in 1876; the Russian explorer E. de Markoff in 1888; the New Zealander Hardwicke Knight in 1936; the Armenian Alim, who displayed a piece of the ark "which had been in his family for centuries."[36] Most important for our survey is the wood found by the French industrialist Fernand Navarra in 1955 and 1969.

This wood brought down from Ağri Daği has come from many locations on the mountain (leading the movie to suggest that the ark was broken by an earthquake into two widely separated pieces). Descriptions of the color have varied widely—red, brown, green, blue, black. It has been described as soft and soggy—and so hard that a bullet or dagger would not penetrate it. In any case, no piece of the wood before Navarra's find is available for scientific analysis, and therefore no conclusion can be based on any of these accounts. The full case of the survival of Noah's ark of Ağri Daği must, to date, depend on the age of the wood recovered by Fernand Navarra.

During his 1955 expedition, Navarra separated a hand-hewn beam about five feet long from a mass of timbers projecting from beneath a glacier at an elevation of about 13,500 feet.[37] Specimens of it were submitted for analysis at a number of institutions,[38] including the Forestry Institute of Madrid, Spain, which assigned it an age of about 5,000 years. Those who believed that the biblical account of the flood was literally true—and that the flood occurred around 2450 B.C.E.[39]—seemingly had their beliefs confirmed. The ark not only had survived, but had at last been undeniably reovered. Radiocarbon analysis, however, did not support such an early date for the wood.

In 1969 Navarra returned to the mountain with members of a group calling themselves the Search Foundation, and more beams were recovered.[140] Specimens of this wood were also submitted for analysis, and the results are now available.

A.   The Radiocarbon Method of Dating

Radiocarbon dating, developed after World War II by Dr. Willard F. Libby at the University of Chicago, determines the age of things that lived during the last 20,000 to 30,000 years by measuring the amount of carbon 14 they contain. Carbon 14 is an unstable (radioactive) heavy form of carbon with an atomic weight of 14 (normal stable carbon has an atomic weight of 12). The half-life of carbon 14, formerly thought to be 5,568 years, has been revised to 5,730 years by recent calculations. This means that an ounce of carbon 14 is reduced by decay to half an ounce in 5,730 years; half the remainder decays during the next 5,730 years, leaving a quarter of an ounce; and so on.

Carbon 14 forms constantly in the earth's upper atmosphere, and then combines with oxygen to form a variety of carbon dioxide that mixes with the earth's atmosphere and enters all living things through plant photosynthesis. When a plant or animal dies, there is no further intake of carbon 14. That which was present at death goes on disintegrating at a constant rate, so that the amount of carbon 14 remaining is proportional to the time elapsed since death. Based on the carbon 14 content of living matter today and the half-life (disintegration rate) of carbon 14, it is possible to calculate the age of an organic sample.

The actual laboratory procedure for radiocarbon dating involved burning the sample to reduce it to pure carbon and then measuring its radioactivity (rate of atomic disintegration) in a form of geiger counter. The measurement is expressed as the number of carbon 14 disintegration per minute per gram of carbon. Contemporary living samples have a 15.3 for this value; it is 7.65 for samples 5,730 years old; and it is 3.83 for samples twice that age. The actual sample is compared with these values to determine its age. The margin of error (expressed as "$\pm$ X years") is no more than 10 percent back to 1000 B.C.E. and 20 percent to 3000 B.C.E.

1.   Radiocarbon Analysis of the 1955 Specimens

Five laboratories have subjected Navarra's wood to radiocarbon (C^{14}) analysis, with the following results:

The National Physical Laboratory, Teddington, Middlesex, England, found the wood to be 1,190 ± 90 years old—resulting in a date of 760 C.E.[141] ("corrected" 5,730 half-life date: 790–770 C.E.).[142]

The University of California at Los Angeles (UCLA) gave 1,230 ± 60 years—or 720 C.E.[143] ("uncorrected" 5,568 half-life date).

The University of California at Riverside gave 1,210 ± 90 years—or 740 C.E.[144] ("uncorrected" 5,568 half-life date).

Teledyne Isotopes (formerly Isotopes, Inc.), Westwood, New Jersey, tested the wood. I have not been able to secure a published report of this test, but have confirmed it by telephone with James Buckley of Teledyne. His memory was that the test results differed "by a couple of centuries" from those of the other labs.[145] This alleged divergence, along with the Geochron report (below), may have contributed to the statement that radiocarbon test results place the wood between 1,300 and 1,700 years of age—that is, around 300–700 C.E.[146]

Geochron Laboratories, Cambridge, Massachusetts, gives an age of 1,690 ± 120—resulting in 260 C.E. However, since the sample was "inadequate" (only one half the amount of wood needed to fill the smallest counter), this test result may be questioned.[147]

Statements sometimes appear that tests of Navarra's wood were conducted by two other laboratories. However, the reported University of Pennsylvania Radiocarbon Laboratory's test[148] appears to have been done on the wood recovered by Navarra in 1969. A University of California at San Diego (La Jolla) test was mistakenly reported in *Science News* (vol. 111, pp. 198–99).

2. *Radiocarbon Analysis of the 1969 Specimens*
    Two institutions have reported thus far on the wood Navarra recovered fourteen years later. The University of Pennsylvania gives the age of this as 1,340 ± 50 years—dating it to 650 C.E. ± 50 years (if "corrected" by dendro-dated samples and based upon 5,730 half-life).[149] (See table 2.) Geochron Laboratories gives 1,350 ± 95 years—600 C.E. If converted to the 5,730 half-life and "corrected," that result would be 640–620 C.E.[150]

3. *What Does This Radiocarbon Analysis Show?*
    The challenge to their theories that these test results present is apparently ignored by some ark-searchers,[151] quickly dismissed by others,[152] and occasionally explained as the result of repairs to the ark![153] That

TABLE 2

REPORT OF RADIOCARBON LABORATORY,
UNIVERSITY OF PENNSYLVANIA

| P–1620 | Mount Ararat | 1340 ± 50 |
| | | *AD 650 ± 50 |

Wood sample from tree belonging to white oak group *(Quercus sp)*, id by B F Kukachka, Forest Prod Lab, US Dept Agric, Madison, Wisconsin. Found at + 4000m under 30cm ice and moraine, exposed by thawing 10m ice pack, on SW face of Mount Ararat, Turkey (39° 20′ N, 44° 00′ E). Sample coll 1969 and subm by SEARCH Foundation Inc, Washington, DC. For previous date from same site see NPL–61, 1190 ± 90 (R, 1965, v 7, p 161; Navarra, 1956).

University of Pennsylvania (P) Radiocarbon Laboratory report No. 1620, showing results of tests performed on Navarra's 1969 wood specimen. (Reproduced with permission from Bernard Fishman, Hamish Forbes, and Barbara Lawn, "University of Pennsylvania Radiocarbon Dates XIX," *Radiocarbon* 19, no. 2 (1977): 188–228, at p. 213.)

NPL–61 is a test performed by the National Physical Laboratory and published in *Radiocarbon*, vol. 7; the reference to Navarra is his *Noah's Ark, I Touched It.*

1340 is the B.P. (Before the Present, counting from C.E./A.D. 1950) age, based upon the old 5,568 half-life calculation for C^{14}. The asterisk means that the given C.E./A.D. date (650) has been calculated from the revised half-life (5,730) and then corrected by dendrochronological data.

Navarra would have had the bad luck, on both his expeditions, to find only hypothetical repair timbers is apparently quite acceptable to many ark-searchers. Only occasionally does one find a systematic objection to the limitations of radiocarbon analysis.[154]

One common objection is that the results of tests on Navarra's wood differ so widely that they must be dismissed—or more generally, that they indicate the unreliability of the method itself.[155] In response, it must be pointed out that of the four verified tests on the 1955 wood, three are in very close agreement. The maximum difference is only forty years (and with an expressed margin of error of ± 60 to ± 90 years).

The fifth anaylsis, by Teledyne, as well as that of Geochron, could well be accounted for in the following fashion. The radiocarbon analyses do not indicate the date of the entire beam found by Navarra, but only of the small pieces that Navarra removed and shipped to the various labs. Moreover, the labs usually will have removed a still smaller section (about ten annual rings)[156] for the actual analysis. Thus, dates from the various tests might differ by as much as the entire growth-age (diameter) of the beam that Navarra removed from the mountain—that is, by years, perhaps even centuries. Navarra's documents are very imprecise in this regard. He seems to have submitted a cross-section of 13 cm. (about 5 inches), with annual rings varying in thickness from 2 mm. to 3 mm., to the National Museum of Natural History in Paris.[157] Provided that the specimens submitted elsewhere were from the same cross-section (which is not stated to be the case), this alone would allow for a variation in results of around thirty-two to sixty-five years. This, when added to a possible sixty- to ninety-year margin of error, goes a long way toward bringing the Teledyne and Geochron results into line with the strong consensus.

One more fact may account for the Teledyne and Geochron results. Navarra cut the single beam that he recovered from the mountain into four (?)[158] pieces for easy removal. The whole beam diminishes radically in diameter (that is, in number of annual rings) from one end to the other. Thus sections removed at random for radiocarbon analysis could differ in age by many years. Until we have precise details as to the spacial relationship of the various test specimens, objections to the divergence of the Teledyne and Geochron tests are pointless.

As to the 1969 results, which agree very well with each other, it is actually no surprise that they differ by about 100 years from the results for the 1955 specimens. After all, we are dealing with two separate beams (trees?), and it is not even self-evident that they are from the same structure. In any case the tests indicate the date at which the particular annual rings being tested grew, not the date at which the entire beam was placed in a structure. In short, objections to the radiocarbon tests, if they are based on the Teledyne and Geochron divergencies, cannot be taken seriously. On the contrary, there is an amazing agreement.

Another objection has been that the great heights at which the wood has so long remained (about 13,500 feet) might have had an effect upon the accuracy of the test results. Exposed to a higher amount of cosmic radiation (because of less atmospheric shielding) and hence to a higher level of C^{14}, the wood might appear younger than it actually is.[159]

However, in an unrelated test, pieces of wood from near sea level and from around 10,000 feet elevation, and both the same age as verified by count of annual rings, have contained the same amount of C^{14}. This means that altitude will have had no effect upon the accuracy of the Navarra wood test result.[160]

Another objection holds that Navarra's wood may have been subjected to contamination by water-soluble C^{14}, and that this may have contributed to a false radiocarbon reading.[161] However, the early test conducted at Teddington, where, apparently, no decontamination procedures were followed, agrees closely with that at UCLA where specific steps were taken to remove secondary materials—that is, to meet this very objection. Teddington gives 790–770 C.E.; UCLA gives 720 C.E.[162] Hence C^{14} contamination has been minimal. In any case, stringent decontamination procedures are now standard prior to radiocarbon analysis.

4. Can We Depend on Radiocarbon Analysis?

Radiocarbon scientists generally explain the divergence of C^{14}-derived dates from absolute dates by the following major factors:[163] (a) the change in the production rate of C^{14} in the earth's atmosphere, which is caused by variations in cosmic-ray intensity. These variations depend upon the interplanetary magnetic field, solar flares, supernova variations, and so forth.[164] (b) changes in the C^{14} production rate, which are caused by variations in the earth's magnetic field, ranging from 1.6 of its present value about 400 B.C.E. to .5 of its present value about 4000 B.C.E.[165] (c) change in the C^{14} balance between the oceans and the atmosphere caused by changes in global climate.[166]

These and other lesser factors have been carefully studied and voluminous statistics compiled in order to allow compensation for them in radiocarbon age determinations. For example, there is a latitudinal difference in the amount of C^{14} in the atmosphere, caused in part by the concentration of the oceans in the southern hemisphere. It is about 4 percent less at 42 degrees south than at 42 degrees north, since the greater expanse of ocean means greater absorption. Contemporaneous samples from the two hemispheres have indicated that the ones from the south will test out about forty years older than those from the north.[167]

The most reliable and wide-ranging correction for all these factors, now standard procedure in testing wood, is comparison of C^{14}-derived dates with dendro-dates (annular ring counts) of the same specimens.

DENDROCHRONOLOGICAL DATES

INDIVIDUAL C¹⁴ DATES FOR DENDRO-DATED SAMPLES

• C¹⁴ DATES OBTAINED BY THE UNIVERSITY OF ARIZONA, TUCSON.
○ C¹⁴ DATES OBTAINED BY THE UNIVERSITY OF CALIFORNIA, SAN DIEGO, AT LA JOLLA.
• C¹⁴ DATES OBTAINED BY THE UNIVERSITY OF PENNSYLVANIA, PHILADELPHIA.

DEVIATION OF C¹⁴ DATES
YEARS

Figure 11. Comparison of dendrochronological dates (that is, "true" age as determined by annular ring count) with radiocarbon dates for the same samples. For example, dendro-dated samples from 2000 B.C.E. tend to give a radiocarbon reading which deviates about 350 years on the average. That is, one would need to add about 350 years to the radiocarbon age in order to approximate the "true" or "corrected" age. Thus, Navarra's 1969 specimen of "ark wood," with a radiocarbon age of 1340 (based on the 5568 half-life of C¹⁴), multiplied by 1.03 (to give the more refined 5730 half-life) for a radiocarbon age of 1380 (= 570 C.E.), needs correcting about 80 years according to this chart. That is, 1380 (refined radiocarbon age) minus 80 (dendro-correction) yields 1300 years before the present (B.P. age), counting from 1950 C.E. The final result for Navarra's specimen is thus 650 C.E. (See table 2.)

Chart reproduced from MASCA Newsletter, Vol. 9, No. 1 (August 1973), p. 19, courtesy of the University Museum, University of Pennsylvania. Refinement of the scale is discussed by Minze Stuiver, "A High-Precision Calibration of the AD Radiocarbon Time Scale," Radiocarbon, 24 (no. 1, 1982), pp. 1–26. This study, based in part upon data from sequoias from the Pacific Northwest and oaks from Germany, suggests an even later date for Navarra's 1969 specimen.

Dendrochronologists, working primarily with the annular rings of bristlecone pines, now have a reliable chronology stretching back about 7,500 years.[168] The results, roughly, are that for samples dated by annular ring count to 1000 B.C.E. and later, radiocarbon dates will be accurate within about 100 years; dating from about 2000 B.C.E., the adjustment is about 350 years; from 3000 B.C.E. it is about 600 years; from 5000 B.C.E. it is about 800 years.[169] For material from earlier periods (beyond the range of the dendrochronological check), the divergence probably would be greater. (See fig. 11.)

As this applies to Navarra's wood, it is useless to point out that radiocarbon dates are sometimes in error by 800 years,[170] since the date to which that margin of error applies is far removed from that of the Navarra test results. Radiocarbon dates in the period 450–974 C.E., as checked by tree-ring samples, are accurate within eighty years. To make matters worse for the ark-searchers' position, therefore, radiocarbon dates during this period are about eighty years too *old*; Navarra's wood, when "corrected," is even *younger* than the tests indicate.

It is likewise to no avail to point out that archaeologists often make little use of radiocarbon tests for dating objects.[171] This is simply because the archaeologist, for strata within the historical period, needs dates that are accurate within a few decades—a century at most—and radiocarbon tests do not yield such precise results, especially for items older than 1000 B.C.E. For their needs, other techniques (e.g., ceramic chronology) are more precise. The limitation is fine precision, not gross error.[172]

The dendrochronological check on radiocarbon dating is not without its own problems, the main one being that some species of trees may, under certain climatic conditions such as late frost, produce more than one ring per year.[173] Fortunately, however, this has been "extremely rare" in the carefully checked history of bristlecone pines.[174]

In sum: while the radiocarbon method often produces results that are not precise enough for archaeologists working in regions with well-established chronologies, and while further refinements are necessary and possible, it is still the most reliable determination of age. For archaeologists studying prehistoric times, it is often the only available method of dating.

B. Other Methods of Dating Navarra's Wood

Color and density change was used by the Forestry Institute in Madrid, Spain, which estimated the wood to be about 5,000 years old. The color was black; the density 1.100. The species of tree was identified as a white oak (*Quercus pedunculata* Ehrh.), said to have an average density while living of .800–.850. Thus the change in density during its years atop the mountain would be approximately .275.[175]

The Department of Anthropology and Prehistoric Studies of the University of Bordeaux, France, dated the wood by degree of lignitization, which is an initial state in the formation of coal. This led to their opinion that the specimen dated to "a remote antiquity." The Madrid Forestry Institute's identification as *Quercus pedunculata* was specifically dismissed in favor of another species of white oak, *Quercus cerris* L., said to have an average density while growing of .925. Another oak, *Quercus castaneifolia* Mey., with a density of .938, was suggested as a second option.[176]

No method or criteria show up at all in the reported 4,500-year age[177] allegedly assigned to the wood by the Center for Forestry Research and Analysis, Paris, France. Their documents, as published by Navarra,[178] make no mention even of date. They did identify the wood as *Quercus robur* L., again an oak.

Finally, an "expert" at the Cairo Museum, without conducting any scientific tests, is said to have assigned an age of 4,000–6,000 years.[179]

The movie *In Search of Noah's Ark* (see below, sec. VII) summarizes the methods that the producers feel are valid in dating Navarra's wood:[180] degree of lignite formation;[181] gain in wood density; cell modification;[182] and degree of fossilization (silicification?). The results of each type of test, it is said, agree that the age of the wood is about 5,000 years—placing it well back to the period of Noah and his ark.

1. How Accurate Are These Methods?

The extent to which fossilization of wood—and related degradation processes—takes place will depend on several environmental factors, including available moisture, contents of the moisture (amounts and kinds of minerals, pH level), aeration (exposure to wind), temperature, and sedimentary setting, including pressure applied and the extent to which oxygen is excluded.[183] It also depends on the length of time during which the environmental factors have been in effect.

For example, environments may differ so radically that some 12,000-year-old specimens may be more fossilized than others that are also 12,000,000 years old.[184] Or the initial stages of siliceous fossilization may, under favorable conditions, be observed in as little as thirteen years.[185] Further, one must know not only the relationship of the various factors but also whether they have remained constant throughout the entire time that the wood was exposed to them. Thus, simple linear degradation formulas for computing the age of a wood specimen are not possible (such as: X-extent of fossilization, or related condition, indicates that Y-amount of time has passed).

Such a formula for dating Navarra's wood could be worked out only if *(a)* all the environmental factors that operate at the 13,500-foot elevation of Aĝri Daĝi were known; *(b)* the history of the mountain were fully known, so that we could be certain that the environmental factors have remained constant or could know exactly when and to what extent they have changed—we know, for example, of two volcanic eruptions; *(c)* a control specimen were available—a piece of wood subjected to conditions similar to those on Aĝri Daĝi and found to fossilize at such-and-such a rate. Since none of these three conditions has been met, attempts to date Navarra's wood by the extent of fossilization and related conditions are totally meaningless.

As for the dark color of the wood, Dr. Francis Kukachka of the United States Forest Service, Wood Identification Bureau, Madison, Wisconsin, remarks: "The dark color and hardness of the wood is characteristic of white oak wood which has been exposed for a long period of time to water containing iron. The tannin in the wood reacts with the iron, producing the characteristic color and hardness and apparently makes the wood very resistant to natural degradation."[186] Kukachka is speaking of the 1969 wood, but presumably the same would apply to the 1955 specimen. In a phone call on November 4, 1977, Dr. Kukachka told the present writer that he has seen specimens of white oak that had reached a dark color equal to that of Navarra's wood after having been immersed in water in a natural setting for no more than 100 years. Presumably, therefore, change of color, as an alleged means of dating the wood, is worthless.

The change-in-density criterion for dating is subject not only to the limitations just discussed but to another as well. The species of the wood being examined must be determined beyond all question, since the average-density-while-growing is the basis of the computation. The widely quoted Madrid age—5,000 years—assumes that the species is *Quercus pedunculata* (average density .825, i.e., density change .275). But the Bordeaux report, seldom quoted in this regard, specifically rejects the Madrid identification and proposes instead *Quercus cerris* (average density .925, i.e., a density change of .175). Assuming a linear rate of degradation, this alone would seem to reduce the age of Navarra's wood to 3,200 years.[187] And the problem is even more severe. Since each individual tree of a species has an individual environment while growing, it is precarious to quote an "average density" for a species. Variations may be rather extreme—indeed, so much so that density range cannot be a reliable guide to species identification. Thus an age computation based upon density change, ignoring all the previous limitations, would be accurate only to the extent that the specimen, while growing, conformed to the assumed average density.

But is even this the end of the density-change problem? According to the Madrid report,[188] the specimen submitted for analysis had two consistencies: a soft outer area and a hard inner core. The report, in translation, is ambiguous as to whether the present density of 1.100 applies to the whole piece of wood or only to the inner core. In either case, the apparent nonuniformity of the change in density poses problems for determining the age.

I have submitted the documents published in Navarra's book, plus a list of the four criteria on which the movie depends for dating, for evaluation to the Department of Wood and Paper Science of North Carolina State University's School of Forest Resources. The reply[189] included the following summary:

> Degree of "lignitization," gain in wood density, cell modification, and degree of fossilization are most unreliable estimates of aging of naturally exposed wood. The exposure variables are so unknown, and so unpredictable, that to apply steady state laboratory degradation formulas just is not credible for these purposes. Certainly color is the least precise criterion of aging that I could suppose.... I find it impossible to accept an age of 5000 years for the wood specimens in question, but I would accept a date in the early centuries of the Christian era.

Even ardent ark-searcher John Morris, speaking of these same four criteria, considers them to be "highly subjective and unreliable techniques ... rather uncertain estimates ... rejected by most scientists."[190]

C. Other Wood on Ağri Daği

Not only have pieces of wood been brought *down* from the heights of Ağri Daği, a considerable amount has been carried *up* it as well. Consider the following instances:

In 1829 Professor Friedrich Parrot carried up two heavy crosses, five feet and ten feet long, the latter made of beams six inches square. The larger cross was erected at the 16,000-foot level, and the smaller one on the summit.[191]

A wooden cross seven feet high and made of oak was erected high on the western slope by Hermann von Abich in 1845.[192]

The Russian Colonel J. Khodzko erected a seven-foot cross on the summit in 1859.[193]

A "small wooden container" was left at the summit in 1902 by the Russian expedition headed by Ivangouloff.[194]

In addition, we know that there were several larger structures on the mountain, all partially built of wood. These include the Monastery of Saint James at 6,350 feet; the Chapel of Saint Gregory at 8,300 feet; various huts in which Struys stayed during his ascent of the mountain;[195] and a house attributed to Noah.[196]

Obviously, then, a great deal of wood has been carried up the mountain, and our records likely cover but a fraction of the total amount. Is it possible that such wood might be, or even has been, discovered by later expeditions and mistaken for part of the ark?

D. The Ağri Daği Wood—A Final Observation

From tests run so far, we can find no reliable indication that Navarra's wood is older than the eighth/seventh century C.E. Ark-searcher John Morris remarks (but based on other grounds): "The Navarra wood remains highly questionable in origin,[197] and Navarra's claim to have found the ark is at best premature."[198]

VII. THE MOVIE: *In Search of Noah's Ark*

Widely distributed to local theaters and also shown on network television,[199] this popular movie has provided an enjoyable adventure for its viewers, whether ark-enthusiasts or not. Certainly it has aroused wide interest in the search for the ark, and likely will make some converts to the group of ark-searchers.

The movie[200] has the following major parts: *(a)* a reenactment of the Genesis account of the flood, in rather literal terms. The Bible is seen as literal history, and the movie attempts to show how archaeology allegedly has verified it. Geographical and geological evidence for a world-wide flood is cited, as well as flood stories from the literature of other cultures. *(b)* a reenactment of ancient and recent attempts to recover the remains of the ark. The basic assumption is that all the attempts were made on Ağri Daği and that it is the only possible landing-site. *(c)* discussion of the ark's size, contents, sea-worthiness, etc., including interviews with several persons who supply technical information to support the literal truth of the ark story. *(d)* a review of the various photographs that have been claimed to show the remains of the ark on Ağri Daği. *(e)* a review of various tests conducted on the wood recovered by Navarra. *(f)* an analysis of satellite photos of the Ağri Daği area.

In the light of the matters that we have examined in the previous sections, claims made in the movie can be evaluated. For example, *In Search of Noah's Ark* should not have suggested or claimed: *a)* that Sir Leonard Woolley, when he excavated the site of ancient Ur, Abraham's hometown, found evidence of a flood that supports the biblical account. On the contrary, anyone can discover, by reading Woolley's report,[201] that the "flood" at Ur did not even destroy the entirety of that city, to say nothing of the entire world. The movie has repeated an old claim that has by now been widely renounced. (See above, chap. 3.)

b) that "all indications seem to point to a universal deluge." Archaeologically, at least, there is no evidence of such an event,[202] and many experts in the fields of geology, geography, and comparative literature would deny that such evidence is to be found in their areas as well. Such sweeping overstatements are often found in the movie. It has a fondness for citing "the scientific community," "scholars," and "scientists," as if there were strong, if not near unanimous, support for the movie's claims among such groups. This is simply not in accordance with the facts.

c) that ancient attempts to reach the remains of the ark were ended after a number of accidents. No evidence is offered for this statement, and to my knowledge there is none (see sec. III, this chap.)

d) that there is evidence, "as early as 300 B.C.,"[203] presumably from Berossus, that the ark came to rest upon and survived upon "Mount Ararat"—meaning Ağri Daği. Not only is that unlikely, but also no mention should have been made of Nicolas of Damascus or of Josephus in support of this location (see sec. III, this chap.)

e) that there is a city in the vicinity of Mount Ararat whose ancient name means "the place of first descent" (see sec. III, this chap.; also app. 1).

f) that Robert ("Believe It or Not") Ripley, who "has never been proved wrong," found the remains of the Tower of Babel at Borsippa in Mesopotamia and "what natives believe to be" the tomb of Noah in the mountains of Lebanon. Actually, the massive ruins at Borsippa (Birs Nimrud) are several miles removed from what is now known to be ancient Babylon (Babel) where the tower was built. Even a source as "conservative" as Henry Halley's *Pocket Bible Handbook*[204] suggests that the traditional nineteenth-century location at Borsippa should be given up. And, for the sake of consistency, the movie ought to have honored the Armenian claim that the tomb of Noah is to be found near Ağri Daği rather than far away in the mountains of Lebanon. And note that Ripley is not quoted as having located Noah's tomb, but only as having found a tradition about its location. Clearly, he is not likely to be "proved wrong" about that. But exactly what the movie was trying to prove by such cleverly worded material is far from clear to me.

g) that explorer James Bryce found wood at the 14,000-foot level of Ağri Daği, and thus near other "finds." However, Bryce's own account puts it at about 13,000 feet. In addition, the movie seems far more confident that a part of the ark had been found than Bryce himself actually was. (See above, sec. IV.)

h) that contamination and a changing environment atop the mountain, which allegedly would make radiocarbon dates for Navarra's wood unreliable, may be ignored when other test methods are applied. That is, having brushed aside the radiocarbon results in a sentence or two, the movie asks what reliable methods are available and then suggests extent of fossilization, gain in density, and so forth. In actuality, those methods are even less reliable, and for the very reasons that radiocarbon analysis was condemned. (See above, sec. VI.)

i) that an ERTS satellite "photographed Noah's ark." Even enthusiastic ark-searchers have found that claim impossible to accept. (See above, sec. V.)

j) that the Cummings photo ("unidentified object") and the Holy Ground Mission Changing Center photo are valid evidence, without mentioning the substantial doubts that have been raised about them even among major ark-searchers (see above, sec. V). Moreover, the language of the movie often has a subtleness that might escape the notice of some casual viewers. For example, "*If* the broken ark theory is valid, this [the Cummings photo] *would be* the lower half . . . ."

k) that widespread doubt about the existence of the ark atop Ağri Daği springs from modernistic antibiblicism and lack of faith. On the contrary, most of the doubts have arisen because of the weakness of the evidence and because of ark-searchers' misuse of sources—neither of which the movie bothered to point out to its viewers.

l) that radiocarbon dates for Navarra's wood range from 1,300 years to 2,100 years of age (that is, from 150 B.C.E. to 650 C.E.). While I will not deny that this is true, my own survey of the various labs has led to a quite different range of results: 260 to 790 C.E. (See above, sec. VI.)

In addition, there are other interesting aspects of the movie to be noted. While the narrator was discussing the various laboratory reports (other than radiocarbon) on the age of Navarra's wood, he held in his hand a thick collection of documents, likely totaling several hundred pages. However, the reports, as published in Navarra's book, with no indication that they are shortened versions, total perhaps a dozen pages only.

Some of the nonradiocarbon tests were said to indicate an age for the wood of 4,484 years. However, Navarra's book indicates that this was a radiocarbon test result. In any case, that a laboratory test, radiocarbon or otherwise, would assign such a precise date seems unlikely. Even other ark-searchers have wondered if such a test result was not "contrived with a preconceived date [for the flood] in mind."[205]

Some viewers will have noted with interest, and perhaps humor, the way in which the testimony of the Babylonian priest Berossus is presented. While he would have written in Greek, basing himself upon earlier Akkadian (cuneiform) accounts, the movie shows us an Egyptian (hieroglyphic) text as background while the narrator discusses his account. There are not, to my knowledge, any Egyptian hieroglyphic accounts of the ark's survival. Does this indicate that the writers and producers of the movie do not know one language from another?

The most impressive part of the movie, and the one apparently containing new data, concerns a computerized examination of the intensity with which various parts of the mountain reflect sunlight. The claim is made that an area of the ERTS photo (see above, sec. V), near the snow line where Navarra's wood was supposedly found ("where the ark is believed to be located"), has a reflective pattern that exists nowhere else on the mountain.[206] However, the following problems must be resolved before one can conclude, as does the movie, that this unique light pattern indicates that Noah's ark—or any foreign object—lies there.

Would the area retain its unique reflectivity under different light conditions as alleged (that is, if the sun shone upon it at a different angle or intensity)? Would other areas on the mountain then display unique reflectivity? Only analysis of other photos can answer such questions.

Why did the village of Ahora, and especially its reported tin roof,[207] not display unique reflectivity?

Since an object the size of the ark is admittedly beyond the capacity of the ERTS cameras to capture on film (see above, sec. V), as even ark-searchers admit, how can this pattern of unique reflectivity possibly be the ark?

The nature of an object that displays unique reflectivity cannot be determined merely by noticing the fact that it does reflect light in a curious way. That is, we cannot automatically conclude that the object is foreign to the mountain or that it is wood, whether ancient or modern. Rather, all one can say is that, based on one photo taken at given time and angle, there is an object of unknown identity, which at that moment reflected light in a unique way.

Nonetheless, this intriguing phenomenon calls for further investigation, and it may support the near certainty that a structure of some sort (though not necessarily a boat) lies beneath the edge of the snow on Ağri Daği. (See below, sec. VIII.)

VIII. IF NOT THE ARK, WHAT IS UP THERE?

Where have our investigations led thus far? Are the remains of Noah's ark still hidden beneath the snows of "Mount Ararat"—Ağri Daği—in modern Turkey? If not, what is there on the mountain that excites present-day ark-searchers?

We have examined the accounts of the ancient witnesses—and found there are none prior to the eleventh/twelfth century C.E. Unquestionably genuine photographs of a boat-shaped object that is not a natural rock formation—if any ever existed—are not available at present. Eyewitness reports have turned out to be unreliable, since they contradict each other in major details. That leaves the question of the wood that has been brought down from the mountain, reportedly dating from the time of the biblical flood.

Whatever its origin, the 1,200-year-old wood that Navarra recovered is a significant archaeological find, and it deserves further investigation in order to determine more precisely when, by whom, and why it was placed in such an unlikely spot. Further expeditions have been planned by several groups, but the Turkish government initially forbade them to journey to the mountain.[208] (Now, however, see app. 4.)

The mystery surrounding the wood is, at first glance, deepened by the geography of the mountain itself. At times it can be one of the least hospitable places on the surface of the earth. At the lower levels there are dangerous predators—bears, wild dogs, wolves—and an abundance of poisonous snakes. At the upper levels lack of oxygen can leave one gasping for breath or even incapacitated. There are hidden crevasses above the snow line as much as 100 feet deep; temperatures as low as 40 degrees below zero; wind with velocities up to 150 miles per hour; avalanches of snow and stone that can be triggered by no more than a normal human voice; swirling mists almost daily; extremely unstable footing caused by loose rock debris; terrifying bursts of lightning; and very little water.[209] It is easy to see why the tradition developed that it was impossible to reach the summit[210] or why Parrot's claim to have done so in 1829 was greeted with skepticism.[211] It is hardly surprising, then, that some modern persons have found it easier to believe that Navarra's wood is part of a boat that floated to the heights of the mountain during the Genesis flood than that it is part of some other structure that was carried up the mountain, timber by timber, in more recent times.

However, the harshness of the mountain is occasionally broken. During one brief season of the year, warm winds blow up from the surrounding plains and cause balmy weather to the line of perpetual snow (about 13,500–14,000 feet).[212] Bryce found night temperatures at the 12,000-foot level to be no less than 40 degrees F., and was able to climb to the top clad only in a light coat.[213] Lynch's Kurdish porters slept unprotected on the open ground at the 12,000-foot level, and he found the temperature at the summit to be around 20 degrees F.[214]

Thus, while on the one hand, determined adults have been defeated or killed by the mountain, on the other hand, Navarra's eleven-year-old son climbed to the snow line in 1955,[215] and Montgomery's son, also eleven, almost reached the summit in 1970.[216] Armenian Georgie Hagopian has related that at the age of ten, he and the necessary supplies were carried by his uncle "for the roughest part of the ascent."[217] Various persons have been able to carry heavy wooden crosses beyond the snow line and even to the summit (see above, sec. VI). Parrot was able to lead horses and oxen, laden with food and firewood, to the 13,000-foot level.[218] There is nothing physically improbable, then, in the proposal that persons may have carried or hauled heavy timbers to the snow line and used them to build some sort of structure. And it is useful to remember that other structures have been erected on the mountain, although at lower altitudes.

It has been said that the species of wood that Navarra recovered does not grow "within 300 miles of the mountain,"[219] or that the timbers were found "150 miles from the nearest tree."[220] (The latter statement likely means: 150 miles from a tree of the same species, since trees of various sorts are found nearby, for example, on the adjoining Little Ararat.) This alleged distance is seen by some persons as proof that the structure, or "boat," was built elsewhere, possibly in Mesopotamia, and was carried by the waters of the flood to the top of the mountain. However, the following evidence argues against that conclusion.

a) The species of Navarra's wood is far from clear. It has been variously identified by wood scientists as one of the following white oaks: *Quercus robur, Quercus pedunculata, Quercus cerris*, and *Quercus castaneifolia* (see above, sec. VI). The problem is caused by the fact that some species of white oak are difficult, if not impossible, to differentiate in a deteriorated condition. Therefore, it seems questionable, if not impossible, to assert that the species of Navarra's wood does not grow within a certain distance of the mountain.

b) Even if the wood grew only at a distance from the mountain, there is nothing improbable in the suggestion that the timbers were brought there overland. Assyrians, Babylonians, and Egyptians, for example, regularly bought massive cedar trees in the mountains of Lebanon and transported them hundreds of miles, by land and water, for use in their own lands.[221]

c) In fact, all the species suggested for Navarra's wood (above), rather than growing only at a great distance from the mountain, seem to grow nearby. Even Balsiger and Sellier[222] quote testimony that white oaks grow "abundantly in the peri-Mediterranean region" and make no mention of any alleged distance between Ağri Daği and where the wood must have grown. The *Encyclopaedia Britannica* gives the following information: *Q. robur* "is a native of most of the milder parts of Europe and of the Caucasus Mountains of Asia"; *Q. cerris*, "the Turkey oak . . . abounds all over the Turkish peninsula, on the Taurus ranges, and in many parts of southern Europe."[223] More detailed information comes from Edmond Boissier's standard reference work: "*Q. pedunculata* is found in Anatolia, Cappadocia, Turkish Armenia in the Province of Musch (just north of Lake Van, and adjoining Airarat); *Q. robur* in the Armenian Province of Musch; *Q. cerris* in the Amanus Mountains and in northern Anatolia; *Q. castaneaefolia* in the Transcaucasian Province of Talysch."[224]

It would be precarious for even an expert on the trees of northeastern Turkey to state emphatically that such-and-such a species does not grow within a specific distance of Ağri Daği. Certainty would require an on-the-spot examination of every square mile of territory within that distance. It is doubtful that such surveys have ever been made for the area, and in any case the present writer has not found evidence that an expert has voiced an opinion about the range of the species of Navarra's wood. How much more skeptical ought one to be, therefore, concerning off-the-cuff remarks about this matter by American-born ark-searchers who may qualify as little more than tourists to the area of Ağri Daği.

d) Even if none of the species mentioned above now grows within some distance of the mountain, there is no reason to think that this was always the case. We know, for example, that depletion of forests in the Ancient Near East began as early as 2500 B.C.E. and was especially pronounced in the last century.[225] In the case of Ağri Daği, we have specific testimony from medieval Arab geographers that, during their time, it was heavily forested. For example, al-Istakhri mentions that nearby villagers cut firewood on its slopes, and al-Mukaddasi (al-Makdisi) says that more than 1,000 villages were located on its flanks.[226] Both wrote during the tenth century C.E.

There is no need, therefore, to propose that the timbers that Navarra found have been transported any distance—either by land or by flood waters. They may have been fashioned from trees felled on the lower elevations of Ağri Daği.

To return to that mysterious structure. What might it have been, if not Noah's ark? Until there is further investigation, certainty in this matter is impossible. In the meanwhile, several plausible conjectures have been, or may be, offered.

Could it have been a chapel,[227] perhaps to commemorate the ark's supposed landing site? We know definitely of two religious structures further down the mountain—the Monastery of Saint James (Jacob), located at 6,350 feet and named for the bishop of Nisibis who sought the ark on Ararat (see above, sec. III), and the Chapel of Saint Gregory, situated at 8,300 feet and named for the monk who brought Christianity to Armenia. They seem to have been founded around the ninth to the eleventh centuries,[228] and they were destroyed in the earthquake of 1840. While an additional chapel at the 13,000- to 14,000-foot snow line, where Navarra found his wood, would be more difficult to build, it is well to remember that the Byzantines, at roughly the same time, were erecting chapels at far more difficult spots—for example, on the jagged rock peaks of islands in the Aegean Sea.

Could it have been a replica of the ark, constructed some time after Ağri Daği came to be regarded by the local population as the landing place? "The industrious monks of the monastery, wishing to further their own livelihood by the tourist trade, may have built something up on the mountain that with great difficulty could be seen and shown to be the 'Ark'"—so wrote the respected American archaeologist, G. Ernest Wright.[229] This explanation would seem to rely upon the hearsay eyewitness accounts that there is a boat-shaped structure on the mountain (see above, sec. V).

Noorbergen, believing that a replica would be mentioned in Armenian records, has searched various archives, including the Jerusalem Armenian Convent. No such evidence was found.[230] In the view of the present writer, such an absence of literary evidence proves nothing. Had such a replica been constructed, the monks would have tried to avoid any record of their activity.

Could it have been a replica of the house that, says tradition, Noah built on the mountain after disembarking from the ark? The French Dominican Jordanus reports, in the fourteenth century: "In a certain part of the mountain is a dwelling which Noah is said to have built on leaving the ark."[231] But since he goes on to talk of the vine that Noah planted, placed by tradition near the village of Ahora on the lower elevations of the mountain, it is not at all clear that he understood the "house" to be near the snow line.

Could it have been a hut for the use of hermits or climbers on the mountain? Several of these are reported by the Dutchman Jans Struys in the seventeenth century.[232]

Could it have been timbers carried up the mountain by recent ark searchers? (See above, sec. VI.)

The second and third suggestions about the origin and purpose of the wood, if not the first as well, presuppose that Ağri Daği had already come to be regarded by the local population as the landing site of Noah's ark. But, as we have seen, there is no literary evidence for such an opinion prior to the eleventh century C.E., whereas Navarra's wood seems to come from the seventh/eighth century. Might this indicate that the timbers were, after all, not connected with the ark story but, rather, were part of some unknown structure from an earlier period, as in the suggestion that it might have been a hut?

However, we must remember that the radiocarbon tests indicate only the date of growth of the particular annular rings being tested.

They do not indicate how much longer a tree continued to grow—that is, the date at which it was felled for timber or at which it died a natural death. Even less so do they indicate when a piece of timber would later have been used or even reused in erecting a building of some sort. More specifically, the timber found by Navarra in 1955 represents a tree that has been hewn until, apparently, only heartwood remained. The specimen received for analysis by the National Center of Scientific Research had a cross-section (diameter across the grain) of 13 cm.—about 5.2 inches.[233] The University of Bordeaux estimated that the total heartwood of the tree, before it was hewn, had a diameter of at least 50 cm.—about 20 inches.[234] Since, according to the National Center analysis, the annular rings had a thickness of 2 to 4 mm. each, the age of the heartwood section alone would be a minimum of eighty-three years.[235]

But what would the diameter of sapwood that surrounded these eighty-three years of growth have been? That is, what was the total age of the tree? Precision in this matter is impossible, since there are so many unknown variables—exact species, soil conditions, nature of growing seasons, etc. However, Balsiger and Sellier, *presumably* after having consulted competent resource persons about the matter, report that "Navarra's sample came from a tree about five feet in diameter with a height of about 150 feet."[236] *If so*, then the total age of the tree would be about 250 years.[237]

If the radiocarbon tests were conducted from specimens at the center of the heartwood, then (using the Teddington test results as an illustration, see above, sec. VI) the tree began to grow about the year 780 C.E. ± 90. Adding 254 years, it would have been felled about the year 1034 C.E. ±90. Only after that date could the structure on the mountain have been erected. This early eleventh-century date would seem to agree very well with other relevant data: (*a*) the two chapels erected lower down on the mountain about the eleventh century; (*b*) the literary evidence that Ağri Daği was regarded as the ark's landing place only after the eleventh/twelfth century.

It is curious that the wood was found precisely at the elevation that marks the upper limit possible for construction. It is thus at the precise height, and from the exact time period, that we would expect for an ark replica, Noah's house replica, or the chapel on the mountain. And since the perpetual snow line fluctuates slightly from season to season, depending upon the intensity of the previous summers and winters, it is not unlikely that a structure erected just beneath the line would later become encased in ice and snow.

HAS NOAH'S ARK SURVIVED?

In conclusion, have we solved the mystery of Noah's ark on "Ararat"? Almost certainly not to the satisfaction of all ark-searchers and other interested persons, but at least a reasonable solution has been proposed. Only further on-the-spot investigation will solve the matter.

FIVE

THE "PRIMEVAL STORY"
(Genesis, 1–11)

I. THE LITERARY CONTEXT OF THE FLOOD STORY
AND ITS IMPLICATIONS

The biblical account of Noah the sailor runs from Genesis 6:5 to
9:19. However complete it may be as a description of an episode in
Israel's sacred story, it is part of a larger literary construction. Thus its
meaning is related to that which comes before and that which comes
after it. Indeed it is an integral part of a collection of materials that have
come to be called the "primeval history" or the "primeval story" (Gen.
1–11), meaning that it is concerned with the "earliest" things.

What is it that sets this material apart frm the rest of Genesis and
earns it a special title? What is the nature of the transition from the
"primeval story" to the "patriarchal story"? While the answer may not
be readily apparent to the casual reader, it will emerge after a few moments of careful reading and reflection on the following topics.

A. The Horizon (or Outlook) of the Material

Whereas the accounts that begin in Genesis 12 focus upon the life
and election of the people of God (and thus would be of interest primar-

ily to hearers in that group), those in chapters 1–11 are concerned with the origins of all things and thus with the beginnings of the human race. There is no hint, as the story gets under way, that it is moving toward the particularity of Israel's patriarchs. It is only at the very end, when the genealogy of Shem is repeated (11:10ff.; cf. 10:21ff.), that the reader begins to suspect that a selectivity is at work. Otherwise chapters 1–11 could stand on their own, of wide interest to readers in the Ancient Near East, and not continue into chapter 12. Indeed it has occasionally been proposed that these chapters (perhaps in an earlier form) did not always stand before the patriarchal accounts.

This difference in focus of the "primeval" and the subsequent accounts is perhaps reflected in Israel's liturgical materials. Thus, when Joshua summoned "all the tribes of Israel to Shechem" (24:1) in order to remind them of their identity and to elicit a pledge of allegiance to their God, he begins his recitation of the sacred story with the migration of Abraham and stresses the exodus event in particular. (It is thought by some interpreters that Joshua 24 served as the model for a regular covenant-renewal ceremony in Israel, and thus is a modified liturgical document.) Similarly, the book of Deuteronomy commands that each Israelite landowner shall make an annual trek to the central sanctuary and recite a creedlike summary as the first sheaf of his wheat harvest is dedicated to the Lord (26:1ff.). That summary begins with the homeless wandering of the patriarchs and moves quickly and in detail to the central event of Israel's religious life: the deliverance from Egypt, followed by the gift of the "promised land." The "primeval" events thus may seem to us to be conspicuously absent from the recitals.

There are, however, other liturgical materials that focus upon God's primeval work. The Psalms, formal liturgical pieces for use in the Temple, contain lyrical praises of God's creation (e.g., Pss. 19, 33, 104, 136). Nonetheless the Psalms often link praises of the Creator with those of the Lord of history (Ps. 136).

B. Theological Theme of the Material

Subsequent stories often relate Israel's faithlessness to the promise and to the covenant (i.e., ingratitude for God's prior graciousness and election): Abraham's departure for Egypt (Gen. 20), murmurings in the wilderness (Exod. 16; Num. 11), societywide injustice (Isa. 1), etc. The "primeval" accounts, however, stress the fallibility of the human being: humans constantly strive to break the bounds that have been set for them as creatures; they are rebels, whose sovereign must deal with them in ways that are appropriate to their status. There seems to be a reflection upon human kind, with its potentialities and limitations, that stands prior to reflection upon the nature of the people of God. Indeed, it has occasionally been proposed that these illustrative materials had their origin in a pre-Israelite (non-Yahwistic) stage of reflection.

C. Wide Cultural Distribution of the Material

Not only are the accounts in Genesis 12 and following almost entirely about the Israelites; they were also preserved exclusively within that culture. We would not expect the neighboring Ammonites, to say nothing of the more remote Babylonians, to have literature about Abraham or Moses. By contrast, much of the "primevel story" has similarities with literature throughout the Ancient Near East. For example, there are parallels between the creation account in Genesis 1:1–2:4a and a Babylonian account known as Enuma Elish; between the Garden of Eden account in Genesis 2–3 and a Sumerian text concerning the deities Enki and Ninhursag; and between the account of Noah's flood in Genesis 6–9 and the aforementioned Mesopotamian accounts (see above, chap. 2).

It is not merely that the "primeval" stories concern topics of interest to all cultures (e.g., "How did it all begin?" or "What is the relationship of humans to other creatures?" or "How did civilization arise?"), such that we need not be surprised at the widespread literature concerning them. Rather, it is the close similarities in content and sequence that are evident in the Bible and in Ancient Near Eastern literature that are of interest. What accounts for this reality? Has one culture borrowed stories from another, and if so, which? Is there a common antecedent tradition behind local variations? What accounts for the local variations? Given great freedom to shape the material, was it likely to have been considered "history" by those who did so? In any case, can the modern interpreter hope to discover "history" in it?

D. Literary Structure of the Material

The literature that begins at Genesis 12 is basically narrative, although it may incorporate a number of other types (e.g., a blessing at 14:19–20; regulations governing daily life at Exod. 20:22–23:19; and a speech at Deut. 1:6–4:40). The "primeval story," by contrast, is unique in that it consists of a genealogical framework into which narrative has been inserted. It is the chain of "begats," beginning in chapter 4 and extending through chapter 11, that gives the larger story its continuity.

Genealogies in the world of the Bible, however, do not necessarily have the same function that they have for the modern Western reader. They may relate the biological history of an individual or they may relate a relationship between groups. Not only was there a Mr. Judah, but also the tribe called Judah (and so on, for each of the sons of Jacob). That is, a group may take its name from the individual who is supposedly its ancestor. Thus, all Israel is said to be descended from Mr. Israel (an alternative designation for Jacob, for which see Gen. 32:28). Was there, however, a Mr. Egypt, the ancestor of all Egyptians (10:6), a Mr. Asshur (Assyria) from whom all Assyrians descended (10:22), a Mr. Shem from whom all Shemites (speakers of a Semitic language) derive (10:22), and even a Mr. Human Being (which is the meaning of the designation "Adam," which usually has the definite article before it, "the *'adam*") from whom all human beings descend (4:1; 5:3)? Or, is it that some "ancestors" are the projection of group-names backward to a supposed individual, i.e., are they the personification of the group? Similarly, note that various cultural achievements are handled in the same way: the first "forger of all instruments of bronze and iron" was named Tubal-cain (4:22), the noun "cain" (*qayin*) itself means "metal-worker." That is, all blacksmiths go back to Mr. Blacksmith, just as city-building is traced back to Enoch (derived from the verb *ḥ-n-k*, apparently indicating the dedication of a foundation-stone).

If the genealogies in the "primeval story" have an agenda which distinguishes them from modern "family history" (i.e., they are not concerned with the history of biological individuals), this raises the question of the proper interpretation of the narrative accounts (including the flood story) that are subordinate to them. Are they "history" in the modern sense of the term? (To that question we shall turn later.)

E. "Unreality" of the Material

If the world as the modern reader knows it may be defined as "reality," then the world of Genesis 12 and following at least approximates it. There one finds recognizable human beings doing things in accordance with the customs of the time. To be sure, an occasional extraordinary occurrence is recorded (as when divine beings drop in for lunch, in chap. 18). The world of the "primeval story," by contrast, is quite unlike anything that the average modern reader could imagine: a human creature is divided into two persons (2:21–23), a serpent talks (3:1), fruit can make one immune from death (2:17; 3:19), persons marry when no one exists with whom to marry (4:17), the human lifespan approaches 1,000 years (5:27), divine beings have intercourse with human females and produce children (6:1–4), a great flood covers the earth to a depth greater than the highest mountains (7:19), and the sky above in which the deity dwells is so near that a human structure becomes a threat (11:1–9).

The aforementioned five characteristics are among the reasons why interpreters of the Bible have isolated the "primeval story" as a literary unit, worthy of study within itself. At the same time, characteristics A through D raise questions about the origin and composition of the material, and characteristics C through E arouse our curiosity about the degree to which the "primeval story" means to report strict "history." To those matters we now turn.

II. WHERE DOES A RELIABLE REPORT OF "HISTORY" BEGIN?

Does the Bible, from beginning to end, contain an objective, verifiable account of "what really happened"? Was it always the intent of those who transmitted the material to report only that which was patently evident to the unbiased observer? Would all observers of the situations that are described have agreed as to the "facts" of the matter? Even if the details have become blurred with the passing ages, is there nonetheless a historical "nucleus" behind each of the accounts? Is there a discernible transition-point from unverifiable to verifiable data, from literature that is detached from time and place to literature that has a concern with "history"?

About these matters a lively debate has taken place among interpreters of the text during the nineteenth and twentieth centuries. It is, at the present writing, most evident in the United States in the struggle for control of the bureaucracy of the Southern Baptist Church, with the "conservative" wing proclaiming a belief in the "inerrancy" of the Scriptures. It is the purpose of the present chapter to summarize, however briefly, the range of opinion about where historical "happenedness" begins.

A. Does Reliable History begin with the Primeval Story?

The issue is not so much whether there really was a creation (as opposed to the eternality of matter), as it is whether Genesis 1 was intended to give the sequence and details, and perhaps whether there are sufficient data even to assign a date to this event. As for the subsequent stories in Genesis 2–11, this position asserts that they happened in a datable sequence.

Attempts to date these happenings relied initially upon the biblical genealogies: "Mr. X lived a stated number of years, and fathered a son named Y," and so on. By beginning at an independently verifiable date, perhaps one could work backward with the aid of such lifespans and arrive at the date of the flood or even of the creation of Adam on the sixth day of the world. An influential calculation of this type was done by the Irish archbishop James Ussher in his *Annales Veteris et Novi Testamenti* (1650–54), with the conclusion that creation took place in the year 4004 B.C.E. This and related dates were thereafter placed in the margin of some English Bibles, notably editions of the KJV. (For compilations of the ages, see Halley, pp. 32–33, 70, 83. He refers to Ussher's dates as the "received chronology," but has some reservations about "the earliest dates.") Slightly earlier (1642) John Lightfoot had reckoned that the creation of the human creature had taken place on October 23, 4004 B.C.E., at 9 A.M.

Even more minute in its ability to detect discrete events in the early text of Genesis are the marginal notes of the Scofield Reference Bible. If Genesis 1:2 could be translated, "And the earth became [rather than KJV, "was"] without form," then this could imply that the perfect earth of v. 1 became corrupt, fell under divine judgment, and was re-created at an unspecified later date when "the Spirit of God moved upon the face of the waters" (v. 2b). What was the occasion for the judgment on the "prehistoric" earth? Likely the rebellion of Satan against the Most High God, as supposedly related in Isaiah 14:12 and Ezekiel 28:12 (so the Scofield notes to Isaiah 45:18 and Genesis 1:2). To some interpreters, such a "first" earth would allow for the vast geologic ages that modern earth-sciences have proposed. In general, however, this interpretation of Genesis 1:2 has been of interest to a very small number of interpreters only, because of grammatical and other objections. It is rejected, for example, by the note at Genesis 1:2 in *The Ryrie Study Bible*.

The attempt to assign a date to any of the events in the "primeval story" encounters serious difficulties, as interpreters since the time of

Archbishop Ussher have come to realize. Should one accept the traditional Hebrew (Masoretic) text represented in the English Bible, as did Ussher? If so, one calculates 1,656 years from Adam to the flood. However, the Samaritan Pentateuch (also an ancient Hebrew text) gives a total of 1,307 years for the same period, and the Greek Bible (Septuagint) of the early church has instead 2,242 years. (Comparative tables, and a useful discussion, may be found in *IDB*, I: 580–99.)

The problem with using the ages of the pre-flood individuals to calculate absolute dates goes deeper than the manuscript differences. Consider the following table based upon Genesis 5 according to the traditional Hebrew manuscripts (Masoretic Text) upon which most English versions are based.

It is immediately obvious that these ages are not random, contrary to what one might expect if they were reliable reports of history. Note the following curiosities, as a minimum: *(a)* two of the figures have a son in their sixty-fifth year, exactly one-half the figure for Adam; *(b)* events happen exactly on multiples of 100 (500, 600, 800 (twice), and 300; *(c)* each figure (save for the lifespan of Methusaleh, which is determined by the flood: he cannot survive it) is divisible by five, or is such a figure to which seven has been added. Thus, every number (save Methusaleh's age) will end in 0, 5, 7, or 2.

TABLE 3. AGES OF PRE-FLOOD INDIVIDUALS

Name	Age at Time of First-born	Remaining Years of Life	Lifespan
Adam	130	800	930
Seth	105	807	912
Enosh	90	815	905
Kenan	70	840	910
Mahalalel	65	830	895
Jared	162	800	962
Enoch	65	300	365
Methuselah	187	782	969
Lamech	182	595	777
Noah	500 (flood begins in Noah's 600th year)	450	950

That the number 7 might occur regularly in such a list is hardly surprising: it and a few other numbers (see app. 3) occur throughout the Bible with such regularity that one may conclude that they have some idealized, mystical significance rather than a straightforward numerical value. Note the use of 7 in the flood story alone: 7 days (Genesis 7:4, 10; 8:10, 12); 7 "clean" pairs of birds (7:2–3); God speaks to Noah 7 times (6:13; 7:1; 8:15; 9:1, 8, 12, 17); the Hebrew verb *shahat* ("to destroy") is used 7 times (6:17; 9:11, 15; 6:12 (RSV: "corrupted," twice); 6:13; 6:11 (RSV: "corrupt"); the word "covenant" occurs 7 times (9:8, 11, 12, 13, 15, 16, 17); etc. (See Cassuto, II: 32, for other instances.) Any standard age with an extra 7 would denote divine blessing, as when Sarah is said to live 127 years (Gen. 23:1), apparently the Egyptian ideal (120) plus 7. One case of reckoning with 7 is especially conspicuous: Lamech's 777. In the case of Kenan, the composer may have had the common biblical 70 in mind: 70, 840 (70 × 12), and 910 (70 × 13).

What, however, are we to make of the curious divisibility by five? In order to grasp that principle the following parallel table of the pre-diluvian kings should be noted (Text W-B 62, Sumerian King List).

TABLE 4. PRE-DILUVIAN KINGS OF MESOPOTAMIA

Name	Length of Reign	Sexagesimal Expression of Reign
Alulim	67,200 years [apparent error for 68,400: see above, chap. 2, n. 4]	$(60^2 \times 18) + (60 \times 40)$ [apparently $60^2 \times 19$ is meant]
Alalgar	72,000	$60^2 \times 20$
—kidunnu	72,000	$60^2 \times 20$
—alimma	21,600	$60^2 \times 6$
Dumuzi	28,800	$60^2 \times 8$
Enmenluanna	21,600	$60^2 \times 6$
Ensipazianna	36,000	$60^2 \times 10$
Enmenduranna	72,000	$60^2 \times 20$
Ubartutu	28,800	$60^2 \times 8$
Ziusudra	36,000	$60^2 \times 10$
	456,000, corrected to 457,200	$(60^3 \times 2) + (60^2 + 7)$

Here one notices repetitions just as one did in the list from Genesis 5, and one remembers the Mesopotamian system of computation in base-60 (the dimensions of Utnapishtim's boat, for example: see above, chap. 2). Now, one may wonder, are the ages in Genesis somehow a modification of base-60, just as were the dimensions of Noah's Ark? Obviously the Bible will have modified them from multiples of 60^2 to 60. Conspicuous possibilities are: Adam's 930 years $= (60/2)^2 + 60/2$; Enosh's 90 years $= 60 + 60/2$; Enoch's 300 $= 60 \times 5$; Noah's 600 $= 60 \times 10$; Kenan's 840 $= 60 \times 14$; Noah's 450 $= 60/2 \times 15$; Methuselah's 187 $= (60 \times 3) + 7$. Nonetheless, this leaves the vast majority of the numbers unexplained.

It is the multiple instances of divisibility by five that seems to provide the key to most of the figures in the Genesis list, once we realize that base-60 is involved (Cassuto, I: 259–264): five years contain 60 months. If the Bible's mode of operation has been to reduce the Mesopotamian lifespan by reckoning in base-60 months rather than in base-60^2 years, then each age would be a multiple of five years! The Table for Genesis would then look like this:

TABLE 5.   AGES OF PRE-FLOOD INDIVIDUALS (MODIFIED)

Name	Age at Time of First-born	Lifespan
Adam	130 (60 × 26 months)	930 (3[60^2] + [60 × 6])
Seth	105 (60 × 21)	912 (3[60^2] + 60) months + 7 yrs
etc.		

To suspect, however, that the biblical writer is playing the base-60 (in contrast to the Babylonian use of 60^2) and with months (in contrast to Babylonian years) is not to solve the mystery of the specific ages. It has not been a simple matter of taking the Babylonian figures, dividing by 60 and then again by 12. In two cases, however, one may offer a conjecture as to the specific age.

The first is the lifespan of Enoch, namely, 365 years. That figure is, by accident or design, the number of days in a (solar) year, and is, curiously enough, assigned to the seventh person in the genealogical list. The seventh generation in Semitic genealogies (*IDBS*, pp. 354–356), and in those of other societies as well,[1] is often singled out for comment or depicted as a spectacular one. This may be why the text says of Enoch that he "walked with God; and he was not, for God took him" (5:24). It is interesting and perhaps relevant to note that, in the pre-diluvian King List (W-B Text 444), entry number 7 is Mr. Enmenduranna of Sippar (who reigned 21,000 years, i.e., [60² × 5] + [60 × 50]). This king, we are told elsewhere (Heidel, p. 141), was summoned into the presence of the gods and taught divine mysteries with which he returned to the realm of humans. Is there a faint echo of this in Enoch's "walk with God"? (For the same description of Noah, see below, chap. 6.) In the much later book of Enoch, we are told of Enoch's tour of the heavenly realm.

As for Enmenduranna's city of Sippar, it is a well-known cult center of the sun-god, who completes a heavenly cycle each 365 days. Is it possible that Enoch's 365 years, rather than being an accurate biological age, is a remnant from an ancient pre-Yahwistic, pre-Israelite story that the biblical writer has adapted for his own purposes?

The other specific age in the Genesis 5 list about which one may conjecture an origin is Lamech's total of 777 years. As a mighty man, boasting of his power of revenge, it is not surprising that his age would be assigned a series of 7s ("a perfect seven," we might say). One may suspect, however, that another factor is at work. The biblical writers assigned a numerical value to each consonant (but not vowel) of the alphabet. This would be comparable, in English, to a = 1, b = 2, c = 3, etc. The total numerical value of a name was sometimes computed and significance derived from it. Thus the total numerical value of the name Nero Caesar (n-r-w-n q-s-r) is 666, the "number of the beast" in Revelation 13:17–18. (See *IDB*, IV: 381–82.) With this system in mind, consider the name Methuselah, the seventh successor to Adam (Gen. 5:21). The total of the consonants of his name (i.e., its gematria, *IDB*, III: 566) is 784, that is 777 + 7. If one turns to the corresponding (semiparallel) genealogy in Genesis 4, where the same (or related) names occur in a slightly different order, it is Methushael who preceded Lamech. The gematria of his name is exactly 777. However, it is to his son Lamech that an age of 777 years is assigned, and he is the seventh-born in that genealogical list.

Furthermore, should one assume that the genealogies in the "primeval story" are complete, as did Ussher, or is it possible that one or more generations have dropped out by accident? An instance of this would seem to be Genesis 10:24; 11:12–13, where Arpachshad is said to be the father of Shelah. Where, then, does Luke 3:36 get the idea that Shelah was the son of Cainan who was the son of Arphaxad? From the Greek Bible, with either the traditional Hebrew text having skipped a generation or the Greek Bible having added one. Can this have happened other times?

Do the Hebrew words ordinarily translated "son" or "father" always have those precise genealogical meanings, or might the former, for example, mean "grandson" or even "descendant"? Matthew 1:8 records that "Joram (was) the father of Uzziah," whereas in actuality he was the great-great-grandfather (2 Kings 8:24; 11:2, 21; 12:21; 14:21).

As a consequence of these and other problems, the genealogies have been generally abandoned as a means of calculating the date of biblical events. Chronological uncertainty, however, need not necessarily lead to doubts as to historicity.

Are there external (extra-biblical) criteria by which the historicity of events in the "primeval story" may be established, or by which they might even be dated? This also has been debated, but to date there is no widely accepted evidence for the historicity of any of the events as related there.[2] For purposes of the present volume, this is of importance only with respect to the story of Noah's flood, the historicity of which has been examined in detail in a previous chapter.

When such lack of widely convincing evidence is added to the questions raised by the nature of the "primeval" literature itself (see above), the transition between it and the patriarchal literature becomes all the more conspicuous.

B. Does Recoverable History Begin with the Era of the Patriarchs?

In the late nineteenth century, questions concerning the historicity of the patriarchal narratives began to evidence a hitherto unknown skepticism. How could such detail have been transmitted from high antiquity? Do not the narratives have the form of literature that, in other cultures, is described as legend (having, at most, a historical nucleus)?[3] Perhaps the classic judgment of the time was that of Julius Wellhausen: "... we attain to no historical knowledge of the patriarchs, but only of the time when the stories about them arose in the Israelite people; this later age is here unconsciously projected, in its inner and its outward features, into hoar antiquity, and is reflected there like a glorified image" (p. 319). That is, in the biblical accounts of the patriarchs, we can learn nothing more than the opinions of those who formulated the narratives (which, in Wellhausen's opinion, was in the ninth century B.C.E. at the earliest). Thus Abraham "might ... be regarded as a free creation of unconscious art" (p. 320).

Early in the twentieth century, however, a wealth of cuneiform texts was recovered by excavations in the Near East, which shed light on the events and customs of the Middle Bronze Age (ca. 2000–1500 B.C.E.) to which the patriarchs, if historical figures, might reasonably be assigned. Foremost among those texts were those from Mari (eighteenth century) and Nuzi (fifteenth century). In such texts one encountered evidence that various of the patriarchal names were indeed in use (e.g., *Abi-ram* for a person; *Ter-ah* for a place) and that patriarchal actions might reflect ancient practice (e.g., adoption of one's wife as sister, possibly reflected in Gen. 12:11–13). Furthermore, it was plausible to conclude that there had been an expansion of Mesopotamians (Amorites) into Syro-Palestine (sometimes designated as "the Amorite migration") of which the biblical migration of the patriarch Abraham might have been a part.

Thus the influential historian John Bright (*A History of Israel*, 1959) could express what had long been the sentiment among American scholars in particular: "... it has become increasingly evident that a new and more sympathetic evaluation of the patriarchal traditions is called for" (p. 62). "We can assert with full confidence that Abraham, Isaac, and Jacob were actual historical individuals" (p. 82). He begins his volume (now in the third edition) with "The Age of the Patriarchs," and thus he does not concern himself with the events of the "primeval story."

Such affirmation of the historicity of the patriarchs as persons, or of the authenticity of the customs that the narratives reflect, does not automatically necessitate belief in the historicity of each event that the narratives relate, for example, that God physically appeared to Abraham and even stopped in for lunch at his place (Gen. 18).

A brief summary of the point of view currently under discussion may be found in the article "Patriarchs" in *IDB*, III: 677–78.

C. Does Recoverable History Begin with the Emergence of Israel as a Sociopolitical Entity in the Land of Canaan?

For some such interpreters, the emergence would be at the time of Moses and begin with the exodus from Egypt (thirteenth century B.C.E.). For others, it would be at the founding of the monarchy at the time of Saul and David (eleventh century).

As more cuneiform texts were deciphered, it was evident that the patriarchal names were in use over a wide period of time, and not merely in the Middle Bronze Age. The same was true of the customs, which seemed to parallel those of the patriarchal stories, and thus there was no necessary reason to suppose on those bases that the accounts had been handed down from antiquity. Furthermore, some of the alleged parallels, upon closer inspection, turned out to be far less convincing than had been at first supposed. In particular, this was the case with alleged adoption of a wife as a "sister" in the texts from Nuzi. (For the affirmation of such relationship, see Speiser's comments on Gen. 12:10–20; for a more recent analysis of the data, see Greengus, pp. 5–31. A convenient summary of the present situation may be found in *IDBS*, pp. 645–48, which may be contrasted with the tone of the previously cited article in *IDB*.)

There are serious problems with the reconstruction of events during the period of Moses and Joshua as well. When did the exodus take place? Was it one major event, or a series of smaller departures? Was the wilderness itinerary (as reported in Exodus and Numbers) actually the annual migration route of groups who lived in the Sinai peninsula? Was the entirety of Israel involved in these events, or only a part? Were all twelve of the "tribes" involved in the conquest of Jericho, or was it the Benjaminites alone, and their tradition later became the core-narrative that was adopted by all of the other tribes? Did the land of Canaan fall into Israelite hands as the result of a sudden and catastrophic onslaught (as the book of Joshua suggests), or did the transition from Canaanite to Israelite control take place gradually and perhaps with a minimum of conflict (as the book of Judges seems to imply)? Did Israel emerge primarily from the oppressed socioeconomic classes of city-state Palestine, rather than from an influx of former slaves from Egypt? (The range and shift of opinion may be sensed by reading the articles "Israel, History of," secs. 2–3, in *IDB*, and "Canaan, Conquest and Settlement of," in *IDBS*.)

Thus Martin Noth, able biblical scholar and archaeologist, in his famous *The History of Israel* (1958), entitles part 1 as: "Israel as the Confederation of the Twelve Tribes." Such uncertainty prevails about earlier "events" (exodus, patriarchs, "primeval story") that they cannot, he implies, serve as the point of departure for commenting upon the history of Israel.

D. Is History, in the Modern Sense of the Term, Characteristic of Any Part of Scripture?

The concern that gave rise to the biblical literature is not to report "the bare facts," although such facts may form a part of its narrative, says this position.

The modern concern for "objective" reporting is often traced back to the Greek historian Thucydides (fifth century B.C.E.) in his study of the Peloponnesian War. He realized that the accuracy of many accounts of the struggle had been tarnished by failing memory, by loss in transmission of data, and by romanticized self-interest. Thus he remarks, "I did not even trust my own impressions . . . the accuracy of the report being always tried by the most severe and detailed tests possible" (I.22). The need for such caution will be well known to many contemporary persons. Those who have served on a jury, for example, will have heard eyewitnesses to an event give conflicting accounts of "what happened." Documents may have been introduced as evidence that were ambiguous as to syntax and vocabulary, and in any case what they "said" may not have been what the writer "meant." Thus the most that one can hope for is a conclusion of "guilt beyond a reasonable doubt."

By contrast with the modern concern for objectivity, the Bible was not concerned to distinguish "what really happened" from the impressions of the proper observer and recorder. It is overtly written from a theological point of view. Thus it speaks of God's involvement in a way that, even if it is true, could not be demonstrated to the impartial observer. For example, when the Pharaoh's chariots got stuck in the mud and his soldiers drowned in the sea, Miriam sang:

> Sing to the Lord,
> > for he has triumphed gloriously;
> > the horse and his rider,
> > he has thrown into the sea.

> [Exod. 15:21]

That may well be true! However, it is doubtful that the Egyptians saw any reason to believe that it was so. Rather, it is a faith stance, grounded in Israel's prior proclamation of a deity who had acted in history in their behalf.

While this most skeptical (or realistic?) of the positions does not regard the Bible basically as a "history" book, it does acknowledge that some accounts in the text relate recoverable and objective history. The books of Kings, for example, contain precise dates and data, which may be quite accurate. For example, we read that the city of Jerusalem was destroyed by the Babylonians, a claim that no historian would see any reason to doubt: there is independent literary attestation, archaeological evidence of destruction of the city at the proper time, and the reality of the exiled Judeans in Babylonia. For events in Moses' life, however, verification becomes more difficult and the details of the accounts are more detached from modern reality (e.g., "the waters being a wall to them on their right hand and on their left," Exod. 14:22). The problem only increases when one studies the patriarchal accounts and even more so for the "primeval story."

III. THE COMPOSITION OF THE "PRIMEVAL STORY"

Until relatively recent times, it was assumed that Genesis 1–11 was the product of a single writer whose work continued to the end of the Pentateuch (i.e., through Deut. 34), and that Moses was likely the author. Indeed, Moses was on the scene relatively early (as the book of exodus opens), is the major actor thereafter, committed some materials to writing (Exod. 24:4; 34:27; Num. 33:2), and the Pentateuch closes with his death. It is hardly surprising, then, that the book of Exodus could later be referred to as "the book of Moses" (Mark 12:26) and Deuteronomy as "the book of the law of Moses" (2 Kings 14:6; cf. Neh. 13:1; Josh. 8:31). Indeed, the entirety of the Pentateuch could be spoken of as "the law which Moses commanded us" (Sirach [Ecclesiasticus] 24:23; cf. Acts 15:21). Such designations possibly are general attributions, much as we refer to "the books of 1 and 2 Samuel," although it is patently clear that Samuel is not the author (i.e., he died at 1 Sam. 25:1). Nonetheless, it may have been generally believed that Moses was indeed the author as well as chief actor (Josephus, *Antiquities*, IV.viii.48; Bab. Talmud, *Baba Batra* 14b). A few ancient interpreters were willing to attribute parts of the materials to others, however.[4]

How, then, could Moses have written of events in Genesis, for which neither he nor any living person was an eyewitness? Presumably, he would have had access to written sources from an earlier time, and God would have guided him in otherwise unknown details. In the former case, the family of Noah would be an indispensable link in the chain of transmission of pre-flood information. In the latter case, one would not expect inaccuracies of any sort, and could rely upon the material as history even if independently unverifiable. Any irregularities, therefore, must be more apparent than real (harmonizable, with proper study and guidance of the Holy Spirit), and any doubts about the historicity of the accounts would reflect a refusal to accept "the Word of God."

A number of problems for this proposal of single (Mosaic) authorship and uniform composition are contained in the text of the Pentateuch, and even within the "primeval story" itself. Some of them were even commented upon by readers in antiquity, but this did not (and perhaps could not) lead to another theory of composition. Among those problems are the following.

A. Use of the Third Person

The third person, rather than the first, was used to indicate the words and activity of Moses. With rare exception, it is "Moses did" or "Moses said," and not "I did" or "I said." Who, then is the writer (or writers?) who refers to Moses in this fashion? The problem becomes acute at Deuteronomy 34:5–6. "So Moses . . . died there in the Land of Moab, according to the word of the Lord, and he buried him. . . but no man knows the place of his burial to this day." Presumably, between the time of the death and that of the reporter, considerable time has passed. Some ancient authorities supposed that Joshua might have been the reporter (since he was Moses' second in command), although the expression "to this day" would seem to suggest a later time. The problem (use of third person) does not arise, of course, within the "primeval story."

B. Awareness of Events That Took Place Well after the Mosaic Age

The writer seems aware of the existence of the monarchy which began more than two centuries after the exodus from Egypt. Thus Genesis 36:31 relates. "These are the kings who reigned in the land of Edom, before any king reigned over the Israelites." Note the use of the past tense: there are now, or at least have been, kings in Israel. The beginnings of that institution, at the time of Saul (about the year 1000 B.C.E.), now lie in the past.[5] Similarly, the writer is aware that the Canaanites were defeated by the incoming Hebrews at the time of Joshua (Lev. 18:26–28): "But you shall keep my statutes . . . lest the land vomit you out . . . as it vomited out the nation that was before you." Again, note the use of the past tense: it is not that the speaker anticipates that this will happen (as Moses would have had to do), but that he states that it has happened (as Moses could not have done).

There are a number of other illustrations (e.g., Gen. 12:6; 14:14), which readers may ponder for themselves. However, no such chronological clues as to the date of the author (or compiler) of the "primeval story" are contained within its material.

C. Repetition of Material

Even the casual reader will be aware of multiple accounts of a given "happening." For example, the Ten Commandments are recited twice (Exod. 20; Deut. 5), if not three times (Exod. 34). Not only are we twice told that Jacob's name was changed to Israel (Gen. 32:28; 35:10), but we are given a different occasion for each instance. Once we realize that Isaac's name is related to the verb "to laugh" (for which, see any Bible dictionary or the note to Gen. 17:19 in RSV), we may be puzzled to find that there are three allusions to how the name came about, and that the one who laughs and the reason for doing so differs in each case: at Genesis 17:15–19, it is Abraham who laughs skeptically; at 18:9–15 it is Sarah who laughs in amusement at the biological ignorance of the visitors; at 21:1–7 it is Sarah and her friends who laugh with pleasure at the child's birth.

Such repetition tends to suggest the work of a collector more than the work of an author. A collector (editor) might gather sources that overlap, whereas an author would repeat only for emphasis, as an aid to memory! While one might plausibly suggest that Moses was such a collector of the "primeval" stories, the fact that the repetitions continue thereafter (including accounts of Moses' deeds and words) indicates that someone other than Moses is the collector.

D. Evidence of Many Small, Complete, Once Independent Stories

If the Pentateuch (Gen.–Deut.) is the product of a collector (rather than a author), we might reasonably expect to find evidence that sources have been used. We would not expect the narrative to flow smoothly from beginning to end: there would be differences in style and vocabulary, perhaps contrasting points of view, and (above all) formal "beginnings" and "endings" of the units that the collector has brought together.

Appropriate openings and conclusions are readily available from contemporary literature, among them: "Dir Sir," "Dearly Beloved," "This indenture, made and entered into," "Once upon a time," "Sincerely yours," "You may kiss the bride," "signed, this 29th day," and "they lived happily ever after." Similarly, the book of Deuteronomy begins appropriately, "These are the words that Moses spoke ...," the book of Numbers with "The Lord spoke to Moses ...," and Genesis with, "In the beginning. ..." No less obvious as a new topic, although not set apart formally, is Deuteronomy 4:44, "This is the law which

Moses . . .," which may once have been the opening of an earlier edition of Deuteronomy. Or, note Genesis 5:1, "This is the book of the generations of Adam," which does not presuppose the existence of chapters 1–4. Indeed, one could begin reading at that point and not be aware that anything had been previously written on the topic. Similar clear beginnings, coinciding which chapter divisions, may be found at 10:1 and 11:1, and less clearly at 6:1. Especially interesting is 1:1–2:4a, where the end of a complete story does not coincide with the end of a chapter or even of a verse. (The chapter and verse divisions are later additions to the text, and thus are not infallible guides to where a once independent story begins or ends.) The completeness of the story is shown by the fact that we come to the end of the seventh day of creation, God "rests," and the text reads, "And that is how the universe was created" (2:4a TEV). This is followed, not surprisingly, by something that sounds like the beginning of a new (different) account: "When the Lord God made the universe," (2:4b TEV).

Careful readers of the Bible have long been aware that a (supposed) single author uses variations in vocabulary. The most conspicuous example is differing designations for the deity. Thus, within the Pentateuch, one finds "God" (Gen. 1:1), "the Lord God" (2:4b), "the Lord" (4:1), "God Most High" (14:18), "the God of your father" (Exod. 3:6), "God Almighty" (6:3), "the Most High" (Deut. 32:8) etc. Ordinarily, much variations would pose no problem, since a single speaker might feel free to mix the designations at random. However, if one suspects (for reasons outlined above) that the material being read is composite (i.e., the product of an editor rather than a single author), then one might wonder if the variations in vocabulary are also a reflection of multiple sources. That is, one source or one unit of tradition might speak of "God," and another of "the Lord," and so on. The suspicion is strengthened when one notices often that, within the boundaries of formal "beginnings" and "endings," the vocabulary may be consistent. Thus, within the bounds of Genesis 1:1–2:4a, the deity is always referred to as "God" (thirty-five times, i.e., 5 × 7, making it deliberate). Within the bounds of the Garden of Eden story (2:4b–3:24), the deity is described as "the Lord God" (twenty times, the only exceptions being when the serpent speaks). In the story of the conflict between Cain and Abel (4:1–16), save for the introductory verse, which ties it to the previous story, the deity is designated "the Lord" (nine times).

An equally conspicuous variation is the designations of the sacred mountain at which Moses received guidelines from the deity. Sometimes it is called "Sinai" (e.g., four times in Exod. 19 and no other designation), and sometimes it is called "Horeb" (always thus in the book of Deuteronomy).

While such variations, within themselves, would not establish beyond doubt that the text of the Pentateuch is composite (i.e., the work of the collector rather than an author), and while the aforementioned formal "beginnings" and "endings" would not, within themselves, forbid a larger unified text, the combination of the two phenomena is quite striking if not compelling. Quite often the vocabulary switches just at the point of formal transition, and is consistent thereafter.

However, the situation is not quite so simple in the entirety (or even the majority) of the Pentateuchal materials. There are many places where the vocabulary seems quite "mixed": within a single story, it is now one designation for the deity, and now another. Note, for example, "Now the earth was corrupt in God's sight . . ." (Gen. 6:11); "Then the Lord said to Noah, 'Go into the ark . . .'" (7:1); "But God remembered Noah . . ." (8:1); "Then Noah built an altar to the Lord . . ." (8:20). If such variations represent once separate sources, they have, in the text as it now stands, been thoroughly combined in alternating layers. Consequently, disentangling them has not been easy and it has not led to universally satisfactory results (as we shall see in chap. 7).

If we may conclude that the "primeval story" (as well as the rest of the Pentateuch) is made up of once independent units of tradition (a creation story, a couple-in-a-garden story, a story of the struggle between two brothers, a great flood account, various genealogies, the story of a great tower in ruins, etc.), then the question arises as to how they were combined into the present coherent whole. Was it done all at once (by Moses or some other)? Was it done in stages? Were there, prior to the present account, only individual stories, or were there earlier collections that have themselves been combined?

Interpreters who began seriously to ponder this matter some 200 years ago soon noticed that some of the accounts had characteristics in common with certain others. "God," for example, is the star actor in Genesis. 1:1–2:4a, exists the scene, and reappears in 5:1–32. Moreover, the two chapters have entire verses in common, for example, male and female in the likeness of God (1:27; 5:1–2), and are concerned with "generations" (2:4; 5:1). After the flood, it is "God" who blesses Noah (9:1), using the same language as 1:28. Consequently, some of the interpreters proposed, about 100 years ago, that there were once two "primeval" stories which later were combined: There was, in effect, a "God" account, and a "Lord"/"Lord God" account. The former began at 1:1

with the creation of all things; the latter began at 2:4*b* with the creation of a garden and of a gardner to care for it. In the former, humans (male and female together) arrive on the scene after all the animals (1:26); in the latter, there is a single human, then all the animals, then the division of the human into male and female (2:7, 18–19, 21–22).

As for the Pentateuch as a whole, those same interpreters perceived its composition to be more complex: there seemed to have been four stages of composition, two of which were evident in the "primeval story," another which becomes evident only with the patriarchal materials, and the last one in the book of Deuteronomy. This approach to the origin and growth of the material has come to be called the Documentary Hypothesis: "documentary," because of the idea that various documents have been combined; "hypothesis," because it is a plausible solution although not demonstrable to the satisfaction of all interpreters.

According to the hypothesis, which became the standard alternative to Mosaic authorship, the Pentateuch took its present shape as the result of the following four groups of tradition-gatherers and tradition-shapers, each seeking to combine once independent units of sacred material into a sustained whole that would shed light on the problems of their present.[6] (See *IDB*, III: 711–27.)

1. *The so-called Yahwist tradition* (*IDBS*, pp. 971–75). This name was assigned to it by modern interpreters because the units of tradition from which it has been built *usually* refer to the deity by the proper name "Yahweh".[7] It is sometimes referred to as the J-Source, because of the supposition that it had taken shape in Judah and because the divine name was spelled Jahweh by the German interpreters who proposed the Documentary Hypothesis. When did this first sustained selection and collection of the old tradition take place? The initial supposition was that it might have been in the nineth century B.C.E., but most subsequent interpreters have proposed that it was during the reign of Solomon (962–922 B.C.E.).

2. *The so-called Elohist tradition* (IDBS, pp. 259–63). The name was derived from the observation, by modern interpreters, that its units of tradition usually refer to the deity by the general designation "God." However, after use of the divine name (Yahweh) is commended to Moses (Exod. 6:1–3), the latter designation occurs in this tradition as well. It is sometimes referred to as the E-Source, because the Hebrew word for "God" is *'elohim* and because it appears to have taken shape in the north where Ephraim was a predominant tribe. It is often dated to the eighth century, although some interpreters suppose it to be a mere supplement

to J (as opposed to having had a prior separate existence of its own).

3. *The Deuteronomic tradition* (*IDBS*, pp. 229–32). This designation refers to the book of Deuteronomy in its entirety, and thus it is sometimes designated the D-Source. (Initially, some interpreters thought that there might be a few scattered parts of it elsewhere in the Pentateuch.) Its growth is complex, with the core-regulations (chap. 12–26) thought to have been put together during the reign of King Hezekiah (715–687 B.C.E.) and much of the remainder to have been proclaimed as part of the reformation of King Josiah (640–609 B.C.E.).

4. *The so-called Priestly tradition* (*IDBS*, pp. 683–87). The title is appropriate, since it is much concerned with cultic matters. It is often referred to as the P-Source (or P-Code), and it seems to have reached its final form during the period of the exile and shortly thereafter (sixth–fifth centuries B.C.E.). (See further detail in chap. 7, below.)

The hypothesis proposes, then, that Israel, in order to maintain its identity as the people of God amidst the challenges of a changing historical situation, drew upon its ancient uncodified traditions in stages. The result was an ever enlarging official version of the "story." (See fig. 12 and table 6.)

In the "primeval story" (Gen. 1–11), it is "sources" J and P alone that occur. According to the hypothesis, their arrangement and sequence is as shown in table 7 (the composition of the flood story, being more complex, is not differentiated in this table; see below, chap. 6).

In addition to the two sections where the sources appear to be quite mixed (6:5–8:22 and 10:1–32), there are occasional small mixtures. For example, there is a numerical note, characteristic of P, amidst the J account (9:28); and possibly a fragment of J's genealogy (11:28–30) amidst the Priestly material.

If the "primeval story" (and indeed, the rest of the Pentateuch) is composed of once independent stories (as their form suggests) and if they were gathered in two stages (as their differences seem to suggest), then one need not be surprised if tensions arise here and there in the total product. That is, those who gathered, arranged, and preserved the stories may have revered them enough, as sacred traditions, that they transmitted them by and large "as is." Tensions need not be smoothed out, if the overall goal of the larger collection was based upon the central idea of a story rather than upon its details. Note, for example, the following illustrations of this reality.

1. In the P account of beginnings, humans (male and female together) are created at the end of the process. In the J account of begin-

THE GROWTH OF PENTATEUCHAL TRADITIONS
(according to the documentary hypothesis)

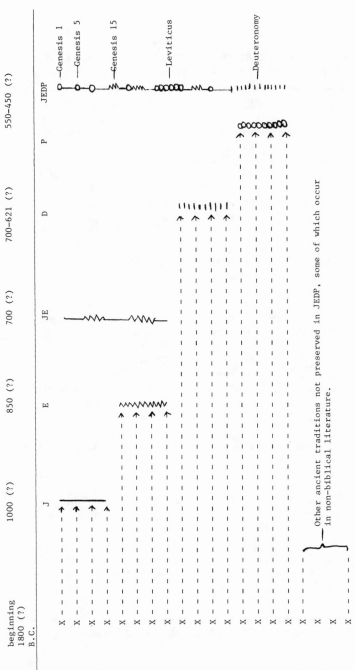

NOTE: Although E and P are shown as separate entities, it may be that they never had a separate existence of their own but rather came about as supplementation of J and JED.

Originally independent (unconnected), orally transmitted (?) stories. Each "X" represents several such units of material.

Other ancient traditions not preserved in JEDP, some of which occur in non-biblical literature.

from Lloyd Bailey, The Pentateuch, p. 48. Courtesy of Abingdon Press.

TABLE 6   SOME CHARACTERISTICS OF THE FOUR COLLECTIONS: J, E, D, P (BASED UPON THE PENTATEUCH AS A WHOLE)

CHARACTER-ISTIC	J	E	D	P
1. usual designation for the deity	Yahweh ("the Lord") (rarely "Lord God") (Gen. 2–3; 4)	Elohim ("God") until Exod. 3 (Gen. 20)	Yahweh your God (Deut. 1:21)	God; God Almighty; Yahweh (after Exod. 6:3)
2. where God's regulations were received by Moses	Mount Sinai (Exod. 19:11)	Mount Horeb (Exod. 3:1)	Mount Horeb (throughout Deuteronomy)	Mount Sinai (throughout Leviticus)
3. the human attitude when the deity appears	comfortable (Gen. 18)	anxious (Exod. 3:6)	afraid (Deut. 5:5)	
4. manner by which the deity is often revealed	in human form (Gen. 3)	in dreams; messengers (angels) (Gen. 20)	voice is heard (no human form) (Deut. 4:12)	voice is heard
5. when the worship of Yahweh began	at the start of human history (but contrast Gen. 4:1 and 4:26)	at the time of Moses (Exod. 3:14)		at the time of Moses (Exod. 6:3)
6. who may serve as priest	members of any of the twelve tribes (Exod. 24:4–5)	members of the twelve tribes	Levites only (Deut. 33:8–11)	Aaronides only (Exod. 28)
7. method of referring to months	by name (Exod. 13:4)		by name (Deut. 16:1)	by number (Gen. 7:11)
8. where Yahweh may be worshiped	multiple places (Exod. 20:24, "in every place . . .")	multiple places	Jerusalem only (Deut. 12:5, "seek the place . . .")	Jerusalem only, as anticipated by the portable sanctuary in the wilderness

(Reproduced from Lloyd Bailey, *The Pentateuch*, p. 40. Courtesy of Abingdon Press.)

TABLE 7   UNITS IN THE PRIMEVAL HISTORY

Location in Genesis	Boundaries and Summary of Contents (of once independent units)	Source
1:1–2:4a	Creation of all things in six days, by bringing order from a watery chaos. Humans are the last act of creation. The deity is referred to as "God."	P
2:4b–3:24	Creation of all living things, with no mention of a time-scale: fertility is created (a garden) amidst barrenness (the desert?). Humans formed in two distinct stages, with the animals between them. The diety is referred to as "the Lord God." The human couple rebels and is expelled from the garden.	J
4:1–16	Two brothers (a metallurgist and farmer who resembles a Canaanite, and a shepherd who resembles an Israelite) struggle, and the deity prefers the latter. In the originally independent story, the world is filled with people (4:14, 17); now they have become the sons of the couple in chaps. 2–3. The deity is referred to as "the Lord."	J
4:17–26	The descendants of Cain (4:17–24) and of Seth; the beginnings of civilization.	J

TABLE 7 (continued)

Location in Genesis	Boundaries and Summary of Contents (of once independent units)	Source
5:1–32	The generations of humanity, from Adam to Noah. The deity is referred to as "God."	P
6:1–4	Sexual interaction of divine beings and humans; shortening of the lifespan; a race of giants.	J
6:5–8:22	The Flood Story.	J and P
9:1–17	The covenant with Noah (all humanity). The deity is referred to as "God."	P
9:18–28	The drunken Noah and his sons and the consequences for life in Canaan.	J
10:1–32	The so-called Table of Nations.	J and P
11:1–9	The Tower of Babel. The deity is referred to as "the Lord."	J
11:10–32	A genealogy: from Shem to Abraham.	P

nings, a human creature precedes the animals, then it is divided into male and female.

2. The story of the two brothers (Cain and Abel), as a once independent account of their struggle, presupposes a fully peopled world (4:14–15, 17). Only when it is combined with the story of the couple in the garden (chaps. 2–3) does the question arise: How can Cain fear, when there is no one to fear? How can he marry, when only he and his parents exist?

3. The genealogy in Genesis 4:17–18 covers six generations, beginning with Cain and concluding with Lamech. That of 5:6–25 covers eight generations, beginning with another son of Adam (Seth) and concluding with Lamech. If we remove the first two generations of the latter

TABLE 8   GENERATIONS IN GENESIS

J (4:17–18)	P (5:6–25)
Cain	Kenan
Enoch	Mahalalel
Irad	Jared
Mehujael	Enoch
Methushael	Methuselah
Lamech	Lamech

(namely, Seth and Enosh), the remaining six are identical with (or are slight variations of) those in the line of Cain as we see in table 8. Presumably it is the same genealogy, with local usage accounting for differences in order and spelling. Some interpreters have suggested that the J account has (for whatever reason) omitted two generations, such that the line would be: Adam, Seth, Enosh, Cain, . . .[8] In that case, one can no longer accept the report in 4:2, 8, 10 that Cain is the "brother" of Abel.

Such divergencies make it difficult to believe that the intent of the "primeval story" was to relate individual biological history of the human race, or even that "history" in the modern sense of that term may be derived from it. Had that been the goal, then presumably the collectors of the accounts, who were no less intelligent than the modern interpreters, would not have let the text stand as it is.

If one can accept the text as it is, with the belief that this is the way the ancient theologians intended it, then one no longer feels it necessary to harmonize its "errors" or to denounce the physical sciences as being antibiblical when they "disagree" with it. It would be equally unfounded for modern scientists and historians to criticize the biblical accounts from the standpoint of their disciplines.

IV.   ASSIGNING A DATE TO THE PENTATEUCHAL SOURCES

The previous discussion and table 6 have listed the proposed sources in the order J, E, D, P and have mentioned a possible date for each. It is now necessary to give a brief account of how those dates were derived, in anticipation of chapter 7, below. There an attempt will be made to relate the message of J and P (as it pertains to the flood story) to the situation of a specific audience. Thus it is not so much that there is a flood story in the abstract (or that a report of "what happened" has come down from the time of Noah) as that the form and meaning of the story was in touch with the needs of specific periods in Israel's history.

Regardless of the process by which the Pentateuch took its present shape (i.e., be the Documentary Hypothesis right or be it wrong), there are occasional clues in the text as to the time during which (or after which) some of its authors and editors lived. Such clues make it clear that Moses' hand (whatever its role may have been) was not the final one. In addition to the aforementioned clues (use of third person, awareness of the decline of the Canaanite civilization, repetitions, and once independent stories), the following evidence should be noted.

There are warnings of a time when the Israelites may be expelled from the land of Canaan (Lev. 26:27–45), just as were the Canaanites before them (Lev. 18:24–25). The content of the warnings so fits what actually took place during the exile (587–539 B.C.E.) and shortly thereafter that many modern interpreters believe that they were actually written *after* that event had happened. Thus they would serve as a warning to the community never again so to act that the land would be lost! The parallels between the warnings and the actual event are as follows. The text says that cities of Israel, under siege, will resort to cannibalism (v. 29), which apparently was the case during the Babylonian attack (Lam 2:20; 4:20); that the destruction of the country would be so thorough that even foreigners would be astonished at it (v. 32), which reportedly they were (2 Chron. 29:8); that the inhabitants of the land would be exiled "among the nations" (v. 32), which was in fact to be the case (2 Kings 24–25); and that ultimately the exiles would be restored to their homeland (v. 45), as indeed they were (2 Chron. 36:22–23).

There are peculiarities of vocabulary that suggest that the setting is the Persian (postexilic) period, i.e., after 539 B.C.E. Those sections, it turns out, belong to the Priestly writings.[9]

Pentateuchal regulations differ concerning who may preside at worship (i.e., serve as priest): members of any of the twelve tribes (Exod. 24:4–5, J), or the entire tribe of Levi only (Deut. 33:8–11), or only those Levites who are descended from Aaron (Exod. 28, P). Furthermore, specification of where legitimate worship may take place also varies: multiple places (Exod. 20:24 J; throughout the books of Judges–Samuel); or at Jerusalem only (Deut. 12:5–7; Ps. 132:11–18). (Consult table 6.)

The question may now plausibly be asked: Were these conflicting regulations concerning personnel and place *simultaneously* in effect, or did they become effective in a chronological sequence that moved from flexibility to restriction? The question is not, *Could* such competing claims have been made simultaneously?" but rather, "Is it *likely* that they were all officially sanctioned from the beginning of Israel's history?" The answer to the latter is "No" (lest there be political and cultic chaos).

The modern, rational supposition would be that there was a developmental sequence, from tolerance to exclusivity: from many altars to one, from multiple priestly families to a single genealogical line. If that is actually the way it happened, then source J would be the earliest and source P the latest, but we would still have only relative dates and not absolute ones.

Should one apply such modern suppositions of developmentalism to the ancient texts, however? Is the way that we may think that is *should* have happened a secure basis for believing that it in fact *did* happen that way? What is needed, given the scarcity of historical data within the Pentateuch itself, is some external evidence by which to test this proposed sequence of regulations. Fortunately, such evidence is to be found in the so-called historical books of the Bible (Joshua–Esther).[10] They provide the necessary "test cases" because they describe known and datable events, for example those connected with the reigns of specific kings.

Of the various cases one might choose, none is clearer than the story of Elijah's "contest" with the prophets of Baal on Mount Carmel (1 Kings 18). In the process of the confrontation, Elijah erects an altar and prepares a bull for sacrifice, and all this in the presence of a larger group of his countrymen. At least two things about the events are striking: Elijah is not of Levitical lineage, to say nothing of being an Aaronide; and Mount Carmel is quite some distance from Jerusalem. How can this be, in view of the restrictions in the Pentateuch? At least three options come to mind: *(a)* Elijah is quite innocent of such regulations, even though they would be central to his country's identity, which certainly would be a curious state of knowledge for a prophet of the Lord. *(b)* He is well aware of such regulations, but decides to ignore them under the circumstances, in which case one might have expected at least some protest from among the more "traditional" citizens in his audience, especially since King Saul, having deviated in such matters, was told by Samuel that God has consequently "rejected you from being king" (1 Sam. 15:23). *(c)* Elijah acted within the guidelines of the time, which had not yet placed restrictions upon either personnel or place of worship. That is, the tradition called J was then operative, but not the ones called D and P. This would seem, then, to have been the case in the mid-ninth century, since Elijah lived during the reign of King Ahab (869–850 B.C.E.).

A century later, the prophet Amos (apparently a Judean) condemns various aspects of the religion of the Northern Kingdom (Israel). However, he does not suggest that the capital (Jerusalem) of his own country is the sole legitimate sanctuary. That is, Deuteronomy is not yet a part of "scripture.'

Another century will pass until, during the reign of Josiah of Judah (640–609 B.C.E.), a sweeping reform will take place. This followed the discovery of "the book of the law in the house of the Lord" (2 Kings 22:8). The resultant reformation included the destruction of sanctuaries and enactment of other requirements that are in the book of Deuteronomy (*IDB*, I: 831–38, at sec. 8; II: 996–99, at p. 997*b*). It is furthermore to be noticed that the Levites, whom Deuteronomy extols as sole priests, are not mentioned in the prophets of the centuries just passed (eighth–seventh): Hosea, Amos, Micah, Nahum, Habakkuk, and Isaiah (1–39). They are mentioned by Jeremiah briefly (who begins his ministry near the time of Josiah's reform), and then they become central in the thought of Ezekiel (who is among the exiles in the sixth century). However, Ezekiel knows nothing of Aaron, upon whom everything depends in the Priestly materials (*IDBS*, pp. 1–3). Presumably, P is just then in the process of formation and promulgation as part of the sacred story.

Based just on the evidence presented above, it is evident as to why J had been assigned a date prior to the ninth century, D in the seventh, and P in the sixth–fifth centuries.

SIX

NOAH IN THE BIBLE

Readers of the English Bible are sometimes surprised to find that it relates events in the lives of two persons named Noah, and not merely of the hero of the flood story. Their names, although the same in the English versions, are clearly distinguishable in the Hebrew original.

The first, and lesser known, is one of the five daughters of Zelophehad (Num. 26:33; 27:1; 36:11; Josh. 17:3). The episode in which she participated was an important one, formative in women's right to inherit real estate. Her name, in Hebrew, is Nōʿāh, with two consonants that are different from that of the hero of the flood (one of them the feminine ending, -āh).

The second, and better known, is the son of Lamech (Gen. 5:28–29). His name, in Hebrew, is Nōᵃḥ, a masculine form with a distinct "ch" sound at the end. When the name was transliterated into Greek (in the Septuagint and in the New Testament), which did not have that sound, the name was shortened to Νῶε (e.g., Matt. 24:37). This was then transliterated into English (e.g., in early editions of the KJV) as Noe, to be pronounced Nō-ĕ. Subsequent revisions of the KJV standardized the spelling to the form that it had used for the name in the Old Testament: "Noah."

This son of Lamech is mentioned in the Bible in four related capacities, which will each be discussed in detail later.

1. A link in the genealogical chain that stretches from Adam to Abraham in the "primeval story" (Gen. 5:28–32; 10:1, 32) and beyond

(1 Chron. 1:4; Luke 3:36). This then provides the framework for the remaining information concerning him.

According to the ages in Genesis 5, Adam died in Lamech's fifty-sixth year, and Noah is the first birth recorded thereafter. Perhaps this was meant to suggest a status for Noah as the second father of the human race, achieved as the ancestor of all those who were born in the post-flood generations.

2. A man of exemplary righteousness, such that he was allowed to survive the great flood that swept his contemporaries away (Ezek. 14:12–20; Heb. 11:7; 1 Pet. 3:18–20; 2 Pet. 2:4–5). Such subsequent praise of him is based upon acclaim at the preface of the flood story itself (Gen. 6:8, 9). However, one aspect of subsequent praise seems to go beyond anything that is explicit in Genesis: that he was "a herald of righteousness" (2 Pet. 2:5), apparently meaning that he exhorted his neighbors to live righteous lives and possibly even warned them of the impending deluge.

3. The hero of the flood story (Gen. 6:5–9:19; Isa. 54:9; Matt. 24:37–39; Luke 17:26–27). Most of the present volume will concern itself with this aspect of the Noah story.

4. The first viniculturist and the discoverer of wine (Gen. 5:29; 9:20–21), whose subsequent drunkenness provided occasion for a curse upon one line of his descendants (Gen. 9:22–27).

I. NOAH THE SAILOR (GENESIS 6:5–9:19)

Regardless of when or by whom the "primeval story" was composed, it is plausible to believe that it was put together from smaller, once independent units of tradition (stories). The overall method of composition was the sequential arrangement of entire episodes: creation, brothers who struggle, divine-human intermixing, and so forth (see table 7).

A. Is It Composite?

In the flood story, however, there is a sudden departure from the whose-unit approach. There is now a curious mixture of vocabulary, style, and content, all within a single story. Here are some illustrations of this reality.

1. *Variations in the designation of the deity,* but not so much at random as by paragraph. There is, for example, "God" within 6:9–22, but "the Lord" within 7:1–5.

2. *Repetitions of a given event or saying.* For example, the deity twice commands Noah to bring various animals into the ark, following which we are told that Noah "did all that God commanded him" (6:22) or that Noah "did all that the Lord commanded him" (7:5). Other repetitions include entering the ark (7:7, 13), the beginning of the flood (7:10, 11), and the death of all land creatures (7:21, 22).

3. *Formal beginnings.* After reading of the Lord's decision to "blot out" humanity (6:5–8), we suddenly find an intrusive introduction at 6:9, "These are the generations of. . . ." It is the type of "standard beginning" to a story that occurs at 5:1 and 10:1, and as a conclusion at 2:4*a* (all of which have been assigned to the P-Source).

4. *Alternative conclusions.* When Noah and his family exit the ark, they are promised that a flood will not thereafter destroy humanity: "While the earth remains seedtime and harvest . . . shall not cease" (8:20–22). Then repetitiously, there is an account of blessing and the promise symbolized by the rainbow: ". . . the waters shall never again become a flood . . ." (9:1–17).

5. *Differences in detail.* One of the most conspicuous is that Noah is told to bring "two of every sort" of animal into the ark (6:19–20), or is it seven pairs of "clean" animals and one pair of the others (7:2)? Curiously, the former is part of a "God" paragraph, but the latter is part of a "the Lord" paragraph.

6. *Certain standard phrases and concerns* are evident, reminding the reader of their occurence elsewhere in the Primeval Story: "male and female. . . according to their kinds" (6:19–20; 7:14–16), reminding one of 1:21, 24, 27 ("P"). There is also a concern with calendar (7:11; 8:4, 13 ,14) and age (7:6), reminding one of chapters 5 and 10 ("P").

To those who had formulated the Documentary Hypothesis, therefore, it looked as if the sources "J" and "P" continued into the flood story, except that now they were closely merged into a single account. Table 9 is a clear but limited illustration of why such interpreters decided that the story was composite, and of the bases upon which the assignment to sources was made.

Once the entire flood story had been divided into its possible sources, the result was approximately as shown in Table 10 (individual scholars might vary slightly in their opinions, of course).[1]

TABLE 9: ILLUSTRATION OF SOURCES

J	P
The *Lord* saw that the wickedness of man was great in the earth, and that every imagination of the thoughts of his heart was evil continuously (6:5).	Now the earth was corrupt in *God's* sight, and the earth was filled with violence. And *God* saw the earth, and behold, it was corrupt; for all flesh had corrupted their way upon the earth (6:11–12).
And the *Lord* was sorry that he had made man on the earth, and it grieved him to his heart. So the *Lord* said, "I will blot out man whom I have created from the face of the ground, man and beast and creeping things and birds of the air, for I am sorry that I have made them" (6:6–7).	And *God* said to Noah, "I have determined to make an end of all flesh; for the earth is filled with violence through them; behold, I will destroy them with the earth" (6:13)
Then the *Lord* said to Noah, "Go into the ark, you and all your household. . . . Take with you *seven pairs* of all clean animals that are not clean. . . *and a pair* of animals that are not clean. . . . For in seven days I will send rain upon the earth forty days and forty nights . . ." (7:1–4).	"Make yourself an ark. . . . For behold, I will bring a flood of waters upon the earth. . . . You shall come into the ark, you, your sons, your wife, and your sons' wives with you. And of every living thing of all flesh, you shall bring *two of every sort* into the ark . . . male and female . . ." (6:14–21).
And Noah did all that the *Lord* had commanded him (7:5).	Noah did this; he did all that *God* commanded him (6:22).
And Noah and his sons and his wife and his sons' wives with him went into the ark, to escape the waters of the flood. Of clean animals, and of animals that are not clean, and of birds, and of everything that creeps on the ground, two and two, male and female, went into the ark of Noah, as God had commanded Noah. And after seven days the waters of the flood came upon the earth (7:7–10).	In the six hundredth *year* of Noah's life, in the second *month*, on the seventeenth *day* of the month, . . . Noah and his sons, Shem and Ham and Japheth, and Noah's wife and the three wives of his sons with them entered the ark, they and every beast *according to its kind* . . . and every creeping thing . . . and every bird. . . . . . .as *God* commanded him (7:11, 13–16).

Given the evidence upon which the Documentary Hypothesis rests (for the entirety of the first five books of the Bible) and the wide consensus among modern scholars as to its correctness, even recent critics have remarked: "The claim is clear and germane—and the concrete textual argument in its favor is utterly stunning" (Kikawada and Quinn, p. 22). Even the pre-flood materials in the "primeval story" seem to support it:

NOAH IN THE BIBLE

TABLE 10:   SOURCES IN THE FLOOD STORY

J	P
6:5–8	
	6:9–22
7:1–5	
	7:6
7:7–10	
	7:11
7:12	
	7:13–16a
7:16b–17	
	7:18–21
7:22–23	
	7:24–8:2a
8:2b–3a	
	8:3b–5
8:6–12	
	8:13a
8:13b	
	8:14–19
8:20	
	9:1–17
9:18–19	

"Clearly if there is effective evidence against the documentary hypothesis, it is going to have to be found outside Genesis 1–5" (Kikawada and Quinn, p. 21).

B.   IS IT A UNITY?

Nonetheless, within the flood story itself there are nagging irregularities. Among them are the following.

1. While the P account seems to be a complete story (that is, one can remove the J materials and there remains a coherent whole), the reverse is apparently not true. Note, for example, the jarring transition

TABLE 11   CHARACTERISTICS OF THE PROPOSED SOURCES IN THE
FLOOD STORY

Characteristic	J-Source	P-Source
1. designation of the deity (usually)	"the Lord"	"God"
2. attitude of the deity toward impending deluge	sorrowful (Gen. 6:6–8)	matter-of-fact (7:11–13)
3. number of animal pairs specified to be brought aboard the ark	Seven pairs of "clean" and one pair of others (7:2)	One pair of each kind (6:19–20)
4. concern for chronology	no	yes (7:11; 8:4, 13a, 14)
5. concern with age of flood hero	no	yes (7:6)
6. a complete story is presented	no	yes
7. deity depicted in human form	yes (7:16b; 8:21a)	no
8. makes allusions to Gen. 1 (P)	no	yes (at 6:20; 7:18–21)
9. makes allusions to Gen. 2–3 (J)	yes (at 6:6–7; 7:2; 8:21)	no
10. duration of the flood, until the earth was dry	Forty days, plus three weeks (8:6, 10, 12, 13b)	a year: from 2/17/600 of Noah's life to 2/27/601 (7:11; 8:14)
11. concern for detail	no	yes (6:15–16, 20–21; 7:20; 8:4)
12. source of the flood waters	rainfall (7:4, 12; 8:2b)	flooding of the cosmic reservoirs, above and beneath: "fountains of the great deep . . . the windows of the heavens" (7:11; 8:2a)

as one reads from 6:8 to 7:1 (J): "But Noah found favor in the eyes of the Lord. Then the Lord said to Noah, 'Go into the ark, . . . '" One moves directly from God's decision to destroy human life to a command to enter the ark. One might have expected some announcement of the flood and the giving of instructions to build a boat, but it is not there. Should one assume, therefore, that J's account of these things has been removed and replaced by the P version (as most interpreters do)? Or may one assume that the J account did not feel it necessary to spell out well-known details (McEvenue, p. 27, n. 15)? A few interpreters, bothered by the assumption that materials have been editorially deleted by P, have proposed that the ages of the two strands be reversed: P becomes the base-text, supplemented by a later J.

2. The statement at the end of 7:16, that "the Lord shut him in," plausibly belongs to the J-Source, thus dividing the verse since it contains a prior reference to "God" (ordinarily, an indicator of the P-Source). In that case, however, it seems oddly out of place: it ought to stand near the conclusion of a J paragraph concerning the entry into the ark. Verse 9 would do nicely: "...went into the ark with Noah, as God had commanded Noah, *and the Lord shut him in.*" More usually, the commentaries suggest that it properly belongs at the end of v. 10 (Speiser).

In any case, one then notices that even the J section, 7:7–10, contains a reference to "God," and this is sometimes attributed to "a later redactor," that is, an editor (Speiser).

How did the supposed J fragment ("and the Lord shut him in") get separated from its supposed original setting (within vv. 7–10)? Did an editor insert the P segment (vv. 11–16a) at the wrong place, for reasons now obscure? One might plausibly think so, if the entirety of vv. 11–16a were P, but then there is v. 12 (J) right in the middle of it!

Things would be a bit neater, of course, if v. 16b were assigned to the P-Source despite its use of "the Lord." That is, the sources are not entirely rigid in their designations for the deity.

Who was it that combined the J and the P materials? Was it the formulators of the P tradition themselves? Or did the P story exist in a the later editor combined the two? Those who propose the latter approach assign the editor (redactor) the siglum R^{jp}. When might this proposed person/group have lived, and what was their purpose? Did they mechanically juxtapose blocks of materal (now a bit of J, now a bit of P)? Or was there a creative use of those traditions (Anderson)? Obviously, modern interpreters are divided on this and other issues relating to the Documentary Hypothesis, and "there is much that we do not know" (Anderson, p. 31).

Such problems with the Documentary Hypothesis,[2] especially within the flood story, have led a few recent interpreters to propose alternative ways of understanding its composition. Is it possible that the flood story is, after all, a single composition (Kikawada and Quinn)?

One of the strongest claims for the unity of the flood story rests upon the perception that it contains instances of a literary form known as a palistrophe, some of which cross the supposed bounds of the sources of the Documentary Hypothesis. A palistrophe is a symmetrical line of thought that covers a series of elements, then retraces its way back over them; the essential element of the construction is "return."[3] Thus, a palistrophe of three elements might be diagrammed as follows:

```
a     b     c     b'     a'     or:     a
                                             b
                                                  c
                                             b'
                                        a'
```

A simple illustration may be found at Isaiah 6:10.

```
a          Make the heart of this people fat,
b               and their ears heavy,
c                    and shut their eyes;
c'                        Lest they see with their eyes,
b'               and hear with their ears,
a'          and understand with their hearts,
            and turn and be healed.
```

An illustration within the Noah material would be at Genesis 9:5 (keeping the RSV wording, but observing the order of the Hebrew text),

```
a          Whoever sheds
b               the blood
c                    of man
c'                   by man
b'               his blood
a'          shall be shed.
```

The question now becomes: Will a given palistrophe be contained entirely within the bounds of alleged J or P material, or will it stretch across the boundaries of such proposed sources? That the J writer might use such a construction, or the P writer, is understandable: but what if a given palistrophe is half J and half P? A proposed illustration (by Kikawada and Quinn, p. 86), is Genesis 6:8–9, where v. 8 is ordinarily assigned to J and v. 9 to P. The order of the Hebrew text is followed.

```
a          ⁸Noah
b               found favor
c                    in the eyes of the Lord.
```

d	⁹These are the generations of Noah.
e	Noah was a righteous man,
e'	blameless he was
d'	in his generation;
c'	with God
b'	walked
a'	Noah.

Based upon this and related evidence, it has been remarked: "Far from being two different accounts, Genesis 6:1–12 could scarcely be more tightly unified" (Kikawada and Quinn, p. 87).

C. Evaluation

How is one to evaluate this methodology and conclusion? At least the following considerations would seem to be in order.

1. Is the beautiful palistrophe that has been constructed from the English text really there in the Hebrew text? Note, for example, the flaw in the d/d' balance: although the English text has "generations"/"generation," the Hebrew words are not the same. The former is *tôledōt*, while the latter is *dōrōt*. The former is more properly rendered as "story" (NEB, NJB, TEV), while the latter is "age" (NAB), "time" (NEB, TEV), "contemporaries" (NJB). Hence in the more accurate NEB the alleged parallel vanishes: "This is the story of Noah."//" (The one blameless man) of his time."

What is sufficient to constitute the "return" which is at the heart of a palistrophe? Reoccurrence of *any* word? Of a *key* word? Of an entire *phrase?* In short, when is the correspondence between members so close that one may reasonably suppose that a palistrophe was intended, and when is it so fluid that the modern interpreter may be imagining it?

2. If ever there is a clear formal opening of a literary unit in biblical literature, it is 'These are the generations of . . . " (see Gen. 5:1; 10:1, 11:10, 27; 25:12, 19; 36:1; 37:2; etc.). It may also serve as a formal conclusion: "These have been the generations of . . ." (e.g., at 2:4*a*; 10:32). To find it *inside* a palistrophe would be equivalent, in a fairy tale, to finding "Once upon a time . . ." in the middle of the story!

3. Genesis 6:8 does not begin with "Noah" (as the palistrophe outline suggests), but with "But Noah" (so also in the Hebrew text). The conjunction (rendered "but") ties this verse with the previous paragraph. Since God has determined to "blot out man" (6:7), the fate of Noah in v.

8 forms the exception ("But Noah found favor . . ."). There is, then, no unit beginning with v. 8, and hence no possible palistrophe.

4. Verse 9 is not the end of the topic under consideration, since it continues into the next verse (10), as is evident from the conjunction: *"And* Noah had three sons. . . ." Once again, the proposed palistrophe modifies the existing text.

5. In the most ancient divisions of the text (from the period of the Talmud, fourth–fifth centuries C.E.), there is an open space in the text following v. 8. In the opinion of those who read the text at that time, there was a clear transition between v. 8 and v. 9. Similarly the ancient liturgical division of the text, for both the annual and the triennial lectionary of the Pentateuch, comes precisely at this point (and clearly so marked in the margin of the Hebrew text). It is not merely the recent interpreters of the Bible according to the Documentary Hypothesis, therefore, who perceive a break of some sort at the words, "These are the generations."

Quite correctly, then, other recent interpreters who have studied the flood story from the standpoint of composition and style have not discovered a palistrophe here. Thus McEvenue (p. 37) translates and structures 6:9–10 as a unit, as follows:

> [9]This is the story of Noah
> Noah was an upright man
> virtuous he was among his contemporaries
> with God walked Noah
> [10]And Noah begot three sons
> Shem, Ham, and Japheth

This arrangement clearly (and properly) recognizes "This is the story of Noah" as the heading; it preserves the link between v. 9 and v. 10, which is mandated by the conjunction ("and"); and it includes the list of Noah's sons (nearly mandated by the heading, where the word "story" is more literally "generations").

Is it possible that the entire flood story has a palistrophic structure? If so, the Documentary Hypothesis would be in deep trouble at that point. Just such an understanding is proposed by Kikawada and Quinn (pp. 103–4, following Wenham), covering Genesis 4:10*a*–8:19. It is reproduced as fig. 13.

A Noah (6:10*a*) [P]
B   Shem, Ham, and Japheth (6:10*b*) [P]
*C   ark to be built (6:14–16) [P]
D   flood announced (6:17) [P]
E   covenant with Noah (6:18–20) [P]
*F   food in the ark (6:21) [P]
G   command to enter ark (7:1–3) [J]
*H   7 days waiting for flood (7:4–5) [J]
*I   7 days waiting for flood (7:7–10) [J]
J   entry into ark (7:11–15) [P/J]
K   Yahweh shuts Noah in (7:16) [J]
L   40 days flood (7:17*a*) [P]
M   waters increase (7:17*b*–18) [J/P]
N   mountains covered (7:19–20) [P]
*O   150 days waters prevail (7:21–24) [P/J/P]
P   GOD REMEMBERED NOAH (8:1) [P]
*O'   150 days waters abate (8:3) [J/P]
N'   mountain tops visible (8:4–5) [P]
*M'   waters abate (8:5) [P]
L'   40 days (end of) (8:6*a*) [J]
*K'   Noah opens windows of ark (8:6b) [J]
*J'   raven and dove leave ark (8:7–9) [J]
*I'   7 days waiting for waters to subside (8:10–11) [J]
H'   7 days waiting for waters to subside (8:12–13) [J/P/J]
*G'   command to leave the ark (8:15–17, or 22) [P, or P/J]
*F'   food outside ark (9:1–4) [P]
E'   covenant with all flesh (9:8–10) [P]
D'   no flood in future (9:11–17) [P]
*C'   ark (9:18a) [J]
B'   Shem, Ham and Japheth (9:19*b*) [J]
A' Noah (9:19 [J]

Fig. 13. Palistrophic structure, following Wenham, p. 338. (Courtesy of E. J. Brill.) Sources according to the Documentary Hypothesis have been added in brackets, for comparison, and an asterisk placed beside those lines concerning which we shall subsequently ask questions.

What a complex and remarkable composition this appears to be! A single (noncomposite) source might indeed appear to be in evidence if fig. 13 accurately reflects the reality (and the intention) of the text.

Even a quick glance, however, reveals some troublesome (although perhaps not fatal) aspects. Some elements are multiverses (up to seven for D'), while others are surprisingly brief (only part of a verse in a case of A, B, L, L', K', C', B'). The corresponding elements are not of comparable length, for example, C (6:14–16) and C' (9:18a); D (6:17) and D' (9:11–17). Furthermore, parts of the text have been skipped over: 6:11–13, 22; 7:6; 8:3, 14; 9:5–7. Should there be leftovers in such an apparently finely wrought composition? And finally, the definition of some of the elements is so unclear that one can list G' either as 8:15–17 or as 8:15–22. In a composition of this magnitude, with so many potential elements, there is plenty of material by means of which the modern interpreter can enhance a form and make it more compelling. Thus, the more complex the proposed structure, the more exacting must be the controls that are used to demonstrate its existence.

Let us turn now to a closer reading, involving those elements that are marked with an asterisk. If there is an obvious "return" anywhere in the flood story, it would be 6:5–8 and 8:20–22. In the former, the deity decides to destroy humanity because "every imagination of the thoughts of his heart was only evil continually." In the latter, God will not so act again, even if "the imagination of man's heart is evil from his youth." The situation of the beginning is now reversed at the end, the very construction that marks the Mesopotamian flood stories as well (see above, chap. 2). Thus a palistrophic construction for the flood story should begin at 6:5, not 6:10, and these two elements should be parallels (perhaps A and A'). Curiously, 8:20–22 plays no part in the scheme of Kikawada and Quinn, or at most they are an optional conclusion to the element entitled, "command to leave the ark" (G'). This alone, in this writer's opinion, is sufficient to demolish the entire proposed palistrophic hypothesis for the flood story.

Both elements H and I are entitled, "7 days waiting for flood"—a curious repetition, especially when H (7:4–5) says nothing about waiting (although it does mention that the flood is seven days away)—and when I (7:7–10) is concerned with the type of animals that are to be brought into the ark. What accounts for such nonobvious labeling of these two elements? Note the more accurate labeling at I' (8:10–11) and H' (8:12–13), where there is specific mention of "waiting." One can scarcely escape the impression that H and I have been tailored to fit an assumed parallel with I' and H'. A *proposed* palistrophe might demand it, but the text itself does not.

The element O is entitled "150 days waters prevail." However, that is hardly the gist of 7:21–24, which is concerned to state that every living thing outside the ark died in keeping with prior divine announcement (6:7, 13), which curiously is not a theme in the palistrophe. The statement of duration is a mere footnote at the end. Has the definition of O been crafted so as to parallel O'?

Does the element K' really mark a return to K? At 7:16 (K) there is an important theological statement: "Yahweh shuts Noah in." The subject is different, with little importance, at 8:6*b* (K'): "Noah opens windows of ark." Neither vocabulary nor concept is the same.

Does "raven and dove leave ark" (J') naturally suggest a palistrophic "return" to "entry into ark" (J)? In the former case, it is not an exit from the ark that is the issue, but the sending out of two animals only, in order to see if dry land has appeared. In the latter case, it is *all* the animals who enter the ark, but the natural equivalent of that would be 8:19 (G'). Furthermore, the story of the flight of the (two) doves curiously has been divided: only one of them has been placed in J'. The other (vv. 10–11) has been labeled "7 days wating for waters for subside" and identified as I'. Has this been done because of the need to find a balance for the element I?

Can one take seriously the proposed "return" of F' to F: "food outside ark" (9:1–4) to "food in the ark" (6:21)? The former really concerns a restriction placed upon humans after the flood: they may now consume meat, which formerly was forbidden to them. And where was it forbidden? At Genesis 1:29, which is the true antecedent of F'. There is, however, another concern in 9:1–4, which the labeling has ignored: the seriousness of murder. Parallels with the Atrahasis Epic (see above, chap. 2) suggest that this is a response to the pre-flood violence, and thus we might be referred back to Genesis 4:1–24. The "return" is thus quite far afield from that proposed by the palistrophe. Would the proposed "return" be any more artificial if element F were expanded to include v. 22, so that one could propose elements "God before the flood" (F) and "God after the flood" (F')?

The proposed element C' is even more far-fetched as a return to C: "ark" (9:18*a*) and "ark to be built" (6:14–16). Note how 9:18*a* actually reads: "The sons of Noah who went out from the ark ..." The alleged connection is but a single word, and not the central one at that.

Abatement of the waters seems to be the concern of 8:3–5, and yet the passage has been divided into three elements (O', N', and M'), two of which are labeled "waters abate." Is this because a parallel had to be found for M, in order for the palistrophe to work?

In sum: a palistrophe has been created (not discovered) by means of deletions (six of them, totaling up to fifteen verses), artificial labeling, premature shortening of proposed elements, and ignoring the most obvious of all possible "returns" (8:20–22 to 6:5–8).

Several of the proposed elements in the palistrophe have crossed the boundaries of those sources that adherents of the Documentary Hypothesis have perceived: J, M, O, O', H', and G'. Compare this list with those elements concerning which, according to the previous discussion, problems are most evident (asterisked): J', M', O, O', H, and G' (among others). This suggests that the proposed palistrophe encounters difficulties at precisely those points where it should if the Documentary Hypothesis has substance.

The compositional unity of the flood story has thus not been demonstrated. It indeed does appear to be composite (i.e., composed of at least two earlier strands), even if the traditional division into the sources J and P is problematic at points.

II. NOAH THE FARMER (GENESIS 9:20–27)

Genesis 9:18–19 seems to be the conclusion of J's account of the flood. If so, it has been displaced (separated from 8:22) by the insertion of the covenant account (P). Note how the wording of 9:19 is appropriate for such a conclusion: "from these the whole earth was populated."

As the completed text now stands, however, 9:18–19 sets the stage for a new episode, that of Noah and his sons (9:20–27). The transition is more radical than it appears at first glance, so much so that some modern interpreters have proposed that the two stories (Noah the Sailor and Noah the Farmer) once circulated independently. Indeed, some of them have wondered if "Noah" is the same person in the two accounts (see below, app. 5).

That v. 20 begins a new story (and possibly a once independent one) is not evident from RSV: "Noah was the first tiller of the soil." The continuity thus seems smooth: this is the same Noah about whom we have been reading all along. NEB, however, has the sound of something new, the beginning of a story: "Noah, a man of the soil, began the planting of vineyards" (similar is the wording of NAB, TEV, JB, NIV).[4] Thus one could begin to read at this point and not have a sense that essential information is missing, namely, that one has begun in the middle of a larger account.

What are the indications of discontinuity, other than the formal beginning, as one moves from v. 19 to v. 20? Among those that have been noticed are the following.

1. In the flood story, the three sons of Noah are married: ". . . come into the ark, you, your sons, your wife, and your sons' wives with you . . ." (Gen. 6:18, P; 7:7, J). In the viniculture story, by contrast, there is no mention of Noah's daughters-in-law. Indeed, his sons seem to live in the same tent with their father, and one might thus think that they are unmarried (von Rad, p. 132; *IDB*, III:555).

Is this, then, a misplaced pre-flood story? Such misplacement in a chronological scheme is not unheard of in the Bible. Consider, for example, that Rachel (wife of the patriarch Jacob) dies at Genesis 35:19, but is nonetheless alive and well in a subsequent chapter (37:10).

Furthermore, in the account as it now stands, Noah is depicted as having a grandson, Canaan (9:22), and thus one might assume that his sons are indeed married. The introduction of Canaan, however, complicates the story even more, as we shall see.

2. The characters in the flood story, and those in the viniculture episode, although they have the same names, do not function in the same way. The characters in the former are depicted as individuals, but those in the latter account are presented as the personification of sociopolitical groups. Whereas we have been reading of the activities of individuals who are the ancestors of the entire human race, we now learn of the fate of specific peoples, and three of them only: Shem (apparently Israel, since Yahweh blesses him), Ham/Canaan (the Canaanites), and Japheth (migrants from the Aegean Sea, related to the Philistines?). The purpose of the viniculture story seems to be to explain the political and/or social relationships of these groups: Why was the once-flourishing Canaanite civilization eclipsed by the other two groups?[5]

What one encounters, then, in the move from v. 19 to v. 20, is a new literary type: from a flood story to an etiology (see app. 5, n. 1). This type of literature, attested in ancient societies around the world, intends to explain some presently existing object or custom by means of an "event" in the past. Thus the present relationship between Canaanites and Israelites is explained by what "Mr. Canaan" and "Mr. Shem"

(Semite) did in primeval time. Likely, neither ancient storyteller nor ancient hearer presupposed that an etiology was, strictly speaking, historical. If modern interpreters want the story to be literally historically true, then that is their problem; it was not the ancient concern when this kind of story was told.

Otherwise put: in Genesis 9:20–27, Shem, Ham, and Japheth are the proposed ancestors of only Israelites, Canaanites, and Philistines (?). It is only when this story is read in the light of the prior flood story (and especially after 9:19) that they also become the ancestors of the entire human race.

There is yet another portrait of the three sons of Noah to be found in the "primeval story." According to Genesis 10, which lists the descendants of Noah under the heading of Shem, Ham, and Japheth, the divisions of humanity are as follows. (a) Shem includes not merely the Israelites, but also such traditional enemies as the Arameans and Assyrians (Shemites/Semites as well),[6] of whom most Israelites would scarcely say, "May the Lord my God bless them" (as is said in Gen. 9:26). (b) The sons of Ham include peoples of Africa, and not just Canaanites. (c) Japheth ranges over a wide area, including the peoples of Asia Minor and Europe. It is obvious, then, that the perception of the sons of Noah in our story (9:20–27) is different from that of the other two accounts. This also suggests that it may have a separate origin.

3. The viniculture account is a strange mixture of prose and poetry (not visible in KJV, but it is in most other English versions). Such a mixture often indicates an edited text rather than the product of single authorship. Note that, according to the prose account, it is Ham who observed his father's drunken exposure and reported it to his brothers (v. 22). However, in the poetic account of the father's curse, it is Canaan who is held accountable. and for no apparent reason (vv. 25–27). This happens when he (Noah) learns "what his youngest son had done to him" (v. 24). If the "youngest son" is Noah's rather than Ham's, (as seems implied) then according to the order in which the sons are listed (Shem, Ham, Japheth: 5:32; 6:10; 9:18; 10:1), the youngest son should be Japheth—but the story clearly does not mean that. Consequently, some modern interpreters have wondered if, behind this episode, there was once a different list of Noah's sons: Shem, Japheth, and Canaan. If so, that would surely indicate that the viniculture story has an independent origin and possibly that it should not be taken as a historical sequel to the flood story.

According to this perspective, the original story ran as follows (with words in parentheses being later editorial clarifications, meant to harmonize the two lists of Noah's sons).[7]

[18]The sons of Noah . . . were Shem, Japheth, and Canaan. (Ham was the father of Canaan.) [19]These three were the sons of Noah. . . [20]Noah . . .[21]became drunk, and lay uncovered in his tent. [22]And (Ham the father of) Canaan, saw the nakedness of his father . . . [24]When Noah awoke. . . [25]he said, "Cursed be Canaan. . ."

Are such editorial explanations necessary, however? The problem with the switch in names (Ham looks, and Canaan is cursed) arises primarily when one reads the text as if it were an account of individuals, rather than reading it as an etiology. That is, if one reads the story from the standpoint of group relationships, the problem may vanish. Perhaps one should not think of it as a historical account of what biological individuals did on one fine day in the Ancient Near East, but, rather, as the projected interaction of peoples in Syro-Palestine (*IDB,* III: 108–10). Ancient hearers would not have clearly distinguished the Canaanites from the larger Hamitic group to which they were assigned. Too them, it would thus be quite intelligible to hear, "And Ham . . .saw the nakedness of his father. . . When Noah awoke . . . he said, 'Cursed be Canaan' . . .." Only when this account was placed in sequence with the flood story, leading to the mentality that the sons of Noah are to continue to be thought of as individuals, would a tension (Ham vs. Canaan) arise that might necessitate editorial clarifications (Westermann, p. 484).

Whatever the relationship of the flood story and the viniculture account may be, there remains the puzzling nature of Ham's offense. What was it that he did to merit such a terrible curse? The text is not explicit in that regard, and this has led to several conjectures.

Was it an excessive consumption of wine, leading to drunkenness? This is a common Christian moralistic interpetation, well illustrated by the following statement (*IB,* I: 552–54): "Drunkenness is as old as history, and as unpredictable. . . . Why did Noah get drunk? . . . the root of the matter may be a desire to escape. . . . The word for our time is 'Be sober, be vigilant' (1 Peter 5:8)." While it may be true that Noah's consumption had negative consequences, that is hardly the point of the narrative. Note that the larger context seems to view the product of the vine in a positive light: at the birth of Noah, in a pun on his name, his father announces: "Out of the ground which the Lord has cursed this one shall bring us relief from our work and from the toil of our hands" (Gen. 5:29; for the nature of the pun, see sec. IV in the present chap.) Indeed, throughout the Bible, wine is regarded as a blessing and as a symbol of a blessed age to come (Hos. 9:10; Amos 9:13–15; Matt. 26:26–29), even though excess is condemned (Isa. 5:11; Prov. 20:1). In our text, there is no condemnation of Noah for any action, and it is clear that viniculture is presented as an advance in the history of civilization. It is Ham/Canaan who is condemned, and nothing is said of his consumption of alcohol.

Did the son indulge in some unmentionable sexual act with his drunken father? Did Ham merely observe the "nakedness of his father," while it was his son (Canaan) who acted in an unmentionable way (i.e., the "youngest son" of v. 24 is Ham's, not Noah's, as some medieval Jewish commentators proposed)? A few modern interpreters have made this suggestion, but it has found little acceptance. It is thus pointless to speculate about that which the text does not express.

Does the text mean to depict the Canaanite civilization as prone to licentiousness, by means of a story about what "Mr. Canaan" (from whom all Canaanites descended) did in primeval time? If so, then is the text suggesting that Israelites (descended from "Mr. Shem") should not accept such values? Such culture-shock on the part of the Israelites is well attested in the Bible (e.g., at Lev. 18:24–30).[8] This is the predominant interpretation of the text among modern critical scholars (e.g., von Rad, p. 133).

It should be noted, however, that the contrast between Ham/Canaan and his brothers is in the way that they respond to their father's situation.

> Ham's sin does not consist in a general shamelessness or in unbridled sexuality, but in dishonoring his father ... then one can no longer say that the text is speaking about anything specifically to do with the historical Canaanite people. It is much more a question of the obligations of the son to take care of his father...
>
> [Westermann, pp. 484–85]

The concern of the passage, then, may be related to that of the fourth of the Ten Commandments ("Honor your father and your mother . . ."). As such, it would be in keeping with a continual theme of the J-Source: the culpability of individuals in the most basic of human relationships (between man and woman in Gen. 2–3, between siblings in Gen. 4, and between parent and child in our text (Westermann, p. 494).

III.   NOAH THE PREACHER (2 PETER 2:5)

One of the basic biblical portraits of Noah falls outside the flood story, and indeed outside the book of Genesis. The author of 2 Peter refers to Noah as "a herald of righteousness" (2:5). While it is true that Genesis 6:9 refers to him as "a righteous man, blameless in his genera-tion," that is somewhat short of one "who preached righteousness" (as TEV translates the text from 2 Peter).

Such a portrait of Noah had already been reported by the Jewish historian Josephus, about the time of the New Testament: "But Noah was very uneasy about what they [his neighbors] did; and being dis-pleased by their conduct, persuaded them to change their dispositions and their acts for the better;—but, seeing that they did not yield to him . . . he departed out of that land." (*Antiquities*, I.3.i., trans. Whiston). Similar claims may be found in other early Jewish literature (e.g., Jubi-lees 7:20–39, ca. 100 B.C.E.) as well as in the writings of early Christians (e.g., Saint Augustine, fifth century) and of Muslims. The author of the Sybilline Oracles supplied Noah with a lengthy speech (1.175–233) in which Noah condemns his society for its belief and acts, and warns of the impending flood.

How might such a tradition concerning Noah have arisen, since it is not contained in the book of Genesis? Did one or more of the following factors contribute to it?[9]

1. In a unit of material (story) that now serves as a prelude to the flood episode, God's displeasure at human activity leads to the judgment that man's "day's shall be a hundred and twenty years " (Gen. 6:1–4). This would seem to set the ordinary upper limits of the individual human lifespan (Westermann, pp. 363–83). If the episode is then read as an integral part of the flood story (rather than as a commentary on mor-tality), one might assume that the 120 years is a period of reprieve until the coming of the waters of the great deluge. Indeed, a number of tradi-tional interpreters have so undertstood it.[10] In that case, Noah would be the likely candidate for one who would warn that pre-flood generation. (For another interpretation, see app. 5, n. 1.)

2. That the Genesis account does not portray Noah as one who was concerned for the spiritual and physical welfare of his contemporaries might raise a question in the mind of readers: "Should he not have warned them?" Would not silence, under the circumstances, be incompatible with one who had been acclaimed "a righteous man, blameless in his generation," and especially with one who "found favor in the eyes of the Lord" (Gen. 6:8)? Pious creativity could thus lead the troubled interpreter to see in the 120 years of Genesis 6:3 a period of grace during which Noah could do the proper thing, and thereby even the deity not be accused of injustice.

3. Comparison of the Genesis account of the flood with the literature of ancient Mesopotamia provides an interesting possibility for understanding Noah the Preacher. When the flood hero Utnapishtim asks his patron deity how he is to explain to his fellow citizens why he is building a great boat (see above, chap. 2), he receives an answer that is both clever and deceitful: he is merely preparing to sail to the realm of his patron in order to escape the displeasure of another deity!

> Thou shalt then thus speak unto them:
> "I have learned that Enlil is hostile to me,
> So that I cannot reside in your city,
> Nor set my f[oo]t in Enlil's territory.
> To the Deep I will therefore go down,
>   To dwell with my lord Ea.
> [But upon] you he will shower down abundance,
> . . . .
> [He who at dusk orders] the husk-greens,
> Will shower down upon you a rain of wheat."
> [Gilgamesh XI, *ll.* 38–47; trans. Pritchard, p. 93][11]

The words rendered "husk-greens" (*kukku*) and "wheat" *(kibtu)* are usually assumed to be a pun on the words for "gloom" and "pain."[12] Thus the hearers would understand that Enlil will rain cereal and wheat upon them, whereas Utnapishtim really meant the gloom and destruction of the flood.

It is hardly surprising that the Genesis account would pass over this section of the traditional story,[13] if the interpretation above is correct, in silence. Thus it merely reports that, after hearing of the impending disaster and receiving instructions for the ark, "Noah did this; he did all that God commanded him." However, literate individuals in ancient Israel, aware of the Mesopotamian version,[14] might be temped to fill in the "missing" section with a response by Noah that was more fitting: Noah the "herald of righteousness."[15]

IV. NOAH: THE NAME BEHIND THE MAN

What does the name "Noah" (Hebrew: $N\bar{o}^a\d{h}$, more properly $N\bar{o}^a\d{h}$) mean? To date, no compelling explanation has been offered and indeed most commentaries pass over the problem in silence.[16] Hebrew dictionaries, however, routinely observe that the name is likely related to the verb "to rest" $(n\hat{u}^a\d{h},$ i.e., the consonants n-w-$\d{h})$. What the name would mean in that case, and why the flood hero should have received it, remains a mystery.

A. *Ziusudra = Utnapishtim = Noah?*

It is plausible to suppose that the name "Noah" might be related in meaning to those of the heroes of the flood stories from Mesopotamia. In the Sumerian version (see above, chap. 2), we read of Ziusudra, whose name is spelled *zi-u₄-sud-rá: zi* ("life") + *u₄* ("day") + *sud* ("to be long") + *rá*, that is, "life of long days." Presumably the name refers to the status granted to him by the deities:

The king Ziusudra
Prostrated himself before An (and) Enlil
. . . .
(Who) gave him life, like a god,
Elevated him to eternal life, like a god.
. . . .
They settled (him) in an overseas country,
in the orient, in Dilmun.
[Lambert and Millard, p. 145; cf. Pritchard, p. 44]

In the Gilgamesh Epic, the survivor of the flood is Utnapishtim: *ūt(a)* ("he found") + *napishtim* ("life"). He is further described as Utnapishtim *rūqu,* "Utnapishtim, the faraway," apparently because he was granted eternal life in the distant realm of the immortals (beyond the known world; Beek, p. 75, map).

Thereupon Enil went aboard the ship.
Holding me by the hand, he took me aboard.

165

He took my wife aboard and made (her) kneel by my side.
Standing between us, he touched our foreheads to bless us:
"Hitherto Utnapishtim has been but human.
Henceforth Utnapishtim and his wife shall be like unto us Gods.
Utnapishtim shall reside far away, at the mouth of the rivers!"

[XI, *ll.* 189–95; Pritchard, p. 95]

Not only are the meanings of the two names roughly the same, but also they are written similarly. (Akkadian is written with Sumerian syllabic values, using the same cuneiform signs.) In order to write "Utnapishtim," one reverses the first two signs of "Ziusudra" (resulting in u_4-*zi*); then gives the first one an alternative phonetic value (*ut* instead of u_4); then understands the second one as an ideogram (i.e., for the Akkadian word for life, *napishtu*), writing it with a phonetic complement for clarification. The result is *ut-zi*^{tim} that is *ut-(napishtim)*^{tim}. Then the Sumerian *sud-rá* is rendered by its Akkadian equivalent, *rūqu*. The result is that Ziusudra ("Life of distant days") is rendered as Utnapishtim rūqu ("He, the faraway, found life").

Might a similar thing have happened when the story was told in the related Semitic dialects of Syro-Palestine (e.g., in Hebrew)? In that case, the options for an explanation are not numerous. Indeed, the only discernible connection would be a meaning of the verb *n-w-ḥ (n-w-ḫ)* that survives otherwise only in Ethiopic: *nōḫa*, "to be extended, long" (and rarely "to rest"). The standard Hebrew dictionaries note the existence of the Ethiopic cognate, but do not connect it with the name of the flood hero. Is it possible, as Driver has suggested, that the name might mean something like "Long (in life)"?[17] That the Ethiopic verb was used in such temporal contexts is clear, for example, from its use to translate Ecclesiastes 8:13, "neither will he *prolong* his days" (see also its use at Deut. 4:40).

Such an explanation of the name is not without its difficulties, since it presupposes (with no evidence otherwise) that there was once a northwest Semitic verb (*n-w-ḥ/n-w-ḫ*, "to be extended") that has ceased to be used and otherwise survives only in Ethiopic. Ordinarily such an expression, in biblical Hebrew, would involve the adjective *'ārōk* ("long," used for designations of time).

Nonetheless, in support of this explanation, it may be pointed out that Noah is said to have "walked with [*hithallēk-'et*] God" (Gen. 6:9.). This is a rare description, said otherwise only of Enoch (Gen. 5:22,24). Modern interpreters have usually understood it to indicate intimate relationship and moral worthiness (Westermann, p. 358; von Rad, pp. 122–23), apparently by comparison with such passages as Genesis 17:1, where the deity says to Abraham, "walk before me [*hithallēk l'pānay*], and be blameless." It should be noted, however, that the prepositions are not the same (*'et* and *le*), and that, in the case of Enoch, quite a different interpretation emerges in the light of cuneiform parallels and in the book of Enoch: he is taken to the realm of the deity (see above, chap. 5). Skinner (p. 159) is likely correct, therefore, when he remarks, concerning Noah's "walk with God": "The expression receives a fuller significance from the Babylonian legend, where Ut-napištim, like the Biblical Enoch, is translated to the society of the gods."

In any case, the Priestly writer, as one might expect, has repressed any mythological implications: Noah is presented as a common citizen, whereas Ziusudra is a king; Noah is assigned a mere 600 years of age at the beginning of the flood, whereas Ziusudra was 36,000 (i.e., reduced from $60^2 \times 10$ to 60×10); and Noah remains a mortal, dying at the age of 950 years, whereas Ziusudra is granted immortality.

B. Mesopotamian Deity or Divinized Human?

An element that may be the grammatical equivalent of *Nō^ah* seems to have been found in a few Mesopotamian personal names. For example, cuneiform texts from the time of the patriarchs mention *Mu-ut-na-ḫa*. The name apparently consists of the word *mutu* ("male," "man") and a proper name. In many such combinations, the second element is a deity, as in the contemporary Babylonian name *Mu-ut-A-na-ta*, "Devotee of (the goddess) Anat." Similarly, at Genesis 5:21, we find Methuselah (*metu-Shelaḫ*), apparently, "Devotee of (the god) Shalaḫ." Again, at Genesis 4:18 we read of Methushael (*metu-Sha'el*), "Devotee of (the god) Sheol."[18] By analogy, might the name *Mu-ut-na-ḫa* mean "Devotee of (the god) Naḫ"? This receives support from other contemporary names such as *Na-ḫi-lum*, "Naḫ is (the) deity," and *Na-ḫi-li*, "Naḫ is my deity."[19]

What would be the possible connection between an apparent Mesopotamian deity Naḫ (more properly, Nāḫ) and the hero of the flood story in Genesis? Is "Noah" merely a nickname, a shortened form of some such full designation as *Na-ḫi-li* (above)?

Such nicknames do occur, as in Coniah (Jer. 22:24; 37:1) for the full Jehoiachin (*IDB* I: 670). Or has Nōaḫ/Nāḫ the human, in a lost version of the flood story, been accorded a semidivine status as were Zi-

usudra and Utnapishtim? Human beings, especially kings, were sometimes granted divine honors and even wrote the word "god" before their
name (*IDB,* III: 14, sec. 7*c*), although this is not attestetd for one of the
flood heroes.

C. Related to the Verb *N-W-Ḥ,* "to Rest?"

What of the supposed connection with the Hebrew verb *n-w-ḥ,* "to
rest"? It has been suggested that the flood story alludes to the name
"Noah" when it uses the verb at 8:4 ("the ark came to *rest*"), when it
uses nouns derived from the verb at 8:9 ("the dove found no *rest,*" KJV),
and even at 6:8 when it uses slight assonance ("Noah found *favor*" [*ḥēn,*
reversing the *n-ḥ*). (See Cassuto, I: 289.)

It is striking that the Akkadian cognate of the verb (i.e., *nāḫu/nuāḫu*)
occurs in the flood text of the Gilgamesh Epic. In its meanings "to relent,
be appeased, subside," it is used to describe the activity of the raging
waters: *i-nu-uḫ tâmtu,* "the sea subsided" (XI, *l.* 131).

Does the name of the hero suggest, then, one for whom the deluge
"abated," or who was granted "rest" at its conclusion (perhaps a faint
echo of Ziusudra's blessing)? Does his name allude to the promise that
"the waters shall never become again become a flood to destroy all
flesh" (9:15)?

Fanciful explanations based upon the verb "to rest" are offered in
postbiblical literature: by providing survivors, he consoled the earth
(Enoch 106–7); by inventing farming implements, he made life easier
(Midrash Agadah on Gen. 5:29); at his birth annual flooding subsided
(Genesis Rabbah, 25:2); etc.[20]

D. Arabic Cognates?

Attempts to explain the name on the basis of Arabic cognates have
also been made. One of the meanings of the Arabic verb *n-w-ḥ (nāḥa)* is
"to lament," and medieval writers told a story illustrative of that basis
for "Noah."[21] Alternatively, the name is explained as "liberality, gener-
osity," on basis of verb *n-ḥ-ḥ (IDB,* III: 556). The former is exceedingly
unlikely, and the latter has not found wide acceptance.

E. Father Lamech's "Explanation"

The biblical text itself appears to draw implications from the name
"Noah." At Genesis 5:28–29 we are told: "When Lamech had lived a

hundred and eighty-two years, he became the father of a son, and called his name Noah, saying, 'Out of the ground which the Lord has cursed this one *will bring us relief [yᵉnaḥᵃmēnû]* from our work and from the toil of our hands.' " Reference thus seems to be made backward to God's curse and the resultant human toil (3:17–19) and forward to Noah's pioneering work in viniculture (9:20), which will facilitate relaxation and festivity. Throughout Israel's history the fruit of the vine has been a symbol of the blessed life and of the messianic age (Amos 9:11–15; Mic. 4:1–4; Matt. 26:26–29).²²

Curiously, however, the writer (at 5:29) did not use the verb *(n-w-ḥ)* from which the name *(Nōᵃḥ)* may be derived. Rather, a unrelated one is used: *n-ḥ-m,* "to console, bring relief." (From the latter, names are also derived in the Bible, among them *Naḥ*man and Me*naḥem.)* Interpreters have long noted this curious incongruity and have explained it in various ways. Hence the rabbis observed: "The explanation does not correspond to the name nor the name to the explanation. The text should have either *Noah*—'this one will give us rest' *yᵉnîḥēnû*—or, *Nahman*—'this one will bring us comfort' *yᵉnaḥᵃmēnû*" (so Genesis Rabbah 25.2; see *IDB,* III: 555–56).

Did the text once contain the "correct" verb *(n-w-ḥ,* "to rest"), just as the Greek Bible (Septuagint) reads ("this one will give us rest"), such that the present Hebrew text (using *n-ḥ-m)* is a corruption (so *IDB,* III: 555–56)? However, the Greek Bible sometimes translates quite freely, in accordance with the context, and thus one need not conclude that the Hebrew text from which it translated actually read "this one will give us rest."

Does the explanation in Genesis 5:29 reflect an alternative (but otherwise lost) name for the flood hero? After all, we have Mesopotamian accounts of both Atrahasis and Ziusudra/Utnapishtim, and the latter is even called Atrahasis (Gilgamesh Epic, XI, *l.* 187). A rabbinic work actually proposed this solution: "And Methuselah called his name Noah, saying, 'The earth *rested* and ceased from acting corruptly in his days,' but his father Lamech called him Menahem, saying, 'This one will bring us *comfort.* . .' " (Sefer Hayyashar, eleven–twelfth centuries C.E.). This view is accepted by Cassuto (I: 288), who suggests that the name "Menahem" is reflected at Genesis 6:6, in a word play, "And the Lord was *sorry.* . ." (where the verb is an aspect of the root *n-ḥ-m,* which, in another aspect, means to "comfort, bring relief," as at 5:29). Just when humans were yearning "to be comforted" because of prior sin (3:17–19), their present sin leads to God's "sorrow" (Cassuto, I: 303).

It is likely, however, that we should not insist upon such a rigid connection between verb and name in the biblical explanation. Since the stories originated in oral form, such connections are more a matter of similarity of sound than they are of the etymological correctness, which the eye might notice in written form. Consider the following similarly loose parallels.

". . . in due time Hannah conceived and bore a son, and she called his name Samuel [*sh'mû'el*], for she said, 'I have asked [verb: *shā'al*] him of the lord' " (1 Sam. 1:20). Strictly speaking, the name means "offspring of god" and has no etymological connection to the verb. Some interpreters thus have proposed that the story must once have been told about the birth of King Saul (*shā'ûl,* literally: "having been asked"), but this is quite unnecessary. There is enough phonetic similarity to satisfy the hearer, who is, after all interested in a good story and not in a lesson in grammar.

2. "Pharaoh's daughter . . . named him Moses (*Mōsheh*), for she said, "Because I drew him out (*māshāh*) of the water' " (Exod. 2:10). The gap between name and suggested explanation is now even more radical. The modern consensus seems to be that the name is Egyptian, which is after all to be expected. It thus would mean "child of," as in the name of Pharaoh Ra-meses ("Child of the god Ra").[23] One would hardly expect Pharaoh's daughter to know the language of one of the several slave groups in her land well enough to make a pun on the Hebrew verb *māshāh*, "to pull." It is later Israelite tradition, then, that has "explained" the name in this fashion.

Based upon such parallels, and there are many more in the Bible, there is no need to emend the text of Genesis 5:29 so that the name and the verb (of the description of Noah) are the same. The present rather loose aural similarity is sufficient for the literary standards of ancient Israel.

Nonethless, the possibility of a closer phonetic parallel presents itself. If the name "Noah" means "Long (of life)," as suggested above, then it may once have expressed that idea fully, using the word for "life" (*hayyîm*). The name would then have sounded something like Nāh-hayyîm, involving all the consonants of the verb that Lamech used to describe the future activity of his son (*n-h-m*).[24] If such was the case, then the name was later shortened to Nah (see above for nicknames), and finally vocalized as Nōah (as if it were an infinitive, a form of name for which there are parallels in the Bible).

SEVEN

SO, WHAT DID IT MEAN?

Thus far our investigation of the story of Noah has been basically historically descriptive: comparison with other deluge stories (chaps. 1–2), examination of possible remains of the flood (chaps. 3–4), and finally the
nature of the early chapters of Genesis (Chap. 5) and their portraits of
Noah (chap. 6). For the historian and literary critic, it might be sufficient to terminate the inquiry at this point.

For those within the synagogue and church at present, however,
there are other questions to be asked. Foremost among them is: What
did the story mean in ancient Israel and what does the story mean to us
now, since we acknowledge the Bible to be normative (more or less) for
our ethical and spiritual existence? Unfortunately, this is an extremely
complex and divisive question, since the answer will depend upon the
very issues that have already given rise to denominational differences.
The present volume is not the place to discuss the general issue of biblical interpretation in detail, and thus we shall here merely summarize a
few aspects of the problem, as a preface to considering the meaning of
the flood story.

I. POSTBIBLICAL UNDERSTANDING

In reaching a decision about what a given text "means" for synagogue or church in the present, is it necessary to know how that text has

been understood in the New Testament, or in the Talmud, or by the
fathers of the church (Does one prefer those of the Greek East or of the
Latin West?), or by the various councils of the church, or by the Protestant Reformers (provided that they agree!)? Are all such opinions
merely a part of the history of interpretation (with no innate authority of
their own), or are they (at least, some of them) part of a continuing
revelation of God's agenda in the text?[1]

One may decide that postbiblical understandings are the result of
God's continuing clarification of what is only implicit in the text. That is,
in addition to the meaning(s) which were intended and understood during the period of the Bible itself, the postbiblical interpreters may have
sensed more than literal (or intended) meanings, which the ultimate author of Scripture (God) has hitherto allowed to remain undetected.
Hence Roman Catholic interpreters have traditionally spoken of the
"fuller sense" (*sensus plenior*) of Scripture.[2]

Conversely, one may decide that only those meanings that were explicit (or at least intended) within the biblical period may lay claim to
divine revelation and thus are authoritative in the present. One must
distinguish the Word of God (even if expressed in human words) from the
human opinion that is expressed in the history of interpretation. Generally this has been a Protestant attitude, although one might appeal to
postbiblical authorities for an understanding of what that intended
meaning was.

For example, is Noah to be accepted as a historical figure (regardless of how he may appear in the "primeval story") simply because the
New Testament speaks of "the days of Noah" (Matt. 24:37)? Does it
then become a matter of faith to believe that there were such "days"?
Did Noah warn his neighbors (2 Pet. 2:5), even though the flood story
itself does not say so? Were his neighbors given 120 years in which to
repent, which, if not expressly stated at Genesis 6:1–4, is the understanding of the Targumim (Aramaic paraphrase of the Bible), of Saint Augustine, and of Martin Luther? Did Ham's offense (Gen. 9:20–27) include
castration of his father in order to prevent further cohabitation with his
mother (Genesis Rabbah 36.7; Babylonian Talmud, *Sanhedrin* 108b)? Is
the serpent in the Garden of Eden a disguise "for a being hostile to God
and an enemy of the human race," i.e., the Devil (so the explanatory
note in the Jerusalem Bible and indeed of most Christian interpreters
before modern times)?

The answers depend, or course, upon whom you ask.

II. Levels of Meaning

The role of postbiblical meanings is only part of a more general problem. There is a spectrum of "meaning," which includes at least the following possibilities (and options for the present?).[3]

First, what did the biblical author intend to accomplish? Notice, for example, that Deuteronomy 15:1–2 mandates the cancellation of indebtedness at the end of every seventh year. The intention is to protect the needy from long-term indebtedness and to provide a new beginning. But what if a loan were really needed and creditors refused to grant it as the sabbatical year approached? In that case, the "spirit" of the regulation would be thwarted by its "letter." Hence Rabbi Hillel (near the time of the New Testament) found a way to honor the intent of the law rather than what it said.[4]

The recovery of this level of meaning, however, is often difficult in the extreme. For example, what Exodus 23:19 says is clear enough: "You shall not boil a kid in its mother's milk." What, however, is its rationale, its larger goal? Is this combination of foods intrinically wrong, so that the prohibition is an end in itself? Or is its aim that of forbidding the adoption of a Canaanite cultic meal? Or is there an expression of sensitivity even to the realm of animals? Since the text does not say, one is reduced to conjecture. Consequently, interpreters are sometimes cautioned against the "intentional fallacy."

Second, what did the biblical author say? While this is a retreat from the slippery realm of the author's intentionality, it still presents the modern interpreter with several problems. Perhaps the text has become corrupt in the long process of transmission.[5] Perhaps there are unusual words whose meaning is no longer clear, or words with more than one meaning and we cannot be sure which was intended.[6] Perhaps there are allusions to then current events, upon which the meaning depends, and about which we know very little.[7] Pehaps the cosmology is so alien to our own that we cannot understand it.

Consider the following illustrations. When the RSV renders Genesis 4:8 as "Cain said to Abel his brother, 'Let us go out to the field.' And when they were in the field . . .," it is following the text of the ancient versions (Greek, Syriac: see note in RSV). Has Cain's remark dropped accidentally from the Hebrew text, which has been followed by the KJV and rendered as "And Cain talked to Abel his brother: and it came to pass, when they were in the field . . ."? Or, is it that the ancient versions have supplied the quote as a clarification of the text? Again, the Hebrew noun *tōlēdôt* can mean both "generations" and "story," but at Genesis 6:9 does it mean the former (KJV, RSV, cf. NAB) or the latter (NEB, JB, TEV, cf. NIV)? What sociopolitical event is described in Genesis 9:25–27 (see above, chap. 6, n. 5)? When Genesis 1:6–8 speaks of a "firmament," does it refer to the troposphere, which once contained the Creationists' vapor canopy (Whitcomb and Morris, pp. 229, 255ff.), or was it thought to be a hard surface that held up a reservoir of water?[8]

There is also the possibility that a given book, or chapter, or paragraph will contain the words of more than one person. To hear what "the" author said, therefore, would necessitate separating the text into its individual parts. Note, for example, that Proverbs 1:1 seems to attribute the entire book to Solomon. That this is not accurate, however, is shown by 30:1 and 31:1. A similar suggestion has been made about many of the biblical books, and a conspicuous example would be the so-called First (genuine) Isaiah (much of chap. 1–39), Second Isaiah (40–55), and Third Isaiah (56–66). (See *IDB*, II: 731–44, at sec. B.) In the Pentateuch, of course, there is the hypothesis that it consists of the compilations J,E,D,P and that the flood story is a combination of J and P. If so, then each source once had its own situation, audience, and agenda. Thus the *authors* must be disentangled before we can listen to an *author*.

Yet another problem lurks to harass the modern interpreter who would become attuned to what "the author" said. While some of the material in the Bible originated in written form at the hand of a single individual (e.g., the letters of Paul), it is generally believed that much of it began in oral form and was transmitted in that fashion for some time.[9] In the latter case, we could not simply speak of what the author said, but only of what an audience heard. This would be most evident in the case of prophetic literature, where the prophet's disciples would gather and arrange whatever they could remember that the master had done and said.[10] In such oral recitation, not only is fallible human memory a potential problem, but also, errors of the ear are well attested in the Bible.[11]

Alas and alack, the end of our troubles is not yet at hand! If J (or P, or Moses, for that matter) is a compiler of ancient traditions (rather than an author, pure and simple: see app. 5, at n. 1), then the question may be asked about the meaning of a story prior to its inclusion in the present context of Scripture. A nice illustration would be Genesis 6:1–4, which apparently was once an independent tradition and not an introduction to the flood story (see App. 5 n. 1). Might one want to inquire as to its meaning, as a unit in itself?

Third, what did the editor (redactor) say? Provided that some books or chapters of the Bible are composite, why were the materials brought together in just this sequence? In those instances where the process was not merely mechanical,[12] what larger and deliberately fashioned ideas emerge for our consideration? Not only would one want to ask: What happens to the meaning of Genesis 6:1–4 when it becomes a preface to the flood story? but also: What happens when the J account of the flood is incorporated into the P account?[13]

Fourth, how is a given text (or episode) understood elsewhere in Scripture? Will the understanding everywhere be the same, or will there be divergencies? In case of the latter, is there a rule of thumb about which is of higher authority? (In the synagogue, it is the Pentateuch that ranks highest; in the church, it is the New Testament.) Who, for example, influenced David to take a census: God (2 Sam. 24:1), or Satan (1 Chron. 21:1)? Does each account have an integrity of its own? Or does one try to harmonize them as does the Living Bible at the first passage: "David was incited . . ."? What is one to make of Saint Paul's use of Hosea 13:14? In the midst of the Assyrian attack upon the remnant of Israel in the eighth century, the prophet apparently announces that God will not save them: "Shall I ransom them from the power of Sheol? Shall I redeem them from Death?" Apparently the prophet refers to political, social, and economic death as the consequence of exile.[14] Paul, however, quotes the text as part of his vision of the transformation of mortals into immortals, when death is defeated at "the victory through our Lord Jesus Christ" (1 Cor. 15:54–57). Has Paul simply misunderstood the prophet? Has he made a free association with the prophet's words, but one that is entirely in keeping with the style of interpretation at the time? Has the true meaning of the prophet's words now been made clear by later revelation?

In terms of the flood story, this level of meaning arises from the portrait of Noah as "a herald of righteousness" (2 Pet. 2:5), and in certain understandings of Genesis 6:1–4.

Fifth, what has the text meant to revered interpreters in the postbiblical age? (This has been discussed at the beginning of the present chapter.)

Sixth, what does the text mean to the individual person? The procedure here is not so much that one must choose among the previous five options as it is that one either deliberately rejects them or is innocent of them. For example, some interpreters have rejected levels of meanings 1–4 because they were addressed to past situations that are quite alien to our own (e.g., "I'm not among the exiles in Babylonia in the sixth century B.C.E., so what could Isaiah 40–55 have to do with me?"); or because such interpreters are skeptical of our ability even to recover the ancient meanings (given the vast chronological, linguistic, and cultural gap that yawns between us and the world of the Bible); or simply because they do not like what the intended meanings would imply for their own lives! Other interpreters have argued that the "Word of God" is not so much the words of the text as it is the compelling sense of a divine presence and an imperative to act that may occur when the text confronts the hearer/reader in the present. Thus the important meaning would be "what it means to me," under the assumption that the Holy Spirit continues to clarify Scripture. And yet other interpreters, focusing upon the literary level, have proposed that *any* and all interpretations that are intellectually stimulating or aesthetically pleasing (i.e., that enhance our "enjoyment" of the text) are "valid" interpretations, whether or not they make any contact with the original concerns of the period of the Bible.

III. CENTRAL THRUST OR SIDE ISSUE?

Another troublesome question on the road to deciding what a text "means" is: Wherein, in a given text, does that meaning lie? Otherwise put: How much text must be taken into consideration before meaning emerges? With respect to the flood story, does one consider the entire account, or individual paragraphs (see the RSV), or sentences, or even individual words? Where did those who produced the account *intend* for meaning to be perceived by an audience: in the total effect, or in as many particulars as the modern hearer might isolate? In much modern preaching, the latter approach seems to be operative.

Consider, for example, how the homiletician treats the flood story in *The Interpreter's Bible* (I: 536–50). At least the following implications for Christian life in the present are drawn from it. (a) Persons now, as at the time of Noah, fail to see "the critical realities." (b) One must not be apathetic, but must, like Noah, act. (c) We must build according to heavenly specifications, as did Noah with the ark. (d) The church, like the family of Noah, must be a redeeming remnant. (e) In moments of despair, we must remember that God does not forget us (since God "remembered Noah," Gen. 8:1). (f) We must be patient, as was Noah when he waited for the waters to subside. (g) We must appreciate all of God's handiwork, since "every living thing" was preserved by divine command. (h) We must cultivate the spiritual life no less than the realm of nature.

All such proposed implications arguably are sage advice. However, they are based upon details in the text, passing incidentals in some cases, rather than the overall "point" being made. Perhaps one should ask: Is any one "meaning" as good as any other, as long as it edifies and meets a need in the congregation? However, if it is edifying to me, apart from the text's own agenda, then I am the final authority of "meaning." In that case, one might as well seek spiritual values in Shakespeare or turn to *The Gospel according to Peanuts*[15] for one's proclamation of "the Word of God."

IV. DID IT HAPPEN?

Another troublesome issue for some readers of the flood story in the present will be that of its historicity. Indeed, it may seem to them to be the question above all others, apart from which there can be no valid discussion of "meaning": "Either one takes the text at face value, or one does not." Thus entire books have been written in order to defend the historicity of the flood account in all its particulars (e.g., Whitcomb and Morris). One would then seek archaeological and geological evidence of a recent worldwide deluge, be lured by claims that the ark might have survived to the present day, be suspicious of claims that the Pentateuchal account was not composed by Moses, and then center the importance of the flood story upon the claim "You can believe a literal reading of the old Bible! Beware of deceivers who would undermine it!" Thus Hal Lindsey has remarked, concerning the potential survival of ark wood atop Ağri Daği: ". . . in this day when the authority and inspiration of the Bible is being rejected, God may give us proof-positive that one of the greatest historical events in this planet's history is absolutely true. This would leave the doubting world with no excuse for their unbelief."[16]

However pressing such historical questions may be to some readers in the present, it may be doubted that it was at the center of concern for those who fashioned and related the flood story. That is, were there per-

sons in ancient Israel who doubted the historicity of the deluge to such
an extent that the account was put forward to silence them? If not, then
what were the concerns of the time, and why should not modern interpreters focus instead on that level of meaning? That is, what is the
Bible's own agenda, and how did what it said so shape the faith and
identity of its age that the community not only survived the travails of
history but handed down the text to future generations?

V. NARROWING THE FOCUS

However brief and incomplete may be this list of the modern interpreter's problems on the way to a decision about "what the text meant,"
it must now serve as the basis for an inquiry about the purpose of the
flood story. I now propose to narrow the focus of the inquiry in accordance with the following decisions.

The question of historicity should be set aside at this point. Such
extra-biblical evidence as there is suggests a local inundation in the valleys of the Tigris and Euphrates (see above, chap. 3), and in any case
such concerns are not central to the "primeval story" (see above, chap.
5). If the concerns of the story are not ours, then that is a reality with
which we must learn to live.

One should deal with the central thrust of an entire story (episode),
rather than theologize (as did *IB*, above) about what may be no more
than passing incidentals within it. This I would take to be in accordance
with the text's own design.

Level of Meaning Six ("What the text means to me," see sec. II,
above) exposes the text to excessive relativism and impressionism, which
is sometimes called "the affective fallacy."[7]

Level of Meaning Five ("What the text meant to revered interpreters," see sec. II, above) I regard as part of the history of interpretation,
i.e., it has no authority concerning what the text *meant*. As a Protestant, I
need not accord such interpreters any authority in what it *means*, either.
The Bible, as interpreted by the best-informed modern scholarship, is the
standard by which the understanding of the fathers of the church and
the Reformers is to be judged.

Level of Meaning Two ("What did the author say?" see sec. II,
above) is a bit complicated for the flood story. The problem is neither

corruption of the text in transmission nor unclarity of its vocabulary. Rather, it arises from the impression that the story is composite (the J-Source and the P-Source of the Documentary Hypothesis). One is handicapped, in determining what the J account of the flood was all about, by the possibility that it is truncated: it may have been edited (with deletions?) when it was incorporated into the later and larger P account (see above, chap. 6). Furthermore, the date of the Yahwist (J) is debated, sometimes hotly, and thus there is resultant difference of opinion about the concerns of the audience for which it might have been formulated. (For the majority opinion, see above, chap. 5.) Nonetheless, this level of meaning will be discussed briefly below.

Our narrowing focus in the search for what the flood story meant could lead us to disentangle the P account and study it. However, since it has incorporated J's material, we shall concentrate upon Level of Meaning Three ("What the editor/redactor said" see sec. II, above). This is all the more desirable, since the larger context of the flood story (i.e., the "primeval story") enables us to close the gap between "What the text said" (Level Three) and "What the text intended" (Level One). We would thus be dealing with the entirety of the text, just as it now stands, and relating it to a well-known period of Israel's history (the exilic and early postexilic ages).

VI. J's Account of the Flood and Its Audience

The formation of the Yahwist's tradition may have taken place near the beginning of Israel's monarchy (near the year 1000 B.C.E.). If so, it was at a time of Israel's internal unification and confident emergence as a power among nations. The long-experienced political and economic precariousness was coming to an end, thanks to the stability and economic bases of the Solomonic state. It would not be surprising to find theological expressions of stability as well. God's ancient promise of land and offspring (Gen. 12) was being realized (*IDBS*, p. 973). The deity, in the long run, seemed demonstrably reliable and to be undergirding Israel's continuity, if not that of the world.

J's account of the flood ends with the theme that had been set out in the beginning. The flood was said to have been necessitated by the realization that "the wickedness of man was great in the earth, and . . . every imagination of the thoughts of his heart was only evil continually" (Gen. 6:5). Now that the flood has cleansed the earth, the question could be raised as to God's agenda in the face of unchanged human nature and attitudes. Will subsequent catastrophic destructions be necessary and thus all of history be a series of discontinuities? Reflecting upon both past and future, the deity decides: "I will never again curse the ground because of man, for the imagination of man's heart is evil from his youth; neither will I ever again destory every living creature as I have done" (8:21). It is not humans who have changed their mode of operation; rather, it is the deity. Hereafter, history will proceed with continuity and regularity "while the earth remains" (8:22). (To be sure, the deity will try other approaches to the human situation, culminating in the call of Abraham in Gen. 12.) It is a state of affairs with which the Priestly account is not content, as will be discussed below.

Mention should be made of two theological nuances that are most obvious in contrast to P as well. First, the deity, when faced with the unrelenting violence of humans, is caught in a painful situation: it results in "sorrow" and "grief" (Gen. 6:5–7, J). By contrast, in the new introduction to the flood story, which P has supplied at 6:9, the report of human violence is followed by a laconic statement of God's intention to destroy (vv. 11–13). This is in keeping with the general style of the Priestly writer: a divine announcement is made and carried out (Gen. 1:3, 9). Nonetheless, by focusing, with repetitious style, upon the condition of the earth (rather than upon God's reaction), P makes it unmistakably clear that the judgment is merited and necessary. The interpreter may well ask: What was there about P's audience that necessitated such straightforwardness?

Second, J's introduction (Gen. 6:5–8) focuses upon God's observations and reactions, and then concludes with the statement that "Noah found favor in the eyes of the Lord." No reason is given for this attitude toward Noah, and it has been conjectured that it reflects a free decision on God's part that a portion of humankind survive (Westermann, pp. 426–27). The P introduction, on the other hand, begins by stressing Noah's character, both in social ("righteous") and cultic ("blameless") terms. A strong contrast is then drawn between Noah's piety and the lack of it among his neighbors: it is his status upon which the future of humanity depends! Surely Westermann is right when he observes, "P is obviously addressing his contemporaries" (p. 412). What was their situation, that this emphasis on Noah's character was needed?

VII. The Situation and Purpose of P

If the Priestly materials took their present shape (i.e., became a part of the sacred story, or Scripture) during or shortly after the exile (sixth–fifth centuries B.C.E.), what was the situation of the community at that time? What were the needs of the community to which the expanded text might have addressed an answer?

The disruption of Judean life that took place in the year 587 B.C.E. was nearly total (*IDB*, II: 186–88). The Babylonian conquest of the nation, including destruction of the capital city, went beyond the realms of government, economics, and social structure. Not only were many citizens killed in battle, diseases rampant, crops destroyed, and large numbers of persons herded away to a foreign land, but also the religious self-understanding of the society had been shaken to its foundations. The land that had been promised to Abraham and his descendants "for ever" (Gen. 13:15) was now under foreign control. The dynasty that had been considered to be God's channel of blessing to the chosen people, undergirded with unconditional and unending promises (2 Sam. 7), was apparently brought to an end: the current ruler had been taken captive (2 Kings 25:7). The sacred city, which God had chosen as a "resting place for ever" (Ps. 132:14), was now in ruins. Rather than being a blessing to others (Gen. 12:3, RSV) or invoked as a paradigm in prayers (Gen. 12:3, NEB), the exiles were openly mocked by their captors (Ps. 137:1–3). How, then, could the traditional faith be taken seriously? How was one to maintain one's identity in an alien land? How could one even keep the traditional festivals, which required physical presence in the now destroyed and unavailable city of Jerusalem (Exod. 23:14–17; Deut. 26:1–4)? For many of the exiles, the only option was to forsake the faith of their ancestors and adopt Babylonian cultural values and religion. Hence one finds heated opposition to this tendency in the oracles of Second Isaiah (e.g., 45:20–21; 46:1–2, 12–13).

Thus the Bible as it existed at the time (J,E,D, according to the Documentary Hypothesis) provided scant comfort to those who found themselves in this strange new world. It was precisely in those sources that one read of divine sanction for the monarchy, of dwelling in "the promised land," of the one place where God should be worshiped, and of the requirements that one appear regularly each year at the central sanctuary. Thus the worshiper's identity and religious faith was inescapably tied to geography, to sacred space. Clearly something more would be needed if the community were to survive!

Fortunately there were a number of old narratives, perhaps locally reported, which might helpfully address the present situation. There were also ancient practices, regionally observed or even of minor importance to the whole, which were not tied to a specific sacred place. Let us here mention but three such practices, and then turn to the narratives (including the flood story).

First, circumcision, widely practiced in the Ancient Near East, which had not previously been connected with Israel's covenant-identity in societywide, authoritative traditions. Formerly, it seems to have been traced back to Moses' foreign wife, in a very opaque episode (Exod. 4:24–26). Now, in a Priestly account, it is connected with God's promise to Abraham: "This is my covenant . . . . Every male among you shall be circumcised" (Gen. 17:9–10). It is thus a reminder of one's identity, affecting every household, whether one be in Judea or in exile.

Second, dietary restrictions, which were also widely observed in the Ancient Near East, but for a variety of reasons. Now they are gathered up and a uniform explanation for them is given: God either allows a particular food, or God forbids it (Lev. 11, P). Wherever one may dwell, food is a regular concern, and thus the restrictions transcend any time or place. The regulations are portable, thus fitting the needs of the moment.

Third, Sabbath observance, which formerly was only one minor calendric requirement among others. True, one had been commanded to observe it (Exod. 20:8–11, J,E), but now it becomes foremost: even the deity was described as having observed it after the week of creation (Gen. 2:1–4a, P). Indeed, this creation story becomes the preface, since apparently the Bible once began at 2:4b with another creation story (J). Such a frequent, regular, mandatory observance, centered upon memory and imitation of the Lord of creation, and not tied to a particular country or even the Temple, would provide the reflection necessary for the Judean exiles to resist the culture and religion of their Babylonian captors.

These and other practices upon which the exiles began to draw were now transmitted to them as parts of the sacred story. That larger literary context gave the reason for the guidelines, and thus it provided the basis for self-understanding in the present. For example, one was to observe certain dietary regulations, not because of custom or taboo, but because the Lord commanded it (Lev. 11:1–2), because one is to imitate the holiness of the deity (Lev. 11:44), and because it is part of the covenant understanding whereby one expresses gratitude to God: "For I am the Lord who brought you up out of the land of Egypt, to be your God; you shall therefore be holy, for I am holy" (Lev. 11:45).

Thus it is that what we have called Level of Meaning One ("What the author intended to accomplish") and Levels of Meanings Two/Three ("What the author/editor said") fall together for P's regulations. What we are given is not merely ethical guidelines ("law," *halakah*) but the account of God's gracious initiative ("gospel," *haggadah*) to which the guidelines are a proper response.

VIII. P'S ACCOUNT OF THE FLOOD

The contributions of the Priestly writers to the flood story, as well as their characteristics, are listed in Tables 10 and 11 in chapter 6, above. By and large, the internal contributions do not change either the flow or the meaning of the story as it had been presented by J. More significant, however, are P's introduction (Gen. 6:9–22, and especially vv. 9–13) and conclusion (9:1–17). The implications of that introduction for its intended audience will be discussed in a separate section, below.

P's conclusion has two parts, clearly distinct: a blessing (vv. 1–7) and a covenant (vv. 8–18): note the paragraphs in the RSV. Each begins with "God said" and closes with a near repetition of its opening phrases.

The covenant, assuring the continuity of the world hereafter, is not significantly different in content from God's promise at the conclusion of the J account (8:21–22). It does, however, further establish itself in the mind of the reader by repetition and by the use of the term "covenant," using the powerful motif of the rainbow as a perpetual sign of the deity's resolve that "the waters shall never again become a flood to destroy all flesh" (9:15–16).

The blessing may be divided into two parts: (*a*) the command to multiply and exercise dominion over the earth (vv. 1–2, 7), and (*b*) restrictions upon the blessing as it pertains to the taking of life (vv. 3–6). The former will be discussed separately below. The restrictions introduce a jarring discontinuity between the pre-flood and the post-flood worlds. Thus, the great flood is an "epoch divider" in at least two senses. First, after it we begin to move toward a more recognizable "history." Note the vastly reduced lifespans in Genesis 11, in contrast to those of chapter 5. Comparison may be made with the Sumerian King List (Jacobsen), where the first postdiluvian monarch reigns 1,200 years in contrast to the last of the prediluvians who ruled for 18,600 years. Second, hereafter, rigid guidelines are to be observed in relation to God's gift of life, in order that divine sovereignty over it may be maintained.

The two restrictions are related: the consumption of food animals, and the killing of human beings. Prior to the flood, according to the Priestly theologians, the diet of humans was to be as follows: ". . . every plant . . . fruit . . . you shall have them as food" (1:29–30; i.e., humans are to be vegetarian). Now, however, they are confronted with dilemmas with respect to the consumption of meat. In one sense, the concern with the consumption of blood is related to that of the dietary restrictions in Leviticus 11 (P), which have been mentioned above: it is a matter of holiness (separateness) and identity-formation. The major concern, however, is fleshed out in Leviticus 17 (P). Since life is an extension of the power of God (Gen. 2:7), and since the life-force appears to reside in the blood, then blood can be shed only in accordance with the guidelines of the Lord of life. Thus it must be drained from food animals, and the failure to do so in accordance with prescribed rituals at the sanctuary is reckoned as "bloodguilt" (Lev. 17:4),[18] a term elsewhere associated with murder.

The other post-flood restriction concerns murder, an act that is "a direct attack on God's right of dominion . . . direct and unbridled revolt against God" (Westermann, p. 468). Focus upon the deity's rights in the matter is so central that conveyance to the community of an obligation to execute the murderer is only indirectly stated.

The observation that restrictions were placed upon the post-flood generations has invited comparison with the Atrahasis Epic (see above, chap. 3), and therein may lie the key to P's understanding of the flood story. In the story of Atrahasis, it may be overpopulation (Kilmer) that led the deities, after lesser efforts failed, to destroy humanity:

> . . . the land extended and the peoples multiplied.
> The land was bellowing like a bull,
> The god got disturbed with their uproar.
>
> [II, ll. 2–4; Lambert and Millard, p. 73]

Once the flood ends, with unintended survivors, the god (Enlil) resumes his concern:

> (Let there be) . . . women who do not bear [i.e., infertility].
> Let there be . . . the *Pāšittu-demon*
> to snatch the baby from the lap of her who bore it.

Establish *Ugbabtu*-women, *Entu*-women, and *Igiṣītu*-women [i.e.,
    various classes of celibate priestesses],
And let them be taboo and so stop childbirth.
        [III.vii. *ll.* 1–8; Lambert and Millard, p. 103]

Thus the post-flood restrictions in Genesis 9 might likewise be an attempt to address a pre-flood situation (so Frymer-Kensky). The flood had solved the problem for the time being, but now steps must be taken to see that the crisis does not again arise, so that God's promise (covenant) can be announced.

In this manner, one is able to supply content to that which is stated only in the vaguest of terms in the introduction to the flood story: "... the wickedness of man ws great" (6:5, J); "the earth was corrupt ... filled with violence" (6:11, P). The larger and earlier context of the deluge account, namely the "primeval story," then supplies additional clarification: humans, only in their second generation, have already committed murder (Gen. 4:8). By the time of the seventh generation, Lamech feels free to boast:

I have slain a man for wounding me,
    a young man for striking me.
If Cain is avenged sevenfold,
    truly Lamech seventy-sevenfold [4:23–24].

Whereas Cain's continued existence was a decree of the deity (4:15), survival for Lamech was a matter of boastful arrogance for which there is no divine sanction.

IX. The Flood Story and Its Exilic Audience

How would the newly expanded flood story have been understood by the Judeans in exile or as they returned to their homeland? One might assume, at the same time, that the needs of the community will have contributed to the way that the P account took shape and was combined with J in order to speak to those theological needs.

If it is in the "covenant" section (9:1–17) that we find P's major agenda in relating the flood story, then insight may be gained by comparing its emphases with the realities of the late pre-exilic age. Let us begin with its concern for God's sovereignty over human life. Note the increasing prophetic denunciation of the violations of that sovereignty:

There is no . . . knowledge of God in the land;
there is . . . killing . . . and murder follows murder [Hos. 4:1–2].

Because the land is full of bloody crimes
and the city is full of violence [Ezek. 7:23]

. . . and because they have filled this place
with the blood of innocents [Jer. 19:4].

When you spread forth your hands,
I will hide my eyes from you;
. . . .
your hands are full of blood [Isa. 1:15].

See also Jeremiah 7:6; 22:3, 17; Ezekiel 8:17; 9:9; 22:1–3; Hosea 6:9; and so forth (*IDB*, I: 738).

To be sure, there had been earlier prohibitions of murder, for example, as part of the covenant between God and Israel that had been mediated by Moses at Mount Sinai: "You shall not commit murder" (Exod. 20:13, NEB, TEV, NIV). Even so, P's articulation must have been startling to those who first heard it: God's concerns in this area go farther back, at least to the time of Noah, and are binding upon all humanity; even an animal will be held accountable; and now there is specific mention of divinely ordained sanctions; indeed, it is as if God were being attacked. Little wonder, then, that such "violence" (Gen. 6:11; Ezek. 7:23) had led to a "flood" . . . be it of water at the time of Noah, or Babylonians in more recent times. (At this point, it is interesting to note not only that invasion is often depicted in Mesopotamian literature as a "flood," but also that the word itself has that double meaning.[19])

Then there is the other restriction: the prohibition of the consumption of blood. Again, it is not per se anything new: Deuteronomy earlier had sanctioned the consumption of food animals (12:21–23), provided that the blood was drained away. Indeed, the concern is voiced in a story about king Saul (1 Sam. 14:32–35), where an altar was erected in order that it be done properly. Deuteronomy, having reduced the number of legitimate sanctuaries to one, exempts the slaughter of food animals there, as a concession to reality: a potentially long journey to Jerusalem may be avoided and the slaughter take place locally. P, at the conclusion of the flood story, not only reminds hearers of the centrality of the blood prohibition, but pushes its first articulation all the way back to Noah, links it with the prohibition against murder, and thus further establishes God's sovereignty over all of life. The issue is picked up again in Leviticus 17 (also P), where the altar is again introduced as the necessary location for the slaughter of food animals: the "local option" of Deuteronomy would thus seem to be negated. Part of the reason for this may have been to stress the centrality of the Temple for the life of the demoralized refugees who had returned from Babylon: it is for anyone who would eat meat. "Corporate worship," we might say, "is as important for individual and community as is food!" The other reason is made quite explicit in Leviticus 17: negation of a particular form of competing religion ("sacrifice for satyrs").

It was imperative, then, that the Temple (having been destroyed by the Babylonians) be rebuilt, that one be single-minded in one's religious loyalties, and that the Yahwistic faith pervade every aspect of daily life. Clearly that had not been the case in the past, and for it there apparently had been a terrible price to pay.

From the restrictions in the covenant, then, the exiles may have sensed implications for their own time. There were indeed similarities between the sins of Noah's generation and of their own, as there were between the fate of the pre-flood society and of exiled Judah.

The traditional understanding of Israel's existence in the land of Canaan had been that God had promised it to Abraham and his descendants (Gen. 12, J), and that the promise had been fulfilled at the time of Joshua (Exod. 13:11, J). Now, with the incorporation of the P materials into the larger story, an additional perspective on the settlement in the land is put forward: the Canaanite inhabitants had not been treated capriciously by Israel's God, nor had the divine action been merely for the benefit of Israel. Rather, aspects of the Canaanite lifestyle were said to have "defiled" the land and to have led to their expulsion from it. Consequently its new inhabitants (Israel) must be careful not to make the same mistake (Lev. 18:24–30). Indeed, such a fate is threatened: ". . . you shall perish among the nations, and the land of your enemies shall eat you up" (Lev. 26:38).

The exile of Israel, should it become necessary, would provide opportunity for the land to "rest, and enjoy its sabbaths" (Lev. 26:34–35). Might this bring to mind the story of how, at a previous time, "the earth was filled with violence" (Gen. 6:11, P), and how the great flood was necessary in order to cleanse it?

Note how the older story had made it clear that "every imagination of the thoughts of his [humankind's] heart was only evil continually," and thus the deity was "grieved" and decided to take action (Gen. 6:5–8, J). Nonetheless, the new and more extensive introduction by P (vv. 11–13) repeats the observation: "the earth was filled with violence . . . . it was corrupt . . . . all flesh had corrupted their way . . . ." The justification for the divine response is clear beyond all doubt, and the deity moves directly to action. One need hardly be surprised, therefore, that later violence would bring a similarly severe reaction, namely, exile.

That is hardly the entirety of P's agenda, however, and likely not the final understanding of it in the minds of the exiles. After all, the warnings concerning the consumption of blood and murder are not self-standing prohibitions: they are restrictions upon a more comprehensive *blessing*. This would have enabled the exiles to sense a parallel between their hopes of return from Babylonia and the survival of Noah's family.

The prophet Jeremiah, who had lived both prior to and during the exile, not only anticipated what would happen to his society and pronounced it justified, but also believed that there would be a subsequent renewal of the society. The remnants of God's flock would be gathered from among the nations and "they shall be fruitful and multiply" (23:1–3). That remnant, perhaps still in exile, heard a familiar phrase, then, when it encountered P's new conclusion to the flood story: "And God blessed Noah and his sons, and said to them, 'Be fruitful and multiply, and fill the earth'" (Gen. 9:1). Both God's judgment and God's graciousness had been demonstrated previously, and thus in the present one was enabled to believe that the deity had worked not only to "pluck up and break down" but also "to build and to plant" (Jer. 1:10).

Moreover, the people of the remnant may have believed that God's blessing upon humankind after the flood extended to their own time because it was already the renewal of a prior commitment. That is, the words "Be fruitful and multiply, and fill the earth" (Gen. 9:1) were but a repetition of God's commitment to creation (1:28) as expressed in the new preface to the sacred story (i.e., P's creation story, 1:1–2:4a). That the two texts are deliberately linked is made even clearer by the fact that each is followed by an expression of the human relationship to the rest of nature and by regulations concerning food (1:29–30; 9:3–4).

Brueggeman's outline of the blessing, and of its refutation of aspects of exilic and early postexilic life, is as follows (*Vitality*, p. 104).

"be fruitful" .... no more barrenness (cf. Isa. 54:1–3)
"multiply" .... no more lack of heirs (cf. Gen. 17:5–8)
"fill the earth" ...... no more being crowded out
"subdue" .... no more subservience
"have dominion" .... no more being dominated

Thus "the formidable blessing declaration in Genesis 1:28 provides the focus for understanding the kerygma of the whole (priestly) work" (p.

103) and "is precisely the antithesis of the experience of the exilic community" (p. 105), with the result that "reentry of the Promised Land is P's central affirmation" (p. 112).

Last of all, attention should be called to the way that the flood story is introduced in the P account. Rather than describe the sinful situation of the earth in general (as had J), it focuses the hearers' attention immediately upon the character of Noah: "Noah was a righteous man, blameless in his generation." Amidst the corruption of the world, he has managed to maintain God's expectations both ethically ("righteous") and cultically ("blameless"). That status is the foundation of all that is related thereafter. "The kernel of the narrative is that the world is preserved because of one pious man" (B. Jacob, in Westermann, p. 412). Surely during the exile or the difficult struggle for survival thereafter, there were those who realized that the future of Israel (if not of the world) depended upon their fidelity. Long thereafter, during equally trying days, it was said: "For the sake of one righteous man the whole world is preserved in existence, as it is written (at Prov. 10:25), 'The righteous man is an everlasting foundation' " (Babylonian Talmud, *Yoma*, 38*b*).

APPENDICES

ONE

Heinrich Hübschmann, "Armeniaca"

Heinrich Hübschmann, "Armeniaca," in *Strassburger Festschrift zur XLVI Versammlung Deutscher Philologen und Schulmänner* (Strassburg: Verlag von Karl Taubner, 1901), section V, as translated by Ben and Beth Weisbrod, while they were candidates for the M. Div. degree at Duke University (1977).

V. ARM. NAXCAVAN: ἀποβατήριον

In his admirable volume, *Ararat und Masis* (Heidelberg, 1901), F. Murad has attempted to present evidence for a native Armenian flood story, the scene of which is said to have been the majestic Mount Masis[1] located in the Province of Airarat, and which supposedly gave rise to the designation Naxčavan[2] for a city lying approximately 100 kilometers southeast of the mountain (Murad, p. 62). The city, which lay in the province of Vaspurakan according to the *Geography* attributed to Moses of Chorene, was later attributed to the province of Siunikh, and according to Armenian tradition was the residence of Noah after the landing of the ark. Hence the residence came to be called Naxčavan (= Naxijavan), which means "first settling place" (from *nax*, "at first, before, prime," and *ijawan*, "shelter, temporary quarters, station, stopping place": p. 63).[3]

Thus when Josephus (*Antiq.*, 1.92) says of the place where the ark landed: ἀποβατήριον μέντοι τὸν τόπον τοῦτον Ἀρμένιοι καλοῦσιν ἐκεῖ γὰρ ἀνασωθείσης τῆς λάρνακος ἔτι νῦν οἱ ἐπιχώριοι τὰ λείψαντα ἐπιδεικνύοσι "the Armenians call this place 'the Place of Descent' (Ἀποβατήριον) for it was there that the ark came safely to rest, and they show relics of it to this day"], it is natural for one to see therein verification for that [Murad's] explanation of the [Armenian] name and at the same time evidence for the antiquity of the Armenian flood tradition.

By capably dismissing opposing arguments, Murad appears to furnish evidence for his position. While I agree with him on almost all the details, I cannot agree with his central thesis for the following reasons.

1. *The etymology.* Murad's explanation of the name would be correct if the original form of the name were Naxiǰavan or Naxiǰevan, since *(a)* the adverb *nax* (in contrast to *apa*, "thereupon, next, then, afterward") means "beforehand, first of all," and in compound forms it means "before, in advance, previously," or "ahead (Latin: *prae-*), first" [e.g., *nax-atʿor* means "front seat"; *naxoṭ̌oin* means "the first to be greeted"; *nax-a-gah*, "chairmanship, precedence over someone"; *nax-a-stetc*, "first created" (Adam); *nax-cin*, "firstborn"; *nax-asaceal*, "prophesied, predicted"; *nax-a-xnamutʿium*, "providence"; *nax-imacutʿiun*, "to know beforehand"; etc. (pp. 65–66)], and since *(b)* *ĭǰawan* (= *ĭǰawankʿ*) means *"temporary quarters, shelter"* (*so also* *ĭǰavan*, *ĭǰevan*, from *ēǰ*, *ēǰ-kʿ*, "dismount, descend," plus *wan-kʿ*, "shelter-dwelling"; cf. *autʿe-wankʿ*, "quarters for the night"). Thus, in Old Armenian, Naxiǰawan or Naxiǰavan would mean "previous temporary quarters, previous shelter, first shelter," and could be so named in contrast to the later stations passed through by the descendants of Noah in their further migration and expansion.

But, an Old Armenian Naxiǰavan is not attested. Instead, one finds Naxčavan or Naxčuan (and in Murad's view, Naxǰavan), which, in current opinion, "is an abbreviation of Naxiǰavan that resulted from the rapid pace of popular speech" (p. 63). At present, however, abbreviations of this kind have not been demonstrated in Old Armenian, and they are not evident as far as I can see. *Ǐǰavan* (which probably originated from *ēǰavan*[4] according to Armenian rules) would have to retain the *i* in compound with *nax*, just as it retains the *i* in *naximac*, etc. The *i* or *u* which begins words of two or more syllables also is not dropped in the formation of compounds. Murad's explanation of this word, although otherwise correct, fails in light of this rule.

Furthermore, the forms Naxiǰavan, Naxiǰevan, Naxǰavan, [and] Naxǰuan (along with Naxčavan and Naxčuan), are traceable in documents only after the tenth century (p. 103), whereas for earlier times the current form is Naxčavan or less frequently Naxčuan. For example, see Faustus, p. 173; Lazar Pharpetsi, p. 369; Moses of Chorene, pp. 77, 129, 219 (Naxjavan only at p. 57); Moses' *Geography*, p. 609 (Naxčuan); Sebeos frequently (see Murad, p. 103; also in the Petersburgh ed., 1879, pp. 92, 93, 94, 118, 150); Levond (Petersburgh, 1887, p. 24 [according to the manuscript], p. 33 (instead of the Naxijevan of the Paris Press ed. of 1857); Stephanos of Taron (Petersburgh, 1885, p. 115, 120, 124 (instead of the Naxčivan of the Paris ed. of 1859); Thomas Artsruni (Petersburgh, 1887), pp. 78, 92, 105, 128, 195, etc. Thus, in the tenth century, only Joh. Katholikos (Murad, p. 103) frequently uses Naxjavan,[5] and Moses Kalankatuatsi in his third book uses Naxijevan twice.[6] In any case, Naxjavan, and even more so Naxijevan, is a later form of the name, which originated with copyists of late manuscripts of the historians and with modern editors of the older texts.

If, however, Naxčavan is the earliest form of the name,[7] it obviously cannot be explained as "the first settling place" (nax-ijavan). Rather, it becomes an otherwise unknown Naxč- (from Naxič- or Naxuč-), which was perhaps a name, plus (the well-known) *avan*, "market-town, country-town" (between the size of a village and a city),[8] and thus means: Naxic- or Naxuc-market-town. This may be compared with such place names as Anušavan, Aršakavan, Bagavan (Baguan), Zarehavan (Zarehuan), Thornavan, Karčavan, Širakavan, Vataršavan, and Smbatavan.

2. *The [flood] tradition.* F. Murad (p. 67) must acknowledge [the correctness of] the statements of L. Alischan and Gelzer that the Old Armenian authors "up to the eleventh or twelfth century never speak of Mount Masis as the landing place of the ark; rather, when they mention the mountain [of the ark] at all, they designate it as the Qardu Range." However, he will not conclude (in contrast to them) that the oldest [native Armenian] tradition did not recognize Mount Masis as the mountain of the ark. Rather, he sees evidence in the words of Johannes Erznkatsi (ca. 1250–1326) that the connection between the flood story and Mount Masis had been a generally recognized fact from time immemorial: "the Ayrarat-mountain, the high-topped Mount Masis, since it became the resting place of the ark" (Murad, p. 69). [But] that is an unqualified exaggeration of the evidence offered by Johannes Erznkatsi, for it only proves that at his time Mount Masis was generally considered to be the mountain of the ark—not that it had always been considered so.

As to the question of the age of this [flood] tradition, we can only rely upon the evidence of the older texts—which regardless of translation or original—do not connect the flood story with Mount Masis.

The evidence, in which we find the same two versions of the flood story as in the older Jewish, Greek, and Syrian authors (i.e., the Babylonian version in which the ark landed in the land of Qardu-Gordyene, and the biblical version in which it landed " on the mountains of Ararat," Gen. 8:4), is as follows (Murad, pp. 26, 36ff.):

1. Eusebius [third century], *Chronicle* (ed. Aucher), vol. 1, pp. 36–37: "And of the ship (of Xisuthros [= the Babylonian Ziusudra]) which landed in Armenia, a small part still remains in the Gordian (Arm.: Korduaçik') Mountains (range)."

2. Faustus of Byzantium [fifth century] (Venice ed., 1832), p. 22: "During that time, the great Bishop of Nisibis, the Holy Jacob, . . . left his city to journey to Mount Sararad[9] in the Armenian Mountains in the region of Airaratic control (domain)[10] in the canton of Gordukh. . . . And he asked God to let him see the preserved ark that Noah had built which had come to rest on this mountain at the time of the deluge."

3. The story of the Holy Hriphsime and her Companions (Moses of Chorene [eighth century?], *Opera*, Venice, 1865), p. 300: The Syrians say of Mount Soloph in Gordukh that "with the receding of the flood waters, the ark arrived on the peak of the mountains, i.e., of Sararad (*i glux lerinn or ē Sararaday*), and that the sawfish halted the ship by passing through it; the place came to be named Themnis,[11] which means: 'eight souls got off the ark' " (see Murad, pp. 28–29; and cf. 1 Pet. 3:20).

4. Thomas Artsruni [early tenth century] (Petersburgh, 1887), p. 19: "After the completion of the divine command, the ark was carried east by the waves to the middle of the world (*yareveleain? i mïjoç ašxarhi*) and rested on the mountains of Gordukh (*i lerins Korduaç*)."

5. The Armenian translation [fifth century] of Genesis 8:4: "And the ark came to rest on the mountains of Ararat" (*i lerins Araratay*,[12] variant Araraday, for the Greek ᾿επὶ τὰ ᾿όρη τὰ ᾿Αραράτ ["upon the mountains of Ararat"]).

If all these attestations stem directly or indirectly from Greek or Syrian sources (as in Murad's opinion), then the question arises as to whether there was a native Armenian flood story.

The only remaining passage in which the flood is mentioned is Moses of Chorene, *History*, vol. 1, chap. 6, p. 17. He reports from his informants Gorgi, Banan, and Davith (?) that one of these three took part in a Greek-style conversation about the distribution of peoples, and that the cleverest among them, Olompiodoros, had talked about names, He said:

> I want to tell you unwritten stories which have come to us through tradition and which many peasants still tell to this day. There was a book about Khsisuthros [Ziusudra] and his sons, which has not survived to the present, in which they say that the following portrayal is found: After Khsisuthros had floated to Armenia and had landed, one of his sons, named Sim, moved northwest to explore the land. He arrived at a small plain at the foot of an extensive mountain through which rivers flowed to the region of Assyria, lived on the river for two months, and named the mountain "Sim" after himself.[13] Then he returned to the southeast in the direction from which he had come. But one of the younger sons separated, with thirty sons and fifteen daughters and their husbands, from their father [Sim?] and took his dwelling place again on the same river bank,[14] after whose name (Tarban) he (Sim) also named the canton of Taron. But he [Sim?] named the place where he lived "Cronk'" ("Dispersion"), because the separation of his sons from him first began at that place. He [Sim?] turned away and lived, so they say, for some time on the borders of the region of Bactria, and one of his sons remained there. [The people of] the Eastern Lands call the Sem (*sic*) "Zrvan," and the canton they call "Zaruand" to this day. Often the old peoples from the descendants of Aram relate this matter with loud music, song, and dance.

In this account, the names Xisuthros and Sim (= Sem), the equating of Sem with Zrvan, the explanation of Taron from Tarbon, of Zarvand from Zrvan, and the entire intent, are not accounted for by popular Armenian tradition but, rather, prove the learned workmanship of Moses. Also, the assertion that the descendants of Aram mention these matters is, in view of the notorious unreliability of Moses, too ambiguous for conclusions to be drawn from it. Even if this account had a popular basis, which I deny, then the scene of the story would be west and south of Lake Van, and the landing place of Xisuthros, according to the location of Mount Sim (see Moses, p. 80; Aristakes, *Last.*, p. 94) and the above account, would not be Mount Masis in [the province of] Airarat, but in the land of Gordukh!

Thus Armenian literature of the fifth through the tenth centuries knows nothing of Masis as the mountain of the ark. When that identification is made at a later time, it is sufficiently explained as the result of the increasing influence of the Bible, which puts the landing place in the mountains of Ararat (= Arm. Airarat). Since the highest and most famous of these mountains was Masis, [it would be thought that] the ark must have landed there.[15] Since, at the same time, the Old Armenian Naxčavan came to be called Naxijevan, which was explained as the "first temporary lodging," it was natural to connect this city with the misplaced landing of the ark on Masis, so that legend and etymology now supported each other.

Be that as it may, there is no trace of a native [Armenian] flood story and no possibility of an explanation of Naxčavan (or even of Naxjavan) as Ἀποβατήριον.[16] Josephus merely leaves us with his statement that the ark's location was "in Armenia, on the peak of a mountain," and speaks neither of the province Ἀραράτ nor of the mountain Masis nor of the city Ναξυάνα. His assertion that the Armenians named a place ἀποβατήριον in connection with the flood story cannot be considered reliable. He does not name his source, and we have no grounds for accepting it forthwith even if it were Armenian. Even an Armenian could have given him a false account of an Armenian place name, and such would be the case if he had explained Naxčavan to him [Josephus] as the "landing place."

TWO

Faustus' Account

The following evaluation of Faustus' account (see above, chap. 4, sec. III) is based upon pp. 318–36 of Paul Peaters' learned article, "La légende de saint Jacques de Nisibe," in *Analecta Bollandiana* 38 (1920): 285–373 ("Invention de l'Arche").

1. The Syrian origin of the legend is indicated *(a)* by the discovery of the ark by a Syrian bishop in the Gordian Mountains near the Syrian plain; *(b)* in the "Life of Mar Augin," where the legend is placed at Mount Qardu; *(c)* by the earliest reference in Armenian literature, which is that the ark has been found by a Syrian bishop; *(d)* by the fact that early Armenian writers know nothing of Ağri Daği as the landing place.

2. After the legend was translated into Armenian, the landing place was "explained" in two additional ways that introduced confusion. *(a)* "On the mountains of Ararat" (*i lerins Araraday*: Gen. 8:4) was added. Then, the "s" in *lerins* was accidentally copied at the beginning of the next word, resulting in "Sararat." *(b)* A later copyist, aware of the similarity of the biblical name to the district of Airarat, added the expression, "in the region of Airaratic control."

3. Once this late, edited, confusing Armenian version was understood to refer to the province of Airarat, it was natural for the landing place to be sought nearby. But Ağri Daği was not the only, and perhaps not the earliest, candidate. Vincent of Beauvais, in the thirteenth century, places Saint Jacob's adventure on Mount Arach, likely the modern Ala-Göz.

THREE

Nonliteral Numbers in the Bible

Frequently in the chapters above, we have suggested that certain numbers in the biblical text probably should not be taken literally at the point under discussion: they may have an ideal, mystical, symbolic significance, or be "round" numbers (see chap. 2, 3, 5). It may now be in order to provide a more general discussion and a summary.

Let us begin with the phenomenon of frequency of usage. As one reads the text of the Bible, one may be struck with the fact that a few numbers are used over and over again. There is not the kind of randomness that one would expect in life, or in an objective report of the "facts," but rather, an amazing frequency of occurrence for three, seven, twelve, forty, sixty, and seventy. (A convenient summary may be found in the *IDB* article "Number, Numbering, Numbers," III: 561–67. In addition, there is "Seven, Seventh, Seventy," in IV: 294–95, and "Twelve" in IV: 719.) Following are a few instances of each number.

Three: age of certain sacrificial animals (Gen. 15:9); the number of required feasts (Exod. 23:14); a period of purification (Num. 19:12); daily prayers (Dan. 6:10); usage in a dream and its interpretation (Gen. 40:10, 12, 16, 18, 20); the distance to a sanctuary (Exod. 3:18); how long a child was hidden (Exod. 2:2); a period of famine (1 Chron. 21:12); part of a prophetic ritual (1 Kings 17:21); the number of Job's daughters (1:2; 42:13); the diameter of a city (Jon. 3:3); the period of Jesus' death (Matt. 12:40).

Seven: the number of days in a week (Gen. 1:1–2:4); the occurrence of festivals in the seventh month of the year (Atonement, Tabernacles);

festivals of seven-day duration (Passover, Tabernacles); number of sacrifical animals (Num. 28:11); the number of altars in use on a given occasion (Num. 23:1); the number of certain ritual acts (Lev. 4:6; 8:11); ritual objects (Exod. 25:37); locks of hair (Judg. 16:13); amount of punishment (Lev. 26:18); the journey around Jericho (Josh. 6:4); groups of demons (Luke 8:2).

Twelve: the tribes of Israel (Gen. 35:22); the sons of Ishmael (Gen. 17:20); the months of the year; Jesus' disciples; the gates of the heavenly Jerusalem (Rev. 21:12); springs of water (Exod. 15:27); offerings (Lev. 24:5); decoration of Solomon's throne (1 Kings 10:20); legions of angels (Matt. 26:53). In addition, multiples of twelve flourish in the text, e.g., 24,000 (1 Chron. 27:1) and 144,000 (Rev. 7:4).

Forty: age at marriage (Gen. 25:20; 26:34); period of wandering in the wilderness (Exod. 16:35); period of peace (Judg. 3:11; 8:28; 13:1); length of reign (2 Sam. 5:4; 1 Kings 11:42; 2 Chron. 24:1); length of the flood (Gen. 7:4; cf. seven days in Mesopotamian accounts); length of Elijah's journey to Horeb (1 Kings 19:8); time left for Nineveh to repent (Jon. 3:4); period of Jesus' temptation (Matt. 4:2). Multiples of forty abound, e.g., 120 as the allotted lifespan of humans (Gen. 6:3); 480 years (40 × 12) as the time from the exodus to Solomon's temple (1 Kings 6:1).

Sixty: Isaac's age when twins were born (Gen. 25:26); number of sacrificial animals (Num. 7:88); number of cities in a region (Deut. 3:4; Josh. 13:30); daily provisions for Solomon's palace (1 Kings 4:22); length of the Temple (1 Kings 6:2); Rehoboam's spouses and daughters (2 Chron. 11:21); agricultural productivity (Matt. 13:8). Multiples abound, especially thirty (Matt. 13:8), but many of them are hidden in reckoning ages by months rather than by years.

Seventy: those who came to Egypt with Jacob (Gen. 46:27); number of trees at an oasis (Exod. 15:27); Israel's elders (Exod. 24:1); period of mourning (Gen. 50:3); amount of vengence (Gen. 5:24); number of princes (2 Kings 10:1); period of exile for Tyre (Isa. 23:15) and Judah (Jer. 25:11); appointees of Jesus (Luke 10:1); period of time for completion of Greek translation of the Hebrew Bible (i.e., the Septuagint).

Not only does the frequency of such numbers violate the principle of randomness and suggest that some of them were not intended to be literal, but also some of them seem implicitly nonliteral. Thus, Jeremiah's anticipation of seventy years of exile (25:11) does not correspond with reality: 587–539 B.C.E. (i.e., forty-eight years). The duration of the flood is forty days in Genesis, but seven in Mesopotamian literature (i.e., nobody records it as being of "ordinary" duration). Sarah lives not only the Egyptian ideal (120 years), but an extra seven (Gen. 23:1). The number of divisions (satrapies) of the Persian empire is set at 120 (60 × 2, Dan. 6:2) or 127 (60 × 2 + 7, Esth. 1:1), but according to Persian records it varied between twenty and thirty. The seventh-born in the genealogy in Genesis 4 lives 777 years, and the gematria of his father is 777. In the alternate genealogy in Genesis 5, his father's gematria is 777 + 7.

What is the origin of such "special" numbers? Why those discussed above, as opposed to others? The origins have long been lost, and modern interpreters are reduced to conjecture.

Concern for *three* may have arisen from observation of basic categories of world order. Thus the Sumerians especially revered the deities An (the numinous sky and source of fertilizing rains), Enlil (the wind, bringing both enriching showers and airborne soil, and destruction), and Enki (the waters of the earth). The Greeks divided the world into the realms of Zeus (sky and earth), Neptune (sea), and Hades/Pluto (underworld). Subsequent deities functioned within the realms of these primordial realities.

Is it surprising, then, that all humanity might be traced back to three divisions (Gen. 9:18–19), that three great festivals be thought necessary (Exod. 23:14; Deut. 16:16), that the number three occur repeatedly in the specifications for religious objects (Exod. 25:32–33; 27:1, 14), and that there be three cities of refuge (Deut. 19:1–3)? As a unit of measure, it seems to be an approximation for a short distance (e.g., Exod. 3:18).

Concern for *seven* may have arisen from the observation of the major celestial bodies (deities): the visible planets (Mercury, Venus, Mars, Jupiter, and Saturn), plus the sun and moon (all of which appear to move against the fixed background). Thus the realm of the sky-gods was perceived as a sevenfold heaven (hence the plural "heavens" in the Bible [e.g., Gen. 1:1] and Paul's reference to a person who "was caught up to the third heaven" [2 Cor. 12:2]), and this was then extended to the underworld as well. Hence seven mountains were thought to support the dome of the sky. Indeed, so fundamental became the concept that the Babylonians could write the word for "world" (AN.KI, "sky-earth") by writing the number seven (seven cuneiform wedges, arranged thus: ▼▼▼). (Briefly, see the article "Cosmology," with map, in *IDB*, I: 702–9.) From the seven principal directions (mountains), there issued forth a heptad of evil spirits, sometimes called "the seven" and sometimes "the seven gods of the universe."

Is it surprising, then, that Yahweh often threatens sevenfold destruction (Deut. 28:22; Job 5:19; Prov. 24:16) or desires sacrificial animals in groups of seven (Num. 28.11)? That is, older polytheistic concepts and practices have been adapted for use in Israel's monotheistic religion. In some contexts, the number may denote thoroughness or completeness (Gen. 4:15), or it may mark that which is exceptional (e.g., the seventh generation in a genealogy, for which see "Generation, Seventh," in *IDBS*, pp. 354–56). Thus Eber (Gen. 11:14), the ancestor of all Hebrews, is the fourteenth generation since creation (7 × 2) and Abraham is the twentyfirst (7 × 3; but only in the Septuagint's list, which inserts an extra generation, perhaps to make it so; in the traditional Hebrew text [followed by the RSV] he is the twentieth).

Twelve as a special number likely arose from the number of lunations (lunar months) in a solar year, and its religious importance was then reinforced by the zodiacal signs and the mythology surrounding them. It seems to denote completeness, as evidenced by the desire to retain this number of tribes within Israel (hence splitting Joseph into Ephraim and Manasseh) and by the replacement of Judas Iscariot as a discilple of Jesus. It also seems to denote fruition or abundance, to judge from the number of baskets left over after Jesus' miracle of feeding the crowd (Matt. 14:20).

Why *forty* should have been singled out is more difficult to discover. It is often thought to have been an approximation for the average length of a generation, perhaps based upon the statement that certain figures married at this age (Gen. 25:20; 26:34) or that an entire generation died during Israel's forty-year journey in the wilderness. In actuality, however, there is evidence that the average lifespan was only thirty to forty years. Often the number seems to be used a "round" figure for any fairly long distance or period of time.

A concern for *sixty* reflects the influence of Mesopotamian mathematics. It is to be contrasted with the familiar place-notation based upon ten, in which, for example, 586 stands for $(5 \times 10^2) + (8 \times 10) + 6$. In the Mesopotamian sexagesimal system (place-notation based upon sixty), the same configuration (five wedges, eight wedges, six wedges) could stand for: $(5 \times 60^2) + (8 \times 60) + 6$, i.e., 18,486.

Echoes of the sexagesimal system survive in modern times: 60 seconds/minute, 60^2 seconds/hour, (60 × 6) degrees in a circle.

In reckoning chronology and ages in primeval time, certain time-units are routinely used: 60 years (1 *shush*), 600 years (1 *nar*, or 10 *shush*), 60^2 or 3,600 years (1 *shar*), 60^3 or 216,000 years (a great *shar*). Adding a unit of 7 is standard. For example, in the Sumerian King List (Weld-Blundell text 444), the total of eight pre-diluvian reigns is 241,200 years, i.e., $60^3 + (60^2 \times 7)$ or 1 great *shar* plus 7 *shar*.

Is it surprising, then, that the flood is set to begin in the 600th year of Noah's life (60×10), or that Methuselah's son is born in his 187th year ($[60 \times 3] + 7$), or that nearly all the other ages in Genesis 5 are calculated to conform to "round" sexagesimal units? (For further discussion, see above, chap. 2, 5.)

There is, however, seemingly a jarring discontinuity between the prediluvian totals. While Genesis and the Sumerian King List are similar in using base-60 for the length of individual ages or reigns, and while the King-List total clearly reflects it (as shown above), the total of ages before the biblical flood is 1,656, i.e., the flood comes in the 1,657th year. Cassuto has suggested that even here there is a sexagesimal reckoning (I: 261): $1,657 = 1,643 + (7 \times 2)$; the number of days in 1,643 years is 599,695, i.e., just short of 60×10^4 (600,000). That is, just as Seth's age, 912 years, is $(3 [60^2] + 60)$ months $+ 7$ years, so the pre-flood total is 60×10^4 days $+ (7 \times 2)$ years.

It may be, however, that by reckoning from the 1,657th year, Cassuto has complicated things unduly, resulting in the necessity for an approximation (599,695 for 60×10^4). If one reckons from the number of full years that have passed since creation (1,656), the total days is then 604,440, i.e., $(60 \times 10^4) + 60^2 + (60 \times 7 \times 2)$.

Why *seventy* has been singled out as a standard number is also unclear. (7×10? $40 + 60/2$? $60 + 10$?) In any case, its chronological usage to state an approximate duration for exile is well attested. Both Tyre and Judah will suffer for "seventy years" (Isa. 23:15; Jer. 25:11). An illuminating parallel is found in Mesopotamian literature. King Sennacherib of Assyria (705–681 B.C.E.) made an unprecedented attempt to destroy the temples of the ancient and sacred city of Babylon and apparently carried away the statue of its chief deity, Marduk. The priesthood of the latter sought to explain the event as Marduk's self-imposed exile, a form of punishment upon his worshipers which would last "seventy years." However, the next king (Esarhaddon), seeking to improve relations with his neighboring state after only eleven years had passed, returned the statue to Babylon. This he did because Marduk had reversed the order of the cuneiform signs with which the dates had been written: formerly 𒐋𒌋 (60 + 10), but now 𒌋𒐕 (10 + 1)!

In conclusion: while the "standard" numbers of the Bible cannot be relied upon for chronological purposes, particularly in the "primeval story," this does not mean that they are in "error." They reflect the concerns and thought-patterns of the biblical period, and must be appreciated for that reason. The goal is to listen honestly to the text, rather than trying to make it fit our preconceived desire to assign an absolute date to biblical happenings.

FOUR

More on the Search for Noah's Ark

Chapter 5 of the present volume presented and evaluated the activities of ark-searchers in the vicinity of Büyük Ağri Daği ("Mount Ararat") up to 1978. Since that time the search has continued on a near annual basis by one or more groups. It is the purpose of this appendix to report on some of that activity.

I. ASTRONAUT IRWIN'S 1982 EXPEDITION

According to the *New York Times* (Aug. 20, p. A2; Aug. 23, p. A5), an expedition of twelve Americans, led by astronaut James Irwin, ended when Irwin hurt himself in a fall near the summit. Two members, however, managed to reach the top. The expedition was sponsored "by a group in Colorado Springs, Colo."

II. A REPORT ON ABC NEWS (20/20 PROGRAM), 1985

The Noah's ark question was given national television coverage on a segment of the ABC news magazine *20/20*, co-anchored by Hugh

Downs and Barbara Walters, and broadcast on Oct. 17, 1985. It was entitled, "The Mystery of Noah's Ark," and included the following aspects. I have placed my brief responses in brackets.

1. An introductory narrative, stating that "the flood legend" appears around the world. "Narratives may differ from culture to culture, but there is one common denominator: except for one family, mankind perished by the hand of God, as punishment for its sins." [The adequacy or inadequacy, as the case may be, of that statement can be seen by reading chap. 1, above: there apparently is no such common denominator. Sometimes it is not a family that is involved in the flood story, not always a deity, nor is the flood always the result of sinful activity on the part of humans.]

2. The mountain is called "Mount Ararat." [See above, chap. 4, for the problems with that designation.]

3. A group is shown investigating a site "fifteen miles south of Ararat," which the local population has designated "Doomsday Mountain." [The location, its physical appearance, and the statement that it had been explored and rejected earlier as the remains of the ark make it clear that this is the object discussed above, in chap. 4 sec. V ("Recent Photographic Evidence"), no. 2. Photos were carried in *Life* magazine, vol. 49 (Sept. 5, 1960), pp. 112–114.] See above, fig. 9.

The area is shown being investigated by Dave Fasold and Ron Wyatt with the aid of a "molecular frequency generator," which detected iron beneath the surface in the shape of a boat. The investigators "hoped to prove" that it was in fact Noah's ark. Actual excavation, however, was prevented by a local rebellion by a group of Kurds. The investigators hoped that future seasons would solve the question of the object's nature.

[Since iron technology is well attested in the ancient world, but not before the middle of the second millennium B.C.E. and even then only for small wrought objects, to expect to find iron over the entire length of a structure some 450 feet long (see above, chap. 2) and dated to at least 2350 B.C.E. (i.e., Archbishop Ussher's minimal age: see above, chap. 4), is at least surprising. See "Iron" in *IDB*, II: 725.]

4. The activities of another group, associated with Eryl Cummings (apparently the Archaeological Research Foundation, for which see above, chap. 4, sec. V, no. 3). Among that team in 1985, hoping to locate the remains of the ark on Agri Daği, was astronaut James Irwin, who suggested that the discovery of the ark might signal the imminent return of Jesus to earth. The team started to climb the northeast face of the mountain, but their permit was rescinded after two days.

5. The narrator (Tom Jerrell) announced that the Turkish government had sent its own team to investigate the object on "Doomsday Mountain."

III. THE 1986 "SNOW TIGER" TEAM

According to the *Bible-Science Newsletter* (Dec. 1986, pp. 12–13), this was the only group of searchers on the mountain during the summer of 1986 ("1986 Mt. Ararat Expedition," by Charles D. Willis). Some of its members have been on previous expeditions. Interest was focused upon the ice cap "at the base of the al-Judi ridge," just beneath the summit of the mountain (i.e., at the 16,800 foot level). A trench was cut in the ice with chain saws to a depth of sixteen feet, but "the deck of the ark was not hit."

The group also surveyed the area of the Ahora Gorge where most of the other expeditions have concentrated, but concluded that "this cataclysmic area just wasn't where the Ark could have survived."

[Apparently, this was not the only team on the mountain, contrary to claim. According to the *New York Times* (Aug. 31, 1986), a team of seven (including astronaut James Irwin and Dutch television crew) were filming the area from the air. Apparently there was some confusion about their permission to do so, and Irwin "was detained most of today by local Turkish policemen after allegations that he engaged in espionage while searching for Noah's Ark."

[As for Willis' designation "al-Judi" for the upper ridge, this is the first time, in accounts ancient or modern, that the present writer has encountered it. Apparently conflation is taking place, so that designations of other mountains are now being applied to Ağri Daği. As a consequence, ancient texts that challenge Ağri Daği as the ark's landing place would now come to support it.]

IV. CRAWFORD'S 1987 EXPEDITION

A 1987 expedition to the mountain was carried out by the Rev. Edward Crawford of the Edmonton (Alberta, Canada) Bible Presbyterian Church, according to an article in the October 19 issue of *Alberta Report* (p. 44).[1] It yielded "conclusive evidence" of the historical truth of the biblical account in the form of a structure 164 x 27 yards, encased in ice and volcanic debris at the 15,500＝foot level of Aǧri Daǧi, "just where the Bible says Noah's enormous ark landed." His estimate (and photographs) were made from a distance of 800 yards (i.e., nearly one-half mile), since the government of Turkey would not allow him to cross over to the north face of the mountain where the structure was actually located.

[These reported remains of Noah's ark lie a full 2,000 feet up the mountain from Noah's ark as located by Fernand Navarra (see above, chap. 4, sec. VI).]

FIVE

Who Is the "Real" Noah?

That there is a transition in Genesis 9, between v. 19 and v. 20, should be obvious even to the casual reader. In terms of subject matter, one concludes the account of "Noah the Sailor" and begins that of "Noah the Farmer" (see above, chap. 6). The transition is more than in subject matter, however, for it involved literary form: v. 19 sounds like a conclusion, and v. 20 like a beginning. The total effect is such that it has been plausible for a few modern interpreters to conclude that two stories once circulate independently, as did many accounts in the Bible. (See above, chap. 6, and more generally, chap. 5). Such a conclusion is supported by the Mesopotamian literature, where the flook story has an independent status. In the Gilgamesh Epic the account of the great deluge has been inserted into the report of Gilgamesh's heroic deeds and of his search for eternal life.

What would be the effect, within the Genesis story, if the flood story were removed? That is, would there be continuity between what comes before it and what comes after it? In doing so, one would need to discount Genesis 6:1–4. (It is a short unit concerned to explain the limits of human life and why there were once giants in the land as evidenced by huge tombstones from ancient times.[1] The story, in its present context, has been given a new meaning: justification for the flood.) One would also need to discount Genesis 5, since it belongs to the P-Source, and thus would be an insertion into the older J account. That would bring us to the end of Genesis 4, the genealogy of Cain, as the point that might once have been continued at 9:20, the account of "Noah the Farmer." Appropriately, both the genealogy (4:17–26) and the viniculture account (9:20–27) are assigned to the J-Source.

The genealogy is concerned with a series of innovations in human culture: the first city builder (v. 17), the ancestor of tent-dwellers (v. 20), the ancestor of musicians (v. 21), and the first forger of bronze and iron instruments (v. 22). Prior to that, Cain is depicted as the first metallurgist and farmer, and Abel as the first shepherd. (On the nonbiological basis of such genealogies, see above, chap. 5.) It would be entirely in keeping with that context to read, at 9:20, "Noah, a man of the soil, began the planting of vineyards" (NEB). That is, the list of cultural innovations continues with the beginnings of viniculture.

One notices immediately, however, that there is no mention of Noah in the genealogy of Cain, and thus the transition to 9:0 would be a bit abrupt. Instead, one reads, at the end of the genealogy, of the innovations wrought by the sons of Lamech, Noah not among them. In the parallel (inserted) genealogy in Genesis 5, however, we again encounter Lamech, and this time the son who is singled out is Noah, who will "bring us relief from our work." This anticipates the viniculture episode nicely, and provides transition to 9:20. It is possible, if not necessary in order to maintain this point of view, to suppose that, prior to the insertion of the P account (Gen. 5), the genealogy of Cain included a reference to Noah as well (so Westermann, pp. 359–60, 411).

Such reflections make it possible to entertain the following speculative but interesting question, which in fact was raised generations ago (e.g., by Skinner, pp. 133–34, 185–87): Did the name "Noah" belong originally to the farmer, the originator of viniculture? An able recent interpreter has continued this line of thought: "It is possible, however, that the connection of Noah with the Deluge . . . is not original but was made in Syria-Palestine for a figure who entered the area originally as a gardener" (*IDB*, III: 554). In that case, the original sailor, whatever his name, would have become "Noah" when the flood story was inserted into the list of cultural innovations.

Were one to pursue this line of thought, the logical question would not be: Why was the flood story inserted at precisely this point—so that Noah became the hero? Why not a generation earlier, so that it would be Lamech? An answer might be found in the Mesopotamian accounts of pre-flood "events." The Sumerian King List (W-B Text 444)[2] lists eight monarchs and then announces (concerning the hometown of the eighth): "The flood swept thereover." Now, in the genealogy in Genesis

4, Noah is the eighth generation from Adam. It apparently was customary, therefore, to put the flood story after the same number of generations, regardless of one's culture.

If this view is correct (namely, that the name "Noah" belonged to the farmer), then we need not be surprised that a connection of his name with the flood story was not obvious (see above, chap. 6).

What, then, would one make of the Akkadian personal names that seem to suggest that there was a deity named Nah, worshiped in Mesopotamia during the Middle Bronze Age (see above, chap. 6)? Could this deity be related in some way to the name "Noah," if Noah is the supposed originator of viniculture in Canaan? One could note that, in the stories of some cultures in the Mediterranean area, the knowledge of wine-making was transmitted to humans by a deity: Dionysus among the Greeks, and Osiris among the Egyptians. Thus it has been proposed "that the Noah of this passage was originally a Canaanitish wine-god."[3] While this view has not found wide acceptance, it is evident that the biblical tradition wants to place some distance between itself and its neighbors. "Once more the benefits of civilization are traced back to a person, not to the gods (Osiris, Dionysus). The suggestion that Noah may have been originally a Canaanite wine god is certainly not correct" (Westermann, p. 487).

Conversely, if the sailor and the farmer were originally different persons, might the name "Noah" have belonged originally to the first of these? The possibility that the name means "long (of life)," reminiscent of both Ziusudra ("life of long days") and Utnapishtim ("he who found life"), would be supportive.

When all is said and done, what may one conclude? First, such conjectures as these, however alien they may appear to the casual reader of the Bible, have arisen from a close reading of the text and from the desire to take it seriously and to understand it. Even if one disagrees with the solutions, nonetheless the questions have arisen from the text. That must, after all, be one's starting point, and not unreflecting notions about what one thinks it ought to say. Second, there surely is much about the text that we do not understand. Details of its origin and growth are lost in the mists of time, and its concerns are apparently often quite alien to our own. Understanding comes slowly and often with the aid of disciplines that require lifelong study (e.g., the cuneiform literature). Indeed, it is doubtful if some of the mysteries will ever be cleared up.

Notes

INTRODUCTION

1. "Noah: Right!" recorded on Warner Brothers Records (no. 1518: *Bill Cosby Is a Very Funny Fellow: Right!*), followed by sketches entitled "Noah and the Neighbor" and "Noah: Me and You, Lord."

1. CATASTROPHE STORIES AROUND THE WORLD

1. William Henry Brett, *The Indian Tribes of Guiana* (London: Bell & Daldy, 1868), pp. 398–99.

2. Lieut. Tickell, "The Hodésum (improperly called Kolehan)," *Journal of the Asiatic Society* 9 (1840): 694–709, 783–808, at p. 798.

3. An extensive bibliography may be found in Westermann (pp. 384–87), and extensive summaries of deluge traditions may be found in Gaster (pp. 82–131).

4. For the relationship of the contents and theologizing tendencies of flood narratives to the society in which they are expressed, see Westermann, pp. 405–6. He observes that "high" societies have accounts with much detail and a theological base, whereas "primitive" cultures tend to have little more than the coming of the flood, salvation from the flood, and the end of the flood. Then he concludes: "it is not possible to understand the flood narrative in the high cultures either in its polytheistic or monotheistic forms apart from its pre-history in the early cultures."

5. Mircea Eliade, *Patterns in Comparative Religion* (New York: Meridian Books, 1963), pp. 423–25 ("The Myth of Human Androgyny").

6. See, e.g., the work that Westermann cites: E. G. Kraeling, *Xisouthros, Deucalion and the Flood-Tradition* (1947).

7. For an example of such "discovery" by later missionaries in the Marquesas Islands, see Gaster, p. 356, sec. 41, n. 11*b*, and also p. 126.

2. FLOOD STORIES IN THE ANCIENT NEAR EAST

1. This text, at first unrecognized as a part of Atrahasis, may be read in Pritchard, 2nd ed., pp. 99–100, where it is given the title, "Creation of Man by the Mother Goddess."

2. Extensive quotations from Berossus were made by Alexander Polyhistor (first century B.C.E.), whose work also was lost, but quotations of it survive in an Armenian translation of Eusebius' *Chronicles*. Eusebius' remarks about the flood were also preserved by the Byzantine historian Georgius Syncellus (eighth century C.E.). See Lambert and Millard, pp. 134–35.

3. This ancient document exists in several versions, for which see Jacobsen, *King List*. My reference is to Weld-Blundell 62, often referred to in Jacobsen's footnotes, whereas his main text is based upon the much more extensive Weld-Blundell 444 (the beautifully preserved prism in the Ashmolean Museum).

4. Each king's reign is a multiple of 60^2, save the first, which has given rise to the plausible suggestion that the text has become corrupt in transmission. The actual total is 456,000 years, if the first king's reign remains at 67,200 years. My total of 457,200 years is based upon a "correction" of his reign to 68,400 years, i.e., $60^2 \times 19$, which is often proposed (Cassuto, I: p. 258).

5. This is the total in the Masoretic Text (the traditional Hebrew, followed by the English Bible). Other ancient texts (e.g., the Greek Bible) have different totals. (See below, chap. 5.)

6. On Puzur-Amurri as a navigator for the boat, see Heidel (p. 84); for the interpretation that he merely caulked it, see Pritchard (2nd ed., p. 94) and Veenker (p. 217, n. 23). The text in question is XI, l. 94.

7. Such instances are recorded by the Muslim historians Abu-al-Ḥassan ʿAli al-Masʿudi (see vol. 1 of the translation, *Les prairies d'or* and Aḥmad ibn-Yaḥya al-Balādhuri (*Futūḥ al-Buldān*, trans. P. Hitti, *The Origins of the Islamic State*). Summaries, with maps, may be found in Le Strange, pp. 25–29, 41–43, 74.

8. See also Beek, p. 12. For photos, see *Aramco World*, November–December 1966, pp. 18–19 (taken in southern Iraq), and March–April 1968, pp. 32–33 (part of an article entitled "The Great Badanah Flood," concerning Saudi Arabia). See also André Parrot, facing p. 30.

9. More properly, the title is Vi-Daeva-Data, meaning something like "The Law to Turn Away from Evil." It apparently was composed during the period third century B.C.E. to third century C.E., but has elements going back much earlier. An English translation may be found in James Darmesteter, *The Zend-Avesta*, 2nd ed. One might also consult E. Benveniste, "What Is the Significance of Vendidad?" in the W. B. Henning Memorial Volume (London: Lund Humphries, 1970; *nv*). Briefly, see *"Avesta," IDB*, I: 321–22.

10. Other sources, however, state that the period of deathlessness under Yima's over-sight lasted for 1,000 years, including a century in the enclosure (Vara) which was soon to be built (see below). See Darmesteter, p. 14, n. 1.

11. Based upon the observations of Martin Schwartz as part of a symposium on "The Flood Myth: An Inquiry into Causes and Circumstances," held at the University of California, Berkeley, in 1976. Audio Tape no. 336.

12. Darmesteter, 2nd ed., pp. lvii–lx ("Jewish Elements in the Religion"); see also p. 10. Brief discussion of Persian influence upon the apocalyptic thought of the Bible may be found in *IDB*, I: 157–58, 873 ("Dualism"); II: 361–62 ("Gehenna").

3. IS THERE PHYSICAL EVIDENCE OF NOAH'S FLOOD?

1. The techniques for assigning a date to a particular level of habitation were not nearly as refined as they are at present. Thus one made a judgment based upon the accumulated depth of debris, architectural style, and ceramics (shape, decoration, and method of production). It is not surprising that some of the early assignments of date have subsequently been revised. For a specific instance bearing upon the date of a flood deposit, see the discussion of Kish in the present chapter.

2. A "biblical" chronology could be constructed by adding the ages of persons in a genealogical list. E.g., "When Adam had lived a hundred and thirty years, he became the father of . . . Seth" (Gen. 5:3). If one had a fairly secure anchor (beginning point), such as the date of the founding of the Solomonic Temple, one could then work backward a generation at a time. The standard computation of this type was by James Ussher, Irish archbishop of Armagh (1581–1656 C.E.), who thus set creation at 4004 B.C.E. and the deluge at 2349 B.C.E. Later interpreters would have serious reservations about such reconstruction, as we shall see in the present chapter, in chap. 5, and in app. 3.

3. For a brief discussion of the location and extent of Shinar (Sumer and Akkad?), see *IDB*, III: 332–33.

4. A brief summary may conveniently be found in *IDB*, II: 278–84. More detail, in a popular style, may be found in Parrot. More up-to-date is Mallowan. Beyond that, one should consult the excavation reports for the individual sites.

5. Woolley dug a number of pits in the mound and found that the water-deposited silt varied in thickness. Subsequently, popular accounts would relate that one or the other of these figures was *the* thickness of the deposit, resulting in contradiction and in confusion for the reader.

6. *Antiquaries Journal* 9 (October 1929). This journal carried preliminary reports of the expedition. For a popular summary by the excavator, Woolley, see his *Excavations at Ur* (London: Ernest Benn, 1954). For details, see the multi-volumed excavation report, *Ur Excavations*, especially vol. 4.

7. Popular accounts sometimes put the thickness of the deposit at five feet (e.g., Halley, p. 78). This seems to be a mistaken understanding of the fact that the deposit lay 1.75 meters below plain-level. For discussion, see the writings of André Parrot and Mallowan; for details, see Watelin and Langdon, *Excavations at Kish* (multi-volume). Even the excavators differ in reporting the thickness of the upper deposit: either 40 cm. or 30 cm. Usually they will mention three deposits in all, rather than four (Mallowan, p. 78).

8. For the document involved, see Jacobsen, *King List*, pp. 76–77.

9. Erik Schmidt, "Excavations at Fara, 1931," University of Pennsylvania's *Museum Journal* 22 (1931): 193–217; *nv*.

10. "Excavations at Nineveh, 1931–1932," *Annals of Archaeology and Anthropology* 20 (1933): 71–186; *nv*.

11. So André Parrot, p. 50, citing Jordan, *Zweiter vorläufiger Bericht* . . ., Abhandlungen der Preussischen Akademie der Wissenschaften, 1929, p. 20. He then cites V. Christian as having interpreted the stratum "as the mark of heavy inundation" (in *Archiv für Orientforschung* VIII, p. 64.)

12. A. Parrot, pp. 50–51. He cites the excavation report, *Tello* (Paris: Albin Michel, 1948), p. 58.

13. For a recent analysis and comparison of Halley's and related works (in their latest editions), see James C. Moyer and Victor H. Matthews, "The Use and Abuse of Archaeology in Current Bible Handbooks," *Biblical Archaeologist*, 48 (September 1985): 149–59.

14. Martin A. Beek, *Atlas of Mesopotamia* (London: Nelson, 1962), p. 12.

15. Mallowan, pp. 73–74. The analyst (H. H. Thomas) had raised the possibility of an eolian origin, but later rejected it.

16. Mallowan, pp. 72, 74, citing results from the Sorbonne and elsewhere (as published in the excavation Report, IV, appendix VI–D, and by V. Malycheff, "Analyse des Limons de Kish et d'Ur," *L'Anthropologie* 41 (1931): 269–71).

17. Woolley, p. 35. See also Mallowan, p. 71.

18. The strata were between the end of the Jamdat Nasr remains and the beginning of those of the Early Dynastic Period.

19. The strata interrupt the remains of the Ubaid (Obeid) culture.

20. Briefly, see the discussion in A. Parrot, pp. 47–49. For more detail, with a very helpful chart for all the sites, see Mallowan, plate XX.

21. However, the authors (Whitcomb and Morris) do not accept the Septuagint's genealogies, since its ages "are obviously false" (p. 475).

22. This list of options, with bibliography, may be found in Whitcomb and Morris, p. 484, n. 1. These are not their own solutions, however.

23. Seuss, *The Face of the Earth*, 5 vols. (Oxford: Clarendon Press, 1904), vol. 1, pp. 17–40, 57–72. This is a translation of his classic *Das Antlitz der Erde*, which appeared in 1885. For summary and negative evaluation, see Heidel, pp. 241–45.

24. This approach to the biblical flood story made newspaper headlines throughout the United States in the 1970s after Cesare Emiliani, of the University of Miami, analyzed sediments from the Gulf of Mexico. A popular account may be found in Fred Warshofsky, "Noah, the Flood, the Facts," *Reader's Digest*, September 1977, pp. 129–34.

25. Van Dijk, *LUGAL UD ME-LÀM-bi NIR-GÁL*, 2 vols. Leiden: E. J. Brill, 1983.

26. Van Dijk's translation of the Sumerian into French is:

> 334. Ce jour-là, l'eau salubre ne sortant plus de la terre,
>   ne montait pas sur les champs,
> 335. puisque, la glace entassée partout, le jour où elle commença
>   à fondre, portait la destruction dans la Montagne,
> 336. (et) puisqu'a cause de cela les dieux du pays étaient
>   soumis à la servitude,
> 337. qu'ils devaient porter la hache et la corbeille,
> . . . .

340. Le Tigre en son plein ne fit pas (encore) m[ont]er sa crue
en haut,

. . . .

344. Personne ne faisant (encore) le nettoyage des canaux,
personne ne draguait les boues,

. . . .

27. Samuel Noah Kramer, book review in *JAOS* 105 (1985): 135–39, at p. 135, n. 4.

28. The precise length of a cubit is uncertain but apparently was about eighteen inches (*IDB*, IV: 837).

29. E.g., at the coronation of King Solomon, the music was said to be so loud that "the earth was split by their noise" (1 Kings 1:40), and Solomon's wisdom was such that "the whole earth sought to be in his presence" (1 Kings 10:24). These instances illustrate nicely that the Bible contains exaggeration, and thus was not meant to be "literally true" in every particular.

30. Vail, *The Waters above the Firmament* (1874, apparently reprinted in 1902); *The Story of the Rocks* (1885); *The Earth's Annular System* (1912). Some of Vail's works are being reproduced, and are the subject of favorable discussion, in various issues of *Stonehenge Viewpoint* (e.g., no. 34, March–April 1980, which has articles entitled "The Vailian Ring-Canopy Theory, the Planet Saturn [Part I]" and "The Ring of Truth").

31. Perhaps the two best-known organizations are the Creation Research Society, a group of scientists in Ann Arbor, Michigan, who publish the *Creation Research Society Quarterly*, and the Institute for Creation Research (ICR) in San Diego, California, with the related Christian Heritage College. The latter group publishes a newsletter (*Acts and Facts*), offers public lectures and debates with "evolutionists" around the world, has a nationwide radio ministry, and has published a number of volumes. Titles by President Henry Morris include *Evolution and the Modern Christian* (1976), *The Scientific Case for Creation* (1977), and (with John C. Whitcomb, Jr.) *The Genesis Flood* (1961). Recently, ICR has sought to aid the introduction of Creationism into the curriculum of public schools, resulting in court cases in Arkansas (1982) and in Louisiana (1985). This has, in turn, generated opposing literature, e.g., the periodical *Creation/Evolution*.

32. Morris, *Evolution and the Modern Christian* (cited above, n. 31), p. 64.

33. Velikorsky, *Worlds in Collision* (New York: Dell Publishing Co., 1950).

34. Velikovsky, *Earth in Upheaval* (New York: Dell Publishing Co., 1955).

35. Velikovsky, *Ages in Chaos* (Garden City, N.Y.: Doubleday, 1952).

36. A brief introduction may be found in William H. Stiebing, Jr., *Ancient Astronauts, Cosmic Collisions* (New York: Prometheus Books, 1984), chap. 3. For more detail, see Alfred de Grazia, ed., *The Velikovsky Affair* (New York: University Books, 1966). The latter contains three essays that had been published in the *American Behavioral Scientist* (September 1963), one of them appropriately entitled "Minds in Chaos."

37. See Edwin M. Yamauchi, "Immanuel Velikovsky's Catastrophic History," *JASA* 25 (1973): 134–39. *JASA* describes itself as "An evangelical perspective on science and the Christian faith."

38. Velikovsky in *Pensée* 2, no. 2 (May 1972): 14, as quoted in *JASA* 25 (1973): 142.

39. Patten, *The Biblical Flood and the Ice Epoch* (Seattle: Pacific Meridian Publishing Co., 1966), as described by Charles McDowell, "The Relationship between Immanuel Velikovsky and Christian Catastrophists," in *JASA* 25 (1973): 140–46, at p. 143.

40. Reviews may be found in *Heythrop Journal* 21 (1980): 180–82 (by W. F. Saggs); *Journal of Semitic Studies* 26 (1981): 275–77 (by A. R. Millard); *Orientalia* 51 (1982): 275–76 (by Jerrold S. Cooper).

41. "The Tenets of Creationism," *ICR Impact Series* 85 (July 1980). The *ICR Impact Series* is a part of *Acts and Facts*, for which see above, n. 31.

42. The full text of the judicial opinion may be found in *Science* 215 (Feb. 19, 1982): 934–38, with the quotation from p. 937. Earlier reports of testimony at the trial may be found in the issues of Jan. 8 (pp. 33–34, 142–46) and Jan. 22 (pp. 380–84). Critical analyses of Creationism may be found in *Science 81* (December 1981) and in *Creation/Evolution* 5 (Summer 1981). Creationist response to the Arkansas decision may be found in *ICR Impact Series* 105 (March 1982).

43. Al Seckel, "Science, Creationism, and the U.S. Supreme Court," *Skeptical Inquirer* 11 (Winter 1986–87): 147–58. The article contains statements by several Nobel laureates, seventy-two of whom have signed a brief opposing the Louisiana statute. See 12 (Winter 1987–88), 184–87 for an approval (by Stephen Jay Gould) of the final decision.

4. HAS NOAH'S ARK SURVIVED?

1. For a discussion of the term "Masis" and the various other designations of the mountain, see P. Gh. Injijian, *Geography of Armenia*, vol. 1, pp. 54ff. (in Armenian; *nv*). The mountain must not be confused with the Masius Mountains of the classical geographers, a range of 5,000-foot peaks lying south and west of the Tigris, now called Jabal Karaja (Karaga Dağ). For the latter, see Heinrich Kiepert, *A Manual of Ancient Geography* (London: Macmillan and Co., 1881), sec. 90, with his *Atlas of Ancient and Classical Geography* (London, 1907), map 19. The similarity of the names may have contributed to the transfer of flood traditions from the area of the Masius range to Masis (see present chap; sec. III).

2. In general, see Boris Piotrovsky, *The Ancient Civilization of Urartu* (New York: Cowled Book Co., 1969); Charles Burney and David Lang, *The Peoples of the Hills* (New York 1972).

3. So Herodotus in his *Histories*, 7.73. See, however, Burney and Lang, *Peoples*, pp. 177–79, who suggest a connection with the Hurrians.

4. The linguistic phenomenon involved is either an interchange of the consonants *r* and *l* (attested in various languages, particularly Semitic) or an inability to distinguish the two (as in the lingua franca of the times, Achaemenian Persian). See George Rowlinson, *History of Herodotus*, 4 vols. (London, 1875), 4: 245 ff. ("On the Alarodians of Herodotus").

5. See Rowlinson, *Herodotus*; Burney and Lang, *Peoples*, pp. 177–78; H. Kiepert, *Manual*, p. 49.

6. Herodotus, *Histories*, 3. 89–94.

7. Kevork Aslan, *Armenia and the Armenians* (New York, 1920), p. 30.

8. Jerome, *Corpus Christianorum: Series Latina*, 73.442.

9. Thus the Septuagint (Greek) translation of Isa. 37:38 and the Vulgate (Latin) translation at Gen. 8:4, 2 Kings 19:37.

10. Kiepert, *Manual*, secs. 40–49; H. F. Tozer, *A History of Ancient Geography* (Cambridge, England: University Press, 1935), pp. 113–14.

11. For later uses of the term "Armenia," in even wider senses, see "Armenia" in *Encyclopaedia Judaica* (1971), 3: 472–75; for the province of Arminiyah during the Abbasid period, see G. Le Strange, *The Lands of the Eastern Caliphate* (Cambridge, England: University Press, 1930), pp. 182–84 (with his map 1).

12. Collections of sources include: Samuel Bochart, *Geographia sacra, seu Phaleg et Canaan* (Lugduni Batavorum: Cornelium Boutesteyn, 1707), 1: 13–21; J. A. Fabricius, *Codex Pseudepigraphs Veteris Testamentii*, 2 vols. (Hamburg and Leipzig: Christian Liebezeit, 1713–33), vol. 1, sec. 33 ("Reliquiae Arcae Noae," *nv*); Theodor Nöldeke, "Kardu and Kurden," in *Beiträge zur Alten Geschichte und Geographie*, Festschrift für Heinrich Kiepert (Berlin: D. Reimer, 1898), p. 73; Louis Ginzberg, *The Legends of the Jews*, 7 vols. (Philadelphia: Jewish Publication Society 1946–47), 5: 186, n. 48; "Deluge," in James Hastings, ed., *Encyclopaedia of Religion and Ethics* (Edinburgh, 1911), vol. 4, esp. pp. 553–55; Theordor Nöldeke, "Der Landungspunkt Noahs," in his *Untersuchungen zur Kritik des Alten Testaments* (Kiel: Schwers, 1896), pp. 145–55. Much more convenient for the average reader (though rather uncritical at points and slanted toward an identification of the biblical Ararat with Büyük Ağri Daği) is the limited collection, in English translation, by John W. Montgomery, *the Quest for Noah's Ark*, 2nd ed. (Minneapolis: Dimension Books, 1974), pp. 61–98, 325–27. Also: S. C. Malan, *the Book of Adam and Eve* (London: Williams and Norgate, 1882), pp. 239–42.

13. Yakut, *Mu'jam al-Buldān*, vol. 2, p. 270, 11. For other classical sources, see M. Streck, "Djudi," in *Encyclopedia of Islam* (1965 ed.) 2: 573–74. The precise location of the range is 27°30′N, 41°30′E. For a description of the area, see William Palgrave, *Narrative of . . . Central and Eastern Arabia* (London: Macmillan and Co., 1865), vol. 1, chap. 3.

14. Regis Blanchère, *Dictionnaire Arabe-Franqis-Anglais* (Paris: G. P. Maisonneuve et Larose, 1967–), vol. 3, pp. 1890–91; "Taiy," in *Encyclopedia of Islam* (1934 ed.), 4: 624a. The deity was apparently named Fals/Fils/Fuls.

15. *Ad Autolycus*, vol. 3, chap. 19 = AND, 2.117.

16. S. Baring-Gould, *Legends of the Patriarchs and Prophets* (New York: J. B. Alden, 1885), pp. 142–43. I have not been able to find a published account of Prevoux's travels. Presumably, however, his Chenna is the small oasis village of Qana (sometimes spelled Kenah by Western travelers, e.g., Palgrave, *Narrative*, vol. 1, p. 100), just north of the 'Aja' range (specifically, at 27°47′N, 41°25′E), and thus within sight of the ark's landing place. However, the Department of Antiquities of the kingdom of Saudi Arabia has informed me that they have no knowledge of this relic at present.

17. Nicholas of Damascus (first century B.C.E.), quoted by Josephus, *Antiquities*, I.3.vi = Loeb Classical Library, 1.95.

18. The traditional identification with the Minni of Jer. 51:27, mentioned along with the kingdom of Ararat, seems doubtful on linguistic grounds (so I. F. Gelb, "Minni," in *IDB*).

19. Cf. Greek βαρίς "tower, elevation"; Persian *barz, burz*, "height, tall"; Old Persian *hara berezaiti*, "high mountain"; Arabic *baraza*, "to come into view, tower up" (said of mountains), *barz*, "hill" (hence: *al-barz*, "the elevation"). See f. Steingass, *A Comprehensive Persian-English Dictionary* (Routledge and K. Paul, 1892), p. 173, col. 2; "Albruz" in *Encyclopedia of Islam*, 1965 ed.; Le Strange, *Lands*, p. 368n. One must not confuse Mount Elbruz with the Elburz Mountains in northern Iran. (For the suggestion that Baris means "exit," which is to be connnected with Noah's departure from the ark, see Samuel Bochart, *Geographia sacra: Phaleg et Canaan* (1707), p. 20 (1.3). For the Caucasus range as the ark's landing place, see Th. Gaster, *Myth*, p. 129. It should also be noted that βαρίς can mean "boat," which, while interesting, seems improbable as a basis for naming the mountain; cf., however, κιβωτός ["box, boat"] as a city name in site no. 4, below.)

20. Carveth Wells, *Kapoot* (New York: R. M. McBride, 1933), p. 219.

21. This carra (Κάρραι) is often considered to be too far to the southeast to be the famous city of Harran (Χαρραν; Κάρραι). The text is often emended to Gordyene

(Καρδοῦ; see the Loeb ed.), an area mentioned in other ancient sources as the ark's landing place (see site 3*b*).

22. Josephus, *Antiquities*, XX.2.ii (Loeb ed., 20.24–25).

23. Hippolytus, *Refutation of All Heresies*, 10, chap. 26 = ANF, 5, 149.

24. Julius Africanus, *Fragments . . . of the Chronology*, 4 = ANF 6, 131. Parthia was generally to the east of Mesopotamia, but occasionally extended its influence to the area of Greater Armenia. Thus Julius' reference allows for a number of possibilities.

25. Located at 35°45′N, 45°15′E; 8,600 feet tall, snow-capped, and visible for 100 miles. For the general geography in Assyrian sources, see Maximilian Strech, "Armenien, Kurdistan und Westpersien n.d. Keilinschriften," *ZA*, 15 (1900): 257–382 (esp. pp. 272ff.). For the specific identification of Mount Nisir and discussion of the area, see E. A. Speiser, "Southern Kurdistan," *AASOR*, 8 (1926/27): 1–42 (at pp. 17–18).

26. Strabo, *Geography*, 16.1.24 = Loeb ed., 7, 231.

27. Xenophon, *Anabasis*, 4: Καρδοῦχοι.

28. Ptolemy, *Geography*, 5.13.5; Muller ed., 5.12.2: τὰ Γορδυαῖα ᾿όρη.

29. e.g., *Ber. Rab.* 33.4 (Albeck ed., vol. 1, p. 309); *Tan.* B, I.41; and the Syriac sources cited under site 5.

30. Josephus, *Antiquities*, I.3.vi = Loeb ed., 1.93; see also *Against Apion*, I.19. Berossus is also quoted in this regard by Eusebius of Caesarea (*Praep. Evang.*, 9.12). For general bibliography, see Montgomery, *Quest*, pp. 61–64.

31. Pliny, *Natural History*, 6.16.

32. Epiphanius, *Panarion Haereses*, 1.1.4 (*Epiphanii Episcopi Constantiae Opera*, ed. G. Dindorifius, vol. 1 [Leipzig, 1859], p. 283 = K. Holl, *Epiphanius*, vol. 1, *Panarion*, GCS [Leipzig, 1915], p. 174): ᾿ανὰ μέσον ᾿Αρμείων καὶ Καρδνέων.

33. Epiphanius, Dindorfius, ed., vol. 1, p. 324 = Holl, ed., p. 217 (= *Panarion Haer.*, 18.3.4).

34. L. W. King, "Sennacherib and the Ionians," *Journal of Hellenic Studies* 30 (1910): 327–35, at p. 328, n. 2.

35. Ibid.; for photos, see Gertrude Bell, *Amurath to Amurath* (London, 1911), p. 290.

36. Bell, *Amurath*, p. 292; "Djudi," in *Encyclopedia of Islam*, 1965 ed., for sources.

37. *Encyclopedia of Islam*, "Djudi," 1965 ed., for sources.

38. An idea as old as Bochart, *Geographia sacra* (1707), vol. 1, 3 (p. 18).

39. *Encycloopedia of Islam*, "Djudi", 1965 ed.; see also Arthur Jeffrey, *Foreign Vocabulary of the Quran* (Baroda: Oriental Institute, 1938), p. 107.

40. Nazm al-jawhir, p. 41 = Migne, *Patrologia Cursus Completus(PCC)*, CXI, p. 915, sec. 40.

41. Murūj al-Dhahab, chap. 3; trans. B. Meynard and P. Courteille, *Les Praries d'Or*, vol. 1, p. 74.

42. *the Itinerary of Rabbi Benjamin of Tudela* (London: A. Asher, 1840), vol. 1, pp. 90–91.

43. *Al-Madjmu' al-Mubārak*; ed. and trans. Th. Erpenius, *Historica Saracenica . . . a Georgia Elmacino*, vol. 1, p. 17, as quoted by Montgomery, *Quest*, p. 327.

44. ῾Adjā'ib al-Makhlūkāt wa-Gharā'ib al-Mawdjūdāt; ed. Wüstenfeld, *Kosmographic*, vol. 1, p. 156.

45. Eutychius, *Nazm al-jawhir*, p. 43 = Migne, *PCC*, CXI, p. 915, secs. 41–43.

46. Ibn-Ḥawqal, *al-Masālik w-al-Mamālik*, in the tenth century. Quoted in Montgomery, *Quest*, p. 327.

47. Bell, *Amurath*, p. 293; *Encyclopedia of Islam*, 1965 ed., "Djudi."

48. Bell, *Amurath*, pp. 289–95; W. F. Ainsworth, *Travels in the Track of the Ten Thousand Greeks* (London: J. W. Parker, 1844), nv. For a photo, see Bell, *Amurath*, p. 291.

49. Bell, *Amurath*, p. 292; and esp. W. A. Wigram and Edgar T. A. Wigram, *The Cradle of Mankind* (London: A. and C. Black, 1914), pp. 335–36.

50. Sibylline Oracles, 1.320ff. The site is actually at the headwaters of the river Maender, of which the Marsyas is a tributary.

51. For references in classical sources and for a description of the area, see J. A. Cramer, *A Geographical and Historical Description of Asia Minor* (Amsterdam: Hakkert, 1971), vol. 2, pp. 47–52.

52. Cramer (*Asia Minor*, p. 50) considers the name to be "attached to Apamea probably as a distinctive appellation from the Syrian town of the same name," but he is uncertain as to its meaning.

53. A variety of such traditions is mentioned by James Bryce, *Transcaucasia and Ararat* (London: Macmillan and Co., 1896), pp. 214, 222–24.

54. Josephus, *Antiquities*, I.3.v.

55. Ptolemy, *Geography*, V.13, xii.

56. Victor Langlois, *Collections des historiens anciens et modernes de l'Armenie*, 2 vols. (Paris: Firmin Didot, 1867–69), vol. 2, p. 242*b*, n. 1; p. 328*b*, n. 2.

57. Moses, *History of the Armenians* (Venice, 1881; in Armenian, *nv*); Latin trans. by W. and G. Whiston, *Moses Chorenensis Historia Armeniae* (London: Caroli Ackers Typographi, 1736; not widely available in the United States; *nv*); French trans. in Longlois, *Collections*, vol. 2, pp. 53–175. For a brief discussion of his career and works (with dated bibliography), see "Moses (5) of Khoren" in the *Dictionary of Christian Biography*, ed. William Smith and Henry Wace (London: J. Murray, 1882), vol. 3, pp. 949–50. Langlois' index does not contain an entry "Idsheuan" and at vol. 2, 242*b*, n. 1, he points out that the city of Idchavan (= Idsheuan?) in the province of Airarat is mentioned only by Vartabed.

58. For the beginnings of the debate, see A. Carrière, *Moïse de Khoren et les généalogies patriarcales* (Paris: L. Cerf, 1891, *nv*), and *Nouvelles Sources de Moïse de Khoren* (Vienna: Mechitaristes, 1893, *nv*), proposing an eighth-century date. The traditional date is defended by F. Conybeare, "The Date of Moses of Khoren," *Byzantinische Zeitschrift* 10 (1901): 489–504.

59. See in particular, Hans Lewy, "The Date and Purpose of Moses of Chorene's History," *Byzantion* 11 (1936): 81–96, with a rejoinder (to Adontz) at pp. 593–96. His ninth-century date for Moses is challenged in favor of the eighth by N. Adontz, "Sur la Date de l'Histoire de l'Armenie," *ibid.*, pp. 97–100, with a rejoinder (to Lewy) at pp. 597–99. For more recent affirmation of a late ninth-century date, see the literature cited in Berthold Altaner, *Patrology* (New York: Herder and Herder, 1960), p. 411. See also Cyril Toumanoff, *Studies in Christian Caucasian History* (Washington: Georgetown University Press, 1963), pp. 330–34, who gives nine reasons for assigning the work to the late eighth century.

60. E.g., while Montgomery (*Quest*, p. 66, n.) is happy to quote the remark in the *Oxford Dictionary of the Christian Church*, ed. F. L. Cross, 2nd ed. (London: Oxford University Press, 1974), p. 944, that Moses' *History* "remains a work of the first importance for the primitive history of Armenia," he has neglected to report that this was prefaced by, "though its contents seem much less reliable than older scholars used to suppose, it. . . "

61. Faustus, *History of the Armenians* (Venice, 1933; in Armenian, *nv*); French trans. in Langlois, *Collections*, vol. 1, pp. 209–310.

62. Usually considered a scribal error for "Ararat" (Longlois, *Collections*, vol. 1, p. 218, n. 2). See also below, app. 1 and 2.

63. An English translation of the entire passage may be found in Montgomery, *Quest*, pp. 71–74.

64. Langlois, *Collections*, vol. 1, p. 288, nn. 1–2; vol. 2, p. 107*b*, n. 4. For a detailed study of the various provinces and the cantons of each, see Heinrich Hübschmann, "Die altarmenischen Ortsnamen," in *Indogermanische Forschungen* 16 (1904): 197–490. A summary account may be found in his *Armenische Grammatik* (Hildesheim: Georg Olms, 1962; reprint of the Leipzig ed. of 1897), pp. 403–4, 518–20.

65. Study of the provinces in Armenia is complicated by the fact there have been several systems of boundaries and of designations: those of the Arsacid monarchs; those of the Byzantines, with a revision by Justinian; and those of the Muslims. See briefly, "Arminiya," in *Encyclopedia of Islam*, 1965 ed. ("Divisions); H. Gelzer, *Die Genesis der byzantinischen Themenverfassung* (Amsterdam: Adolph Hakkert, 1966), esp. pp. 64–72; and the works of Hübschmann cited in the previous note.

66. For the sources, see "Kurds" in *Encyclopedia of Islam*.

67. Ptolemy, *Geography*, Müller ed., V.12.2,3.

68. Montgomery; *Quest*, p. 71, n. 3, following Langlois, *Collections*, vol. 2, p. 107*b*, n. 4; vol. 1; p. 288, nn. 1–2, who is following Saint-Martin, *Memoirs*, vol. 1, p. 176, *nv*).

69. I have used Mühler's text.

70. In the type font of some Renaissance Latin editions of Ptolemy, an *i* can easily be mistakenly read for a *t*.

71. Κοριαία in the Greek original: V.12.8 in Mühler but V.13.18 in some others.

72. Κωταία in the Greek original: V.12.9 in Mühler but V.13.20 in some others. For the erroneous Latin reading "Cortaea," on which Montgomery has depended, see Mühler's ed., I.2, p. 947, n.

73. Bell, *Amurath*, p. 294.

74. *(a)* "Hymns on Paradise," I.10 (Ephraem Syrus [trans. Renè Lavenant; Paris, 1968], p. 39; *Corpus Scriptorum Christianorum Orientalium*, 174. *Scriptores Syri*, 78: *Des Heiligen Ephraem des Syrers [Louvain, 1957], with translation in vol. 79, p. 3); (b)* "Commentary on Genesis and Exodus," sec. 6, p. 12 (*CSCO*, 152; *SS*, 71: *Sancti Ephraem Syri* [ed. R. M. Tonneau; Louvain, 1955], with translation in vol. 72, p. 48); *(c)* "Passover Hymns," VII.7 (*CSCO* 248; *SS* 108: *Des Heiligen Ephraem des Syrers*, with translation in vol. 109, p. 57).

75. Cited in Malan, *Adam and Eve*, p. 239, n. 17, citing the Arabic text (in contrast to the Syriac, which places the landing site at Apamea, near Celaenae [site no. 4]). Most of Bar-Hebraeus is yet unpublished.

76. For the complete text, see Montgomery, *Quest*, pp. 80–81.

77. S. C. Malan, *The Life and Times of S. Gregory the Illuminator* (London: Rivingtons, 1868).

78. "Jacobus (4) or James," in *A Dictionary of Christian Biography*, ed. William Smith and Henry Wace (London, 1882), 3: 325–27, at p. 326*b*.

79. Le Strange, *Lands*, p. 94.

80. Translated in Montgomery, *Quest*, pp. 85–86. "Cemanum" appears to be a corruption of the Hebrew word for "eighty" (*shemōnīm*; Syriac: *themānīn*; Arabic: *thamānīn*).

81. Le Strange, *Lands*, p. 98.

82. Bell, *Amurath*, pp. 291–93.

83. Bryce, *Transcaucasia*, p. 222; Bell, *Amurath*, p. 294.

84. E.g., *Sepher Noah*, 155, beginning.

85. For the texts, see Hermann Rönsch, *Das Buch der Jubiläen* (Amsterdam: Rodopi, 1970), p. 293 for Syncellus, *Chronicle*, and p. 305 for Cedrenus, *Synopsis*.

86. Th. Gaster, *Myth*, p. 359; Umberto Cassuto, *Genesis*, vol. 1, p. 105; Bochart, *Geographia sacra*, vol. 1, sec. 3, p. 21.

87. For the Islamic traditions, see "Ceylon" in *Encyclopedia of Islam*.

88. See "Alwand Kuh" in *Encyclopedia of Islam*, 1965 ed.

89. William Foster, ed., *Thomas Herbert: Travels in Persia, 1627–1629* (London: G. Routledge and Sons, 1928), pp. 191, 322.

90. C. P. Tiele and W. H. Kosters, "Ararat," in *Encyclopaedia Biblica*, 4 vols., ed. T. K. Cheyne and J. S. Black (New York, 1899–1903).

91. For a summary of the position, as contained in Lenormant, *Les origines de l'histoire*, (Paris: Maisonneuve, 1880), vol. 2, pp. 1–45, and for a brief refutation, see J. van den Gheyn, "Ararat," in *Dictionnaire de la Bible* (1895).

92. Tim La Haye and John Morris, *The Ark on Ararat*, p. 41.

93. J. Bryce, *Transcaucasia*, p. 250, relates the story of the Persian shah who offered a vast reward for anyone able to reach the top. No one claimed it.

94. For the full accounts, see Montgomery, *Quest*, pp. 82–83, 85–86, 99–100, 106–9.

95. Ibid., p. 110.

96. J. J. Friedrich Parrot, *Journey to Ararat* (New York: Harper, 1859), is a detailed, careful study of the mountain and its surroundings. For a lengthy bibliography of travel in the area and of its topography, see H. F. B. Lynch, *Armenia* (London: Longmans, Green, and Co., 1901), vol. 2, pp. 471–84. Lynch's work is itself a reliable source of information and is not focused on the search for Noah's ark.

97. For a description of the 1840 eruption that blew away a vast strip of the mountain and created the Ahora Gorge, see J. J. F. Parrot, *Journey*, pp. 385–89.

98. La Haye and Morris, *Ark on Ararat*, pp. xi–xii, 56ff.

99. Ibid., pp. 43–49.

100. Montgomery, *Quest*, pp. 158–80, for Stuart's own account. See also René Noorbergen, *The Ark File* (Mountain View, Calif.: Pacific Press, 1974), pp. 106–7, who mentions another expedition in the same time period.

101. Noorbergen, *Ark File*, p. 106, cites the death certificate. Williams' account puts the death in 1918, apparently in error.

102. Bryce, *Transcaucasia*, p. 280.

103. Ibid., p. 281.

104. La Haye and Morris, *Ark on Ararat*, pp. 56–63.

105. Bryce, *Transcaucasia*, pp. 240–44; Lynch, *Armenia*, 1: p. 161 (mentions the unique stand of birches on Little Ararat); Balsiger and Sellier, *In Search of Noah's Ark* (Los Angeles: Sun Classic Books, 1976), p. 71.

106. Bryce, *Transcaucasia*, pp. 240–44; Lynch, *Armenia*, 1: 167, does mention a seasonal stream near the foot of the mountain, as does J. J. F. Parrot, *Journey*, p. 240.

107. Noorbergen, *Ark File*, pp. 107–8.

108. La Haye and Morris, *Ark on Ararat*, pp. 64–67; Montgomery, Quest, pp. 110–12.

109. For considerable detail, see Noorbergen, *Ark File*, pp. 96–102.

110. La Haye and Morris, *Ark on Ararat*, pp. 65–66.

111. For a scholarly discussion, see "Weights and Measures" in *IDB*, IV: 836–37. Arksearchers La Haye and Morris, *Ark on Ararat*, p. 244, list estimates from 17.5 to 24 inches, and prefer ca. 18 inches.

112. Noorbergen, *Ark File*, pp. 99–100.

113. This is the date given in Montgomery, *Quest*, p. 113, who seems to be discussing Hagopian under the assumed name George Tamisian. La Haye and Morris, however, list the date as 1908–10 (*Ark on Ararat*, p. 68). For a long interview with Hagopian, see Noorbergen, *Ark File*, pp. 164–71.

114. La Haye and Morris, *Ark on Ararat*, pp. 73–92; Montgomery, *Quest*, pp. 119–25; Noorbergen, *Ark File*, pp. 82–96.

115. La Haye and Morris, *Ark on Ararat*, pp. 98–101; Montgomery, *Quest*, pp. 125–28.

116. For details, see La Haye and Morris, *Ark on Ararat*, pp. 115–25.

117. A Kurd named Shukru Asena from the vicinity of Büyük Ağri Daği is reported to have given the story to reporter Edwin Greenwald in Istanbul, Turkey. However, the subjec indexes for 1948 of the *New York Times* and of the London *Times* indicate that they did not carry the item, which La Haye and Morris, *Ark on Ararat*, date to Nov. 13.

118. Smith reportedly published two books on the topic: *The Reported Discovery of Noah's Ark* (Orlando, Fla.: Christ for the World Publishers, 1949); *On the Mountains of Ararat in Quest of Noah's Ark* (Apollo, Pa.: West Pub. Co., 1950). Cited by La Haye and Morris, *Ark on Ararat*, p. 125, nn. 1–2.

119. Balsiger and Sellier, *In Search*, pp. 159–60.

120. It is sometimes claimed that various aviators saw or photographed the ark, and that an edition of *Stars and Stripes* in 1943 carried an article about some of them. To date, however, it appears that neither airman, nor newspaper, nor photo has been produced as evidence. See La Haye and Morris, *Ark on Ararat*, pp. 103–7; Dave Balsiger and Charles Sellier, *In Search*, pp. 155–57.

121. For discussion, see Montgomery, *Quest*, pp. 128–31, 252–53; Balsiger and Sellier, *In Search*, pp. 160–61. For a sketch based upon the photos, see Montgomery, *Quest*, following p. 192.

122. See "Noah's Ark?" *Life* magazine, Sept. 5, 1960, pp. 112–14. For discussion, see La Haye and Morris, *Ark on Ararat*, pp. 143–44. For a copy of the photo, see Balsiger and Sellier, *In Search*, following p. 106. For a detailed account by a member of the expedition, see Noorbergen, *Ark File*, chap. 5.

123. For a copy of the photo, see Balsiger and Sellier, *In Search*, following p. 106, with discussion at pp. 164–65; La Haye and Morris, *Ark on Ararat*, pp. 176–78 (with photo on p. 177).

124. La Haye and Morris, *Ark on Ararat*, p. 177 (Morris was a member of the ICR group that tried to locate the object).

125. Ibid.

126. For a copy, see *ibid.*, p. 204 (with a wider area photographed from Skylab, on p. 202); Montgomery, *Quest*, following p. 192 (two photos, one magnified).

127. Balsiger and Sellier, *In Search*, pp. 192–96.

128. Montgomery's own account is found in *Quest*, pp. 316–17, with copies of the correspondence involved at pp. 350–55.

129. Ibid., pp. 355–56; La Haye and Morris, *Ark on Ararat*, pp. 203–5.

130. For the problem, see n. 111, above.

131. As quoted in La Haye and Morris, *Ark on Ararat*, pp. 205–7; Balsiger and Sellier, *In Search*, pp. 194–96.

132. Montgomery, *Quest*, p. 317.

133. For discussion, see La Haye and Morris, *Ark on Ararat*, pp. 190, 214–15. For a copy of the photo, see Balsiger and Sellier, *In Search*, following p. 106.

134. La Hayer and Morris, *Ark on Ararat*, pp. 214–15. Balsiger and Sellier are more cautious: *In Search*, p. 163.

135. La Haye and Morris, *Ark on Ararat*, p. 215.

136. It was viewing this relic that helped encourage Navarra to journey to the mountain: Balsiger and Sellier, *In Search*, p. 167.

137. See Navarra's account in *Noah's Ark: I Touched It* (Plainfield, N.J.: Logos International, 1974), pp. 49–69, with abundant photos. However, the exact location of the "find" is unclear. Navarra allegedly indicated three different spots, several thousand feet apart. See Noorbergen, *Ark File*, pp. 162–63, with the map on p. 155.

138. For copies of their reports, see Navarra, *Noah's Ark*, pp. 125–32.

139. Such chronological reckoning bristles with difficulties, and there are major tensions between the manuscript families (e.g., MT and LXX). See "Chronology, OT," in *IDB* and *IDBS*.

140. *New York Times*, Feb. 27, 1970, p. 39; Mar. 1, 1970, sec. IV, p. 8. For Navarra's diary account, see *Noah's Ark*, pp. 70–94.

141. *Radiocarbon* 7 (1965): 161. The report concludes with the comment: "Evidently not the ark."

142. Radiocarbon dates traditionally have been based upon a 5,568 half-life for C^{14}, but this has recently been revised to 5,730. A 5,568-derived age multiplied by 1.03 yields a 5,730-derived age. In either case, the age of the sample is subtracted from 1,950 to give the before-present date. "Correction" is an adjustment based upon C^{14} dating of tree-ring dated samples (see below). The "corrections" given in this article are courtesy of the University of Pennsylvania; e.g., the 1,190 age multiplied by 1.03 equals 1,225; 1950 C.E. minus 1,225 equals 725 C.E. But with a fifty-year "correction" subtracted, we get: 1225-50 = 1175; 1950 - 1175 = 775 C.E.

143. *Sceince News* 111 (Mar. 26, 1977): 198–99. I have confirmed this by telephone conversation with the director of the laboratory, Professor Rainer Berger. Results will be published as "UCLA Radiocarbon Dates" in a future issue of *Radiocarbon*.

144. Ibid; confirmed by telephone conversation with Professor R. E. Taylor, Department of Anthropology. He and Professor Berger are preparing an article that will examine all the radiocarbon evidence in this matter.

145. Radiocarbon laboratories file test results under a specimen number and under the name of the person who submitted the specimen for analysis (rather than by the location where it was found). This has made retrieval of test results somewhat difficult for me.

146. *Science News* 97 (June 13, 1970): 574, discussing only tests allegedly done at Geochron, University of Pennsylvania, and UCLA. I have not discovered any support for the claim in *Christianity Today* 13 (Sept. 12, 1969): 48, that the wood has been radiocarbon dated to 4,000 years of age. The publisher's foreword to Navarra, *Noah's Ark* (p. xi), lists an age of 1,500 years but does not identify the lab. Page 136 alludes to a radiocarbon age of 4,448 years, but gives no documentation to support it. See Noorbergen, *Ark File*, pp. 135-37, 143, for reasons to doubt that such a test was ever done. Listing Navarra's book as his source, William Stiebing (in *the biblical Archaeology Review* 2, no. 2, p. 17) gives a range of 450–750 C.E. (Thus one can scarcely believe anything concerning this topic that has been published in popular words.)

147. Noorbergen, *Ark File*, p. 142. Confirmed by telephone by the laboratory director, Harold Krueger, The specimen number is Gx 1668.

148. *Science News* 97, no. 24; Balsiger and Sellier, *In Search*, pp. 185–86; *New York Times*, Feb. 27, 1970, p. 39.

149. This result was published in *Radiocarbon* 19 (1977): 213.

150. Noorbergen, *Ark File*, p. 142, identified by the laboratory director as Gx 1667.

151. E.g., Navarra's book makes not mention of them (in contrast to a brief note in the publisher's foreword).

152. Montgomery (*Quest*, p. 255) speaks only of "widely divergent results"; La Haye and Morris (*Ark on Ararat*, p. 132) say that the (unspecified) results "far exceed a proper percentage of error."

153. Cited in *New York Times*, Mar. 1, 1970 sec. IV, p. 8, concerning the 1969 wood.

154. For reasonably informed but dated objections to the method in general (from the point of view of someone sympathetic to biblical chronology, and generally in polemical tones), see John Whitcomb, Jr., and Henry Morris, *The Genesis Flood* (Philadelphia: Presbyterian and Reformed Pub. Co., 1961), pp. 370–79. For detailed up-to-date discussion of the limitations of the method, by readiocarbon scientists, see Ingrid Olsson, *Radiocarbon Variations and Absolute Chronology*, Nobel Symposium 12 (New York, 1970); see also the review by Robert Adams in *JNES* 32 (1973): 253–56. For an excellent general discussion, see J. O. D. Johnston, "The Problems of Radiocarbon Dating," *PEQ* (1973), pp. 13–26.

155. In addition to the sources cited in n. 154, above, see Balsiger and Sellier, *In Search*, p. 190.

156. Olsson, *Radiocarbon Variations*, p. 305.

157. Navarra, *Noah's Ark*, p. 124.

158. So the caption beneath one of the pictures in *Noah's Ark* (following p. 76, on the fourth photo page). However, the caption under the sixth photo page speaks of "the three pieces . . . refitted," as does the text on p. 63 (thus one can scarcely trust even the most elemental statmenets about this entire matter). To make matters worse, the beam as reconstructed bears striking dissimilarities to what is allegedly the same beam still intact atop the mountain (*Noah's Ark*, following p. 76, photo pp. 2–3). This may be due, however, to the perspective from which the various photos were taken, or to Navarra's chopping activity.

159. La Haye and Morris, *Ark Ararat*, p. 132.

160. *Science News* 111 (Mar. 26, 1977): 198, citing research done at the University of California, La Jolla, by Professor Hans Suess.

161. La Haye and Morris, *Ark Ararat*, p. 132; Balsiger and Sellier, *In Search*, p. 189.

162. *Science News* 111 (Mar. 26, 1977): 198–99.

163. In general, see H. E. Suess, "The Three Causes of the Secular C^{14} Fluctuations," in Olsson, ed., *Radiocarbon Variations*, pp. 595–605.

164. R. E. Lingenfelter and R. Ramaty, "Astrophysical and Geophysical Variations in C^{14} Productions," in Olsson, *Radiocarbon Variations*, pp. 513–37.

165. V. Bucha, "Influence of the Earth's Magnetic Field in Radiocarbon Dating," in Olsson, *Radiocarbon Variations*, pp. 501–11.

166. J. Labeyrie, G. Delibrias, and J. C. Duplessy, "The Possible Origin of Natural Carbon Radioactivity Fluctuations in the Past," in Olsson, *Radiocarbon Variations*, pp. 539–47.

167. J. C. Lerman, W. G. Mook, and J. C. Vogel, "C^{14} in Tree Rings from Different Localities," in Olsson, *Radiocarbon Variations*, pp. 275–301, esp. pp. 292–97.

168. See the series of articles under the heading, "C^{14} and Dendrochronology," in Olsson, *Radiocarbon Variations*, in pp. 233–333.

169. Ibid.; H. N. Michael and E. K. Ralph, "Correction Factors Applied to Egyptian Radiocarbon Dates from the Era before Christ," in Olsson, pp. 109–20 (with various charts, including plate 2); E. K. Ralph, H. N. Michael, and M. C. Han, "Radiocarbon Dates and Reality," *MASCA Newsletter* 9 (August 1973).

170. See Balsiger and Sellier, *In Search*, p. 189, who claim even more excessive variations.

171. As do La Haye and Morris, *Ark on Ararat*, pp. 132–33.

172. See the series of articles under the heading "C¹⁴ and Archaeology" in Olsson, *Radiocarbon Variations*, pp. 23–126.

173. W. S. Glock and S. Agerter, "Anomalous Patterns in Tree Rings," *Endeavor* 22 (1963): 9–13.

174. C. W. Ferguson, "Bristlecone Pine: Science and Esthetics," *Science* 159 (1968): 839–46, at p. 840.

175. Navarra, *Noah's Ark*, p. 125–28.

176. Ibid., pp. 128–32.

177. Balsigner and Sellier, *In Search*, p. 185.

178. Navarra, *Noah's Ark*, pp. 132–33.

179. Balsiger and Sellier, *In Search*, p. 185.

180. So also *ibid.*, p. 181.

181. This seems to refer to lignite formation and not lignin loss. Navarra's documents make no mention of this.

182. Presumably degradation is meant.

183. See, e.g., Richard Leo and Elso Barghoorn, "Silicification of Wood," *Harvard Museum Leaflets* 25 (Dec. 7, 1976): 4.

184. Personal communication from paleaobotanists at North Carolina State University.

185. Leo and Barghoorn in *Harvard Museum Leaflets* 25, p. 27

186. Letter to the University of Pennsylvania Radiocarbon lab, as quoted in Noorbergen, *Ark File*, p. 143.

187. $.175/.275 = X/5000$. If Bordeaux's alternative identification is adopted (*Quercus castaneifolia*), the age becomes less still: 2,950 years.

188. Navarra, *Noah's Ark*, pp. 126–27.

189. Written by Professor A.C. Barefoot and dated June 15, 1977.

190. John Morris, "Noah's Ark Goes to Hollywood," in *ICR Impact Series*, no. 47 (May 1977), p. iv.

191. J.J.F. Parrot, *Journey to Ararat*, pp. 167, 172, 174–75, 187, 190, 194–95.

192. Cited in La Haye and Morris, *Ark on Ararat*, p. 54. See Stuart's account of having rediscovered it in 1856 (in Montgomery, *Quest*, p. 178).

193. Ibid. Sixty soldiers and loads of scientific equipment accompanied him, and he spent five days atop the mountain. For an account, see Montgomery, *Quest*, p. 214.

194. Montgomery, *Quest*, p. 214.

195. See Struys' account, quoted in La Haye and Morris, *Ark on Ararat*, at p. 24.

196. Jondanus (fourteenth century) reports this. See Montgomery, *Quest*, pp. 86–88.

197. This is a cryptic remark, perhaps alluding to the charge, sometimes allegedly made by Navarra's associates, that both the 1955 and the 1969 wood specimens involved "fraud" (La Haye and Morris, *Ark on Ararat*, pp. 133–34, 157–60). See Noorbergen, *Ark File*, pp. 161–62, for another such charge.

198. *ICR Impact Series*, no. 47, p. iv.

199. On NBC, May 2 and Dec. 24, 1977.

200. Produced by Charles E. Sellier, Jr., for Sun Classic Pictures, Los Angeles, Calif. It is related to a book of the same title, written by Dave Balsiger and Charles Sellier, Jr., and published by Sun Classic Books, Los Angeles, 1976.

201. Woolley, *Excavation at Ur* (1954). However, Woolley himself did tend to see his discovery as evidence in support of the biblical account. Few subsequent examiners of the evidence have agreed with his interpretation.

202. See the excellent summary in "Flood (Genesis)," IDB.

203. The production notes for the film, entitled *Noah's Ark: The Facts*, contain the following statement: "Ancient accounts report that pilgrims climbed Mt. Ararat as early as 700 B.C. to scrape pitch from a ship believed to be the Ark." However, I am not aware of any statement of the ark's survival from such an early period. Indeed, it seems first to have been reported by Berossus 400 years later. In any case, there is no reason to believe that such accounts refer to Ağri Daği (see chap. 4, sec. III).

204. Halley, *Pocket Bible Handbook* (19th ed.; 1951), p. 82.

205. R. Noorbergen, *Ark File*, pp. 135–37.

206. For a brief discussion, see Balsiger andSellier, *In Search*, pp. 196–98.

207. Ark-searcher John Morris (*ICR Impact Series*, no. 47, p. iv) claims that the spot of unique reflectivity is indeed the schoolhouse roof, located at 5,000 feet elevation, rather than at 14,000 feet as the movie indicates. However, the spot seems indeed to be at the snow line, and thus Morris' claim would be without foundation. He makes a similarly erroneous claim (p. ii) concerning the location of the object in the ERTS photo which Montgomery initially thought to be the ark (see chap. 4, sec, V, above).

208. For the basic story, see *New York Times*, July 19, 1970, p. 11; for speculations as to why permission was refused, see Balsiger and Sellier, *In Search*, pp. 205–7; Montgomery, *Quest*, pp. 294–97.

209. For various accounts of difficulties, see Balsiger and Sellier, *In Search*, pp. 70–74; Montgomery, *Quest*, pp. 271–78; La Haye and Morris, *Ark on Ararat*, pp. 180–87.

210. See above, n. 93; J.J.F. Parrot, *Journey to Ararat*, pp. 163–64.

211. J.J.F. Parrot, *Journey to Ararat, pp. 199–209*.

212. Lynch, *Armenia*, vol. 1, p. 198; J.J.F. Parrot, *Journey to Ararat*, pp. 171, 219; Bryce, *Transcaucasia*, pp. 239–40.

213. Bryce, *Transcaucasia*, pp. 305, 293.

214. Lynch, *Armenia*, vol. 1, pp. 169, 177.

215. Navarra, *Noah's Ark: I Touched It*, pp. 40–69, with photos.

216. Montgomery, *Quest*, p. 276, with photo following p. 192.

217. Cited by La Haye and Morris, *Ark on Ararat*, p. 70.

218. J.J.F. Parrot, *Journey to Ararat*, pp. 170–87.

219. An opinion quoted in the *New York Times*, Feb. 27, 1970, p. 39.

220. La Haye and Morris, *Ark on Ararat*, p. 261.

221. For drawings, based upon Assyrian reliefs, see Martin Beek, *Atlas of Mesopotamia* (London, 1962), plates 42–46.

222. Balsiger and Sellier, *In Search*, pp. 122, 184–85.

223. *Encyclopaedia Britannica* (1956 ed.), see under "Oak."

224. Boissier, *Flora Orientalis* (Geneva: H. Georg, 1879), vol. 4, pp. 1163–64, 1170–71, 1174.

225. See under "Forest," in *IDBS*.

226. See "Agri Dagh," in *Encyclopedia of Islam*, 1965 ed., for sources; see also Le Strang, *Lands*, p. 182; for al-Istakhri's text, see M.J. de Goeje, ed., *Bibliotheca Georgraphorum Arabicorum*, vol. 3 (Leiden, 1906).

227. As suggested in the *New York Times*, Mar. 1, 1970, sec. 4, p. 8, and elsewhere.

228. Navarra, *Noah's Ark*, p. 121, for the later date.

229. Wright, "The Ark Again?" in *Newsletter, no. 3* of the American Schools of Oriental Research (October 1970).

230. Noorbergen, *The Ark File*, pp. 50–53.

231. As quoted in Montgomery, *Quest*, pp. 86–88.

232. Ibid., pp. 102–3.

233. Navarra, *Noah's Ark*, p. 124.

234. Ibid., p. 128.

235. (50 x 10)mm/2 = 250 mm. radius; 250/3 mm. average = 83.

236. Balsiger and Sellier, *In Search*, p. 185.

237. (5 ft. x 12 in. x 2.54 cm x 10) mm. diameter/2 x 3 mm. average (?) per annual ring = 254 years.

5. THE "PRIMEVAL STORY" (GENESIS 1–11)

1. An elderly resident of the county in which I grew up (in western North Carolina) once told me that a cousin in previous generations, being the seventh son of a seventh son, was sought out for his ability to cure certain diseases in children.

2. A possible exception, of course, would be creation itself, now that the debate over origins has been tilted in favor of the "Big Bang Theory" (as opposed to the "Steady State Theory") by the discovery of constant background radiation. That is, one could now speak of creation as an event in time. See "Science and the Bible' in *IDBS*, pp. 789–94, at sec. 3.

3. Briefly, see the article "Legend" in *IDB*, III: pp. 108–10. For more detail, see Gunkel, and most recently Coats (pp. 8–9).

4. Joshua was proposed by the rabbis as the author of the account of Moses' death (Deut. 34). Clement of Rome attributed the (supposedly) unlikely accounts of Noah's drunkenness and Abraham's remarriage to an unknown person. Briefly, see *IB*, I: 185; for more detail, see Bailey, *Pentateuch*, pp. 27–28.

5. For an amusing and desperate attempt to escape this evidence of non-Mosaic authorship, see P. J. Wiseman, *Ancient Records and the Structure of Genesis* (Nashville: Thomas Nelson, 1985; originally published in 1936), pp. 121–23. He points out that the text says that the kings reigned "over" Israel, rather than "in" Israel, and thus it could even refer to the time when "Pharaoh reigned over the children of Israel." In actuality, however, the distinction is not between the English text's "over" versus "in," since the Hebrew text says, literally, "before the reigning of a king belonging to the Israelites." Although this has occasionally been taken to mean Israelite control over Edom (which would put its author even later than Moses), it is quite likely that it means the beginnings of monarchy within Israel as a country (Westermann, *Genesis 12–36*, p. 565).

6. Those who desire more information in this approach than is given below would consult *IB*, I: 185–200; *IO–VC*, pp. 1082–84.

7. While deities in the Ancient Near East could be referred to as "god," each had a proper name as well, e.g., Marduk (of Babylon), and Yahweh (of Israel). A growing concern that the holy name not be casually used led, by the third century B.C.E., to substitute designations for Yahweh. The most common of them was "the Lord," a tradition that has continued in English Bibles to the present day. Thus when one reads "the Lord" at Gen.

4:1, one may safely assume that behind it, in the Hebrew text, are the four consonants ("tetragrammaton") which make up the divine name (y-h-w-h). See *IDB*, II: 409ff.

8. An instance of a missing generation in a genealogy, at Gen. 10:24 and 11:12–13, has been cited above, in the present chapter.

9. Brief discussion may be found in *IDBS*, at p. 685 (sec. 2: "The Completion of P").

10. This methodology was worked out by Wellhausen, especially in his chaps. 1 ("The Place of Worship") and 4 ("The Priests and Levites").

6. NOAH IN THE BIBLE

1. I have here followed the divisions of Speiser. Discussion may conveniently be found in *IB*, I: 536–54 (provided that one should neglect the distinctions there made between J¹, J², etc., which will add to the confusion of those to whom this topic is new). A more straightforward discussion may be found in *IO–VC* (pp. 7–9), available in most church libraries.

2. Three models for understanding the composition of the entire Pentateuch (Gen.–Deut.), with the reasons and problems of each, may briefly be studied in Bailey, *Pentateuch*, chap. 1, part 3. They are the Single Author (Mosaic) model, the Documentary Hypothesis model, and the Complex-of-Traditions model (usually associated with the work of Rolf Rendtorff).

3. For the basic definition, see McEvenue, pp. 29–30. He points out that writers have sometimes misnamed this construction as a "concentric inclusion" or a "chiastic structure."

4. Brief grammatical discussion may be found in Westermann, p. 487. RSV's erroneous "first tiller of the soil" (apparently following KJV), would in any case conflict with the earlier J account of Cain as the first farmer (Gen. 4:2).

5. On the difficulty of deciding upon the period in Syro-Palestinian history when the conditions of the text are met, see Westermann, pp. 490–91.

6. A map showing the distribution of the groups in the so-called Table of Nations (Gen. 10) may not readily be available to readers of the present volume. Helpful is the one found in *IB*, I: 558.

7. See von Rad, p. 131; Speiser, p. 62. The latter mentions the possibility above, and then concludes, "The problem remains unsolved."

8. A learned caution against making comparative moral-value judgments based upon the Bible versus other Ancient Near Eastern literature may be found in Finkelstein's article.

9. I am indebted, at this point, to my former classmate at Hebrew Union College–Jewish Institute of Religion, Ronald Veenker (see bibliography).

10. So Targum Psuedo-Jonathan, various Midrashim (e.g., Genesis Rabbah, Sifre Numbers), some early fathers of the church (e.g., Jerome, Augustine), and some modern interpreters (e.g., Speiser)

11. A brief discussion may be found in *IDB*, II: sec. 3a.

12. The suggested pun goes back to Carl Frank, "Zu den Wortspielen *kukku* und *kibāti* in Gilg. Ep. XI," *ZA* 36 (1925): 218. It is accepted by Heidel (p. 82, n. 170) and Pritchard

(p. 93, n. 190), but questioned by other interpreters. The words *kukku* ("cake; cereal") and *kukkû* ("darkness") are attested, as is *kibtu* ("wheat"), but one only assumes the existence of *kîbtu* ("pain"). The last of these words is not listed in *CAD*, although the possibility of the pun is mentioned (vol. K, p. 498*b*).

13. Not only is it attested in the Gilgamesh Epic, but also partially in Atrahasis (although the existing copy is broken, at III.i.50).

14. A fragment of the Gilgamesh Epic has even been unearthed in Israel (at Megiddo: see *IDB*, III: 338), and one of Atrahasis at Ugarit in Syria (Lambert and Millard, p. 131).

15. For a brief discussion, attributing the omission in Genesis to "cultural differences," see Westermann, p., 399.

16. Even the standard treatment of biblical names has no suggestion to offer, and "Noah" is not even listed in the index to Martin Noth, *Die israelitischen Personennamen im Rahmen der gemeinsemitischen Namengebung* (Hildesheim: Georg Olms Verlagsbuchhandlung, 1966).

17. G. R. Driver, "L'interprétation du texte masorétique a la lumière de la lexicographie hébraïque," in *ETL* 26 (1950): 337–53, at p. 350. The Ethiopic cognate of the Hebrew verb has long been noted by standard lexica, e.g., Brown-Driver-Briggs, *A Hebrew and English Lexicon* (Oxford, England: Clarendon: 1907) p. 628.

18. See the article "Shalah (God)," in *IDBS*, p. 820.

19. For a brief account, see "Noah," in *IDB*, III, at p. 556. For detail, see Julius Lewy, "Nâḫ et Rušpan," in *Mélanges Syriens offerts à M. R. Dussaud*, pp. 273–75, with the comments by Martin Noth in *VT* 1 (1951): 253–59. Evidence for spelling the divine name with a long vowel (Nâḫ rather than Naḫ) may be found in Lewy's article.

20. See the article "Noah" in the *Jewish Encyclopedia* for these and other examples.

21. Ignaz Goldziher, "Zur Geschichte der Etymologie des Namens نوح ," *ZDMG* 25 (1870): 207–11.

22. The other suggestion, less popular among modern interpreters, is that Noah's "relief" refers to the covenant in Gen. 9. In a modified form, this is accepted by Cassuto.

23. See "Moses" in *IDB*, III, at p. 443. Presumably, the full name would have involved the name of an Egyptian deity: "child of (the god) So-and-so." The god-name then will have become lost (deliberately?) in Israelite tradition.

24. In written form, the similarity is even greater. If the name Nâḫ-ḥayyîm is written without division of words (as would have been the case), and with a double-duty consonant (for the two ḥ's, as was done in some periods), and without the so-called *mater lectionis* to represent a long vowel (as it would have been in the early period), then the name would be written: *nḥym* and the verb *nḥm*.

7. SO, WHAT DID IT MEAN?

1. For discussions of the history of interpretation of the Bible, see *IB*, I: 106–41; *IDB*, II: 718–24; *IDBS*, pp. 436–456.

2. Likely, the most obtainable discussion of this topic for the average reader of the present volume will be in the *Jerome Biblical Commentary*, ed. Raymond E. Brown, Joseph A. Fitzmyer, and Roland E. Murphy (Englewood Cliffs, N. J.: Prentice-Hall, 1968); see sec. 71 ("Hermeneutics").

3. See Bailey, *The Pentateuch*, chap. 3, for a larger list of options, discussion, and bibliography.

4. On this so-called Prosbul regulation, see briefly *IDBS*, p. 763*a*; for details, see standard references such as *Jewish Encyclopedia* or *Encyclopaedia Judaica*.

5. A compact but excellent introduction to the topic may be found in *IDBS*, pp. 889–90 (sec. 4*a*: "Unintentional errors").

6. Brief discussion may be found in Lloyd Bailey, "Words and the Translator," *Word and World*, 6 (1986): 266–77, esp. under 'Lexicography," at p. 270.

7. Briefly, see *IDBS*, pp. 301–2 (sec. 5*a*: "Historical Understanding"). More generally, see "The Historical Study of the Bible," in *IO-VC*, pp. 978–82.

8. See the article "Cosmogony" in *IDB*, I: 702–9.

9. See 'Tradition, Oral," in *IDB*, IV: 683–85.

10. See the article "Prophet" in *IDB*, III: 896–919, at sec. B5.

11. See *IDBS*, p. 889 (sec. 4*a*.iv, "Confusion of Words Which Sound Alike").

12. In theory, mechanical arrangements could be (*a*) chronological (e.g., from the earliest to the last of a prophet's oracles); (*b*) topical (grouping together the prophet's oracles on topics X, Y, and Z); and (*c*) for convenience of memory. The last of these is most common in the Bible and is most alien to the modern mentality. See the article "Mnemonic Devices" in *IDBS*, pp. 600–602.

13. On such editorial perspectives, see the articles "Redaction Criticism, OT" and "Redaction Criticism, NT," in *IDBS*, pp. 729–32, 733–35.

14. A detailed discussion of the prophet's concern may be found in Hans Walter Wolff, *Hosea* (Philadelphia: Fortress Press, 1974).

15. Robert L. Short, *The Gospel according to Peanuts* (Richmond, Va.: John Knox Press, 1965).

16. From the preface to La Haye and Morris, *The Ark on Ararat*.

17. On the terms "affective fallacy" and "intentional fallacy," which arose in modern (secular) literary criticism, see W. K. Wimsatt, Jr., *The Verbal Icon* (Lexington: Universtiy of Kentucky Press, 1954).

18. Helpful discussions of Leviticus are difficult to find. Recommended are the *IDBS* and *IO-VC* articles (by Milgrom). For more detail, see Bailey (1987).

19. For the range of meaning of Akkadian *abūbu*, see *CAD*, A/1, 77–81: deluge as cosmic event; personified as destructiveness of deities or humans; as a monster; or as flooding in general. Hence Assyrian monarch Shalmaneser III remarks, "I slew their warriors with the sword, decscending upon them like (the god) Adad when he made a rainstorm pour down" (Pritchard, p. 277). Tiglathpileser I is described as a "burning flame, fierce one, Deluge of battle" (*a-bu-ub tamhāri*: *CAD*, A/1, 79). In particular, see the long composition entitled "Lamentation over the Destruction of Ur," wherein the devastating attack of the Elamites is repeatedly referred to as "the storm."

> The city is being destroyed by the storm.
> . . . .
>
> My possessions verily he . . . has carried off;
> . . . .
>
> My (precious) metal verily they who know not
> (precious) metal have fastened about their hands;
>
> [*ll.* 252*a*, 276–77, 280; trans, Kramer, 1940]

APPENDIX 1. HEMRICH HUBSCHMANN, "ARMENIACA"

1. Cf. Müller-Simonis, *Durch Armenien, Kurdistan, und Mesopotamien*, p. 43.

2. Pronounced Nachtschavan, now Nachitschevan on the maps. Designated Ναξοὺάνα by Ptolemy, located near Armavir and Artašat. A diminutive form is Naxjavanik, a village in the canton of Khašunikh in the province of Siunikh (Stephen *Orb.*, vol. 2, p. 270).

3. Cf. Injijean, *Storagruthiun him Hayast* (Venice, 1822), p. 219 (= *nax ĭjevan* or *nax avan*, etc.).

4. Cf. *ĭjanem*, from *ējanem*; *ĭjic*, gen. pl. of *ejk'*.

5. Thus in the Moscow ed., 1853, e.g., at pp. 61, 117, 179, along with Naxčavan (var, Naxčuan), p. 56.

6. Thus the Moscow ed. 1860, e.g., p. 265.

7. Cf. Leon Alischan, *Sisakan* (Venice, 1893), p. 497; "The oldest and best authors, [Moses of] Chorene and others, always write [the name as] Naxčavan until approx. 12th and 13th centuries." Cf. also np. Naxčŭvān, Naxjuvān, gr. Ναξοὺάνα (in Ptolemy).

8. Thus L. Alischan, *Sisakan*, p. 497.

9. *i learn Sararaday*. Since Sararad is the mountain itself (see Faustus, p. 24, line 5 from the bottom: *i Sararad lerinn*), and not the territory in which it lay, it cannot be translated "on the mountain of Sararad" (Murad, p. 71). With words for province, canton, city, market-town, village, mountain, etc., Armenian usage requires the name either in the genitive case or (esp. when it comes first) uninflected as appositional, e.g., *gavarn Airaratu* (FB, 143; Lax Pharp., 283), or *Airarat gavarn, gavarin*, etc. (quite often) = "the province Airarat." Has Sararad evolved from Ararad = Ararat (see below)? Cf. Murad, p. 84, n.

10. This totally unique and far-fetched expression ("region of Airaratic control") has for long been problematic to me (so also for Murad, p. 84). When Faustus elsewhere mentions the canton of Gordukh (or other canton in Armenia), the phrase "canton of Gordukh" (or "canton of Aloyhovit," etc.) always seems a sufficient description to him, with no necessity for more precise designations. Such as designation would be superfluous if it even mentioned that the canton belonged to the country or kingdom of Armenia. This is already sufficiently indicated in the words "in the Armenian Mountains." Moreover, there never was such a thing as Airaratic rule, but rather, only control by the Arsacid kings who resided in a city in the province of Airarat. Faustus uses the phrase only to indicate that if the ark landed in the canton of Gordukh, it landed, if not in the province of Airarat, then surely in one of the regions of Armenia ruled by Airarat. Thus he obviously intends to harmonize the Babylonian-Syrian account with the biblical, as the Jewish tradition had already done when Ararat (Armenian: Airarat) was identified with Qardu (Armenian: Gordukh). (Murad, pp. 26, 39.) The contradiction between the two accounts was later (eleventh–twelfth centuries) emphasized by an Armenian writer; however, at the same time, the conflict was decided, naturally, in favor of the Bible (Murad, p. 91). I cannot agree that, in the passage from Faustus, Airarat still had the meaning of the old kingdom of Urartu as preferred by Dr. Belck (verbal communication).

11. Cf. Nöldeke, *Festschrift für Kiepert*, p. 77.

12. Did the Armenian translator of Gen. 8:4 comprehend the meaning of Ἀραράτ? Why did he not more clearly translate it as *Airarat* (as did the translator of Jer. 51:27)? In any case, *Ararat* (var.: *Ararad*) is only the transliteration of Greek Ἀραράτ and is a thoroughly un-Armenian word by no means derived from *Airarat* (contrary to Murad, p. 20).

Just as strange is *Ararad* in the phrase *erkirn Araraday*, "the territory of Ararat": 2 Kings 19:37; (Pseudo-) Sebeos (Petersburg, 1879), p. 2; and three times in Moses of Chorene, pp. 22, 23. And Sararad? Cf. Murad, pp. 23, 91–92n., 102.

13. In the canton of Sasun (InJiJ., p. 70), west of Lake Van. Moses has selected this mountain because of the resemblance of its name to the name Sem (the son of Noah), which he here changes to Sim.

14. *i noin getezerbn?* The preposition *i* can only be combined with the dative, accusative, and ablative, but not with the instrumental case.

15. Cf. Murad, pp. 91–92.

16. IJavank', the name of the village in [the province of] Airarat (Elise, [Venice, 1859], p. 139; Murad, p. 63), indeed means "disembark, descend, land": ʾαποβαίνειν (from *ijanel*). However, it is located in the canton of Vanand, far away from Mount Masis, and it has no connection with the flood narrative.

APPENDIX 4.   MORE ON THE SEARCH FOR NOAH'S ARK

1. The information courtesy of John Armstrong of Calgary, Alberta, Canada.

APPENDIX 5.   WHO IS THE "REAL" NOAH?

1. The huge tombstones are now called dolmens (*IDB*, I. 862–63; *IDBS*, pp. 245–47), and it is plausible to believe that Gen. 6:1–4 once served an etiological function. (On the nature of etiologies, see *IDBS*, pp. 293–95, and Chap. 7, above, where I used it to describe Gen. 9:20–27.) The playful question-answer sequence between child and parent, or audience and storyteller, might run like this:

"What are those large free-standing stones?"
"Grave markers."
"Why are they so large?"
"Giants are buried in them."
"What are giants?"
"Mighty men, who lived long ago."
"How did giants come about?"
"Sexual union of divine and human beings."
"Why, then, did they die, if they are semidivine?"
"God set a limit on their existence."

2. For other discussion, see above, chap. 3, n. 3; chap. 6; and app. 3. For publication of Text 444, see Jacobsen.

3. Skinner, p. 183, citing Carl Niebuhr, *Geschichte des Ebräischen Zeitalters*, pp. 36ff.

SELECTED BIBLIOGRAPHY

(Includes basic reading and often cited works; excludes IDB/IDBS articles and most secondary sources in chapter 4)

Anderson, Bernard W. "From Analysis to Synthesis: The Interpretation of Genesis 1–11." *Journal of Biblical Literature* 97 (1978): 23–39.

Bailey, Lloyd R. *Leviticus*. John Knox Preaching Guides. Atlanta: John Knox Press, 1987.

———. *The Pentateuch*. Nashville: Abingdon Press, 1981.

———. "Wood from 'Mount Ararat': Noah's Ark?" *Biblical Archaeologist* 40 (1977): 137–46.

Balsinger, Dave, and Charles E. Sellier, Jr. *In Search of Noah's Ark*. Los Angeles: Sun Classic Books, 1976.

Beek, Martin A. *Atlas of Mesopotamia*. London: Thomas Nelson & Sons, 1962.

Brice, William C., ed. *The Environmental History of the Near and Middle East since the Last Ice Age*. New York: Academic Press, 1978.

Bright, John. "Has Archaeology Found Evidence of the Flood?" *Biblical Archaeologist* 4 (1942): 55–62. Reprinted in *The Biblical Archaeologist Reader*, I (Garden City, NY. Double Day Anchor Books, 1961; pp. 32–40).

Brueggemann, Walter. "The Kerygma of the Priestly Writers." *Zeitschrift für die Alttestamentliche Wissenschaft* 84 (1972): 397–413. Reprinted in Walter Brueggemann and Hans Walter Wolff, *The Vitality of Old Testament Traditions* (Atlanta: John Knox Press, 1975), pp. 101–13.

Cassuto, U(mberto). *A Commentary on the Book of Genesis*. 2 vols. Jerusalem: Magnes Press, 1961, 1964 (Hebrew ed., 1944, 1949).

Coats, George W. *Genesis, with an Introduction to Narrative Literature*. Grand Rapids: Wm. B. Eerdmans, 1983.

Darmesteter, James. *The Zend-Avesta*. Vol. 4 of the Sacred Books of the East (ed. F. Max Müller). 2nd ed. Oxford: Clarendon Press, 1895.

Driver, G.R. "L'nterprétation du texte masorétique à la lumière de la lexicographie hébraïque." *Ephermerides Theologicae Louvanienses* 26 (1950): 337–53.

Eliade, Mircea. *Patterns in Comparative Religion*. New York: Meridian Books, 1963.

Finkelstein, Jacob J. "The Study of Man: Bible and Babel." *Commentary* 26 (1958): 431–44.

Frymer-Kensky, Tikva. "The Atrahasis Epic and Its Significance for Our Understanding of Genesis 1–9." *Biblical Archaeologist* 40 (1977): 147–55.

Gaster, Theodor H. *Myth, Legend, and Custom in the Old Testament*. New York: Harper & Row, 1969.

Goldziher, Ignaz. "Zur Geschichte der Etymologie des Namens ﻥﻮﺣ ." *Zeitschrift der deutschen morgenländischen Gesellschaft* 25 (1870): 207–11.

BIBLIOGRAPHY

Greengus, Samuel. "Sisterhood Adoption at Nuzi and the 'Wife-Sister' in Genesis." *Hebrew Union College Annual* 46 (1975): 5–31.

Gunkel, Hermann. *The Legends of Genesis.* New York: Schocken Books, 1964 (first published in 1901).

Halley, Henry H. *Pocket Bible Handbook.* 19th ed., rev. Chicago, Ill.: Henry H. Halley (Box 774), 1951.

Harmatta, J. "Akkadian Epic Poetry and Its Sumerian Sources." *Acta Antiqua* 23 (1975): 41–63.

Heidel, Alexander. *The Gilgamesh Epic and Old Testament Parallels.* Chicago: Phoenix Books, 1963.

Jacobson, Thorkild. *The Sumerian King List.* Assyriological Studies No. 11. Chicago: University of Chicago Press, 1939.

——. *The Treasures of Darkness: A History of Mesopotamian Religion.* New Haven: Yale University Press, 1976.

Kikawada, Isaac M., and Arthur Quinn. *Before Abraham Was: The Unity of Genesis 1–11.* Nashville: Abingdon Press, 1985.

Kilmer, Anne Draffkorn. "The Mesopotamian Concept of Overpopulation and Its Solution as Reflected in the Mythology." *Orientalia,* new series, 41 (1972): 160–77.

Kramer, Samuel Noah. *Enmertkar and the Lord of Aratta.* Philadelphia: The Uni-

——. "Inanna and the Numun-Plant: A New Sumerian Myth." *The Bible World: Essays in Honor of Cyrus H. Gordon,* (ed. Gary Rendsburg, et al.) New York: KTAV Publishing House, 1980 (pp. 87–97).

——. *Lamentation over the Destruction of Ur.* Assyriological Studies No. 12. Chicago: University of Chicago Press, 1940.

La Haye, Tim, and John Morris, *The Ark on Ararat.* Nashville: Thomas Nelson, 1976.

Lambert, W.G., and A.R. Millard. *Atra-hasis: The Babylonian Story of the Flood.* Oxford: Clarendon Press, 1969.

Langlois, Victor. *Collections des historiens anciens et modernes de l'Armenie.* 2 vol. Paris: Firmin-Didot, 1867–1869.

Larsen, Curtis E., and Graham Evans. "The Holocene Geological History of the Tigris-Euphrates-Karun Delta." *The Environmental History of the Near and Middle East since the Last Ice Age,* (ed. William C. Brice.) New York: Academic Books, 1978 (pp. 227–44).

Lees, G.M., and M.L. Falcon. "The Geographical History of the Mesopotamian Plains." *Geographical Journal* 118 (1952): 24–39.

Le Strange, G. *The Lands of the Eastern Caliphate.* Cambridge, England: University Press, 1930.

Lewy, Julius. "Nāḫ et Rušpan." *Mélanges Syriens offerts à M.R. Dussaud.* Paris: P. Geithner, 1939.

BIBLIOGRAPHY

Mallowan, M.E.L. "Noah's Flood Reconsidered." *Iraq* 26 (1964): 62–82.

Malycheff, V. "Analyse des Limons de Kish et d'Ur." *L'Anthropologie* 41 (1931): 269–71.

McEvenue, Sean E. *The Narrative Style of the Priestly Writer.* Analecta Biblica 50. Rome: Biblical Institute Press, 1971.

Montgomery, John Warwick. *The Quest for Noah's Ark.* 2nd ed. Minneapolis: Bethany Fellowship, 1972.

Navarra, Fernand. *Noah's Ark, I Touched It.* Plainfield, N.J.: Logos International, 1974.

Noorbergen, René. *The Ark File.* Mountain View, Calif.: Pacific Press Publishing Association, 1974.

Noth, Martin. "Noah, Daniel and Hiob in Ezechiel XVI." *Vetus Testamentum* 1 (1951): 253–59.

Olson, Walter S. "Has Science Dated the Biblical Flood?" *Zygon* 2 (1967): 272–78.

Olsson, Ingrid, ed. *Radiocarbon Variations and Absolute Chronology.* Nobel Symposium 12. New York: John Wiley & Sons, 1970.

Parrot, André. *The Flood and Noah's Ark.* London: SCM Press, 1955.

Pritchard, James B., ed. *Ancient Near Eastern Texts Relating to the Old Testament.* 2nd ed. Princeton, N.J.: University Press, 1955.

Rad, Gerhard von. *Genesis.* Old Testament Library. Philadelphia: Westminster Press, 1961.

Raikes, R.L. "The Physical Evidence for Noah's Flood." *Iraq* 28 (1966): 52–63.

Schmidt, Eric. "Excavations at Fara, 1931." *Museum Journal* (University of Pennsylvania), 22 (1931): 193–217.

Schwartz, Martin. Audio Tape No. 336 of a symposium on "The Flood Myth: An Inquiry into Causes and Circumstances," at the University of California at Berkeley, 1976.

Seckel, Al. "Science, Creationism, and the U.S. Supreme Court." *The Skeptical Inquirer* 11 (Winter 1986–87): 147–58.

Skinner, John. *A Critical and Exegetical Commentary on Genesis.* International Critical Commentary. 2nd ed. Edinburgh: T. & T. Clark, 1930.

Sollberger, Edmond. "The Rulers of Lagas." *Journal of Cuneiform Studies* 21 (1967): 279–86.

Speiser, E.A. *Genesis.* The Anchor Bible, Vol.1. Garden City: Doubleday and Company, Inc., 1964.

Stuiver, Minze. "A High-Precision Calibration of the AD Radiocarbon Time Scale." *Radiocarbon* 24, no. 1 (1982): 1–26.

Suess, Edward. *The Face of the Earth.* 5 vols. Oxford: Clarendon Press, 1904.

Teeple, Howard M. *The Noah's Ark Nonsense.* Evanston, Ill.: Religion and Ethics Institute, 1978.

BIBLIOGRAPHY

Thompson, R.C., and M.E.L. Mallowan. "Excavations at Nineveh, 1931–1932." *Annals of Archaeology and Anthropology* 20 (1933): 71–186.

Tigay, Jeffrey H. *The Evolution of the Gilgamesh Epic.* Philadelphia: University of Pennsylvania Press, 1982.

Van Dijk, J. *LUGAL UD ME-LÁM-bi NIR-GÁL.* 2 vols. Leiden: E.J. Brill, 1983.

Veenker, Ronald A. "Noah, Herald of Righteousness." *Proceedings: Eastern Great Lakes and Midwest Biblical Society* 6 (1986): 204–18.

Velikovsky, Immanuel. *Worlds in Collision.* New York: Dell Publishing Co., 1950.

Watelin, Louis Charles, and Stephen Herbert Langdon. *Excavations at Kish.* 4 (?) vols. Paris: P. Geuthner, 1924–193?.

Wellhausen, Julius. *Prolegomena to the History of Ancient Israel.* New York: Meridian Books, 1957 (first published in 1878).

Wenham, Gordon J. "The Coherence of the Flood Narrative." *Vetus Testamentum* 28 (1987): 336–48.

Westermann, Claus. *Genesis 1–11.* Minneapolis: Augsburg Publishing House, 1984 (German ed., 1974).

Whitcomb, John C., Jr., and Henry M. Morris. *The Genesis Flood.* Philadelphia: Presbyterian and Reformed Publishing Co., 1961.

Wilson, J.V. Kinnier. *The Rebel Lands.* Cambridge, Eng.: University Press, 1979.

Woolley, Leonard. *Excavations at Ur.* London: Ernest Benn, 1954.

Yamauchi, Edwin M. "Immanuel Velikovsky's Catastrophic History." *Journal of the American Scientific Affiliation* 25 (1973): 134–39.

Subject Index

SUBJECT INDEX

Kabir Kuh (Mount Ebih), 50
Kish, 29, 31, 32, 33, 34, 35, 36, 37, 212, 213
Kuh-i-Nuh ("Mountain of Noah"), 81

Lagash, 31, 33, 36, 213
Landslide, 50–51
Larak, 36
Lubar (mountain), 79
Lugal-e ud melambi nirgal. *See* Cuneiform Literature Index

Masis (mountain); "Mt. Ararat." *See* Ağri Dağ
Mount Aragats, 77
Mount Baris, 62, 63–64, 79
Movie: "In Search of Noah's Ark," 105–109

Nakhichavan/Nachidsheuan. *See* Ağri Dağ, 190–195
New Eden (magazine), 87
Nineveh, 30, 31, 32, 33, 34, 35, 36, 213
North Carolina State University, 104, 224
Numbers/Numerology, 19, 26, 122–125, 197–202

Palistrophe, 152–158
Pira Magrun (Pir Omar Gudrun), 62, 64, 65
Prophetic Messenger (newspaper), 85

Qardu. *See* Gordian Mountains

Radiocarbon, 95–101, 223

Sexagesimal System. *See* Numbers/ Numerology
Shuruppak, 29, 33, 34, 35, 36, 37
Sippar, 33, 36
Sumerian King List. *See* Cuneiform Literature Index

Tectonic Activity, 46
Tidal Wave, 40
Turkish Expedition, 85

United States Forest Service, 103
Ur, 29, 31, 32, 33, 34, 35, 36, 37, 106, 212
Urartu ("Ararat"), 55–58
Uruk, 30, 33, 34, 35, 36
Utnapishtim. *See* Cuneiform Literature Index

Vapor Canopy, 46–48

Yima, 25–27, 212

Ziusudra. *See* Cuneiform Literature Index
Zoroastrians, 6, 25–27

Index of Cuneiform Literature
(Excluding chapter 2 and Its
Footnotes)

Index of Medieval and Ancient (Non-Biblical) Sources

239

Modern Authors or Persons Cited